'Helping each new generation of school science teachers as they begin their careers is crucial to education. This is the updated, third edition of this valuable textbook. It contains a wonderful range of inspirational chapters. All science teachers, not only those at the start of the profession, would benefit from it, in Australia and beyond.'

Michael J. Reiss, *Professor of Science Education, University College, London*

## Praise for the Second Edition

'This new edition brings much of the expert knowledge about science learning to secondary teachers in a very accessible and useful manner. The chapters on ICT and a "thinking" science classroom directly address two of the new challenges for teachers in the Australian Science Curriculum.'

Peter J. Fensham, *Adjunct Professor of Science Education, QUT and Monash University*

EDITED BY
Vaille Dawson
Grady Venville
Jennifer Donovan

# THE ART OF TEACHING SCIENCE

A comprehensive guide to the teaching of secondary school science

**3RD EDITION**

LONDON AND NEW YORK

First published 2019 by Allen & Unwin

Published 2020 by Routledge
2 Park Square, Milton Park, Abingdon, Oxon OX14 4RN
605 Third Avenue, New York, NY 10017

First issued in hardback 2021

*Routledge is an imprint of the Taylor & Francis Group, an informa business*

Copyright © in the collection of Vaille Dawson, Grady Venville, and Jennifer Donovan 2019
Copyright in individual chapters with their authors 2019

All rights reserved. No part of this book may be reprinted or reproduced or utilised in any form or by any electronic, mechanical, or other means, now known or hereafter invented, including photocopying and recording, or in any information storage or retrieval system, without permission in writing from the publishers.

Notice:
Product or corporate names may be trademarks or registered trademarks, and are used only for identification and explanation without intent to infringe.

Publisher's Note
The publisher has gone to great lengths to ensure the quality of this reprint but points out that some imperfections in the original copies may be apparent.

 A catalogue record for this book is available from the National Library of Australia

Index by Puddingburn
Set in 11.5/14 pt Berkeley by Midland Typesetters, Australia

ISBN 13: 978-0-367-71970-8 (hbk)
ISBN 13: 978-1-76052-836-2 (pbk)

# CONTENTS

| | | |
|---|---|---|
| Figures, tables and snapshots | | vii |
| Contributors | | x |
| About the editors | | xvi |
| Preface | | xviii |

**Part 1**  **Understanding the Art of Teaching Science**

| | | |
|---|---|---|
| Chapter 1 | What is science? | 3 |
| | *Catherine Milne* | |
| Chapter 2 | Facts, laws and theories: The three dimensions of science? | 19 |
| | *Catherine Milne* | |
| Chapter 3 | Constructivist and sociocultural theories of learning | 35 |
| | *Russell Tytler, Joseph Ferguson and Peta White* | |
| Chapter 4 | Conceptual change teaching and learning | 50 |
| | *David Treagust, Reinders Duit and Hye-Eun Chu* | |

**Part 2**  **Implementing the Art of Teaching Science**

| | | |
|---|---|---|
| Chapter 5 | Contemporary science curricula in Australian schools | 69 |
| | *Vaille Dawson and Angela Fitzgerald* | |
| Chapter 6 | Planning in secondary-school science | 84 |
| | *Donna King and Reece Mills* | |
| Chapter 7 | Principles of effective science teaching and learning | 105 |
| | *Denis Goodrum* | |

v

# THE ART OF TEACHING SCIENCE 3RD EDITION

| | | |
|---|---|---|
| Chapter 8 | Science inquiry: Thinking and working like a scientist | 122 |
| | *Grady Venville* | |
| Chapter 9 | Assessment, learning and teaching: A symbiotic relationship | 140 |
| | *Debra Panizzon* | |
| Chapter 10 | Diversity and differentiation in science | 159 |
| | *Gemma Scarparolo* | |
| | | |
| **Part 3** | **Extending the Art of Teaching Science** | |
| Chapter 11 | A toolkit of additional teaching strategies and procedures | 175 |
| | *Jennifer Donovan* | |
| Chapter 12 | Science and safety inside and outside school laboratories | 190 |
| | *Siew Fong Yap* | |
| Chapter 13 | Teaching and learning science with digital technologies | 209 |
| | *Matthew Kearney and Wendy Nielsen* | |
| Chapter 14 | Integrating STEM | 226 |
| | *Linda Hobbs and John Cripps Clark* | |
| | | |
| **Index** | | 244 |

# FIGURES, TABLES AND SNAPSHOTS

## FIGURES

| | | |
|---|---|---|
| 5.1 | Strands, sub-strands, and key concepts of the Australian Curriculum: Science | 80 |
| 8.1 | An example of a variables table | 135 |
| 9.1 | Symbiotic relationship between assessment, learning and teaching | 142 |
| 9.2 | An example of a concept map on the concept of *ecosystem* | 146 |
| 11.1 | A possible hierarchy of teaching terminology | 177 |
| 12.1 | Laboratory safety for a dissection | 193 |
| 12.2 | Laboratory safety features and equipment | 194 |
| 12.3 | Emergency shower, eyewash and fume cupboard | 194 |
| 12.4 | Student-created models as teaching aids | 197 |
| 12.5 | An example of a laboratory code of behaviour | 201 |
| 12.6 | A drone in action on the school oval | 203 |
| 13.1 | The 14 sub-categories of Web 2.0 technologies, one of the many broad categories of learning technologies (used with permission from Bower 2015) | 212 |
| 14.1 | Models of STEM in education (used with permission from Springer, *STEM Education in the Junior Secondary: The State of Play* by R. Jorgensen & K. Larkin [eds], copyright 2018) | 230 |
| 14.2 | Skill lists promoted as 21st-century skills, STEM skills and general capabilities (used with permission from Springer, *STEM Education in the Junior Secondary: The State of Play* by R. Jorgensen & K. Larkin [eds], copyright 2018) | 232 |

14.3 Teacher collaboration and integration models (used with permission from Springer, *STEM Education in the Junior Secondary: The State of Play* by R. Jorgensen & K. Larkin [eds], copyright 2018)     237

## TABLES

7.1   An outline of inquiry-based teaching     108
8.1   A learning sequence that prepares students for more complex forms of practical work in science, based on Lederman (2018)     129
8.2   Questions used to scaffold science inquiry for secondary-school science students     133
9.1   Assessment types and purposes     143
12.1   Useful websites for science teachers and laboratory technicians     198

## SNAPSHOTS

1.1   MMR vaccine and autism     4
1.2   Schoolgirl discovers supernova     4
1.3   Yanyuwa and Garrwa people and cycads     4
1.4   Antibodies and water memory     5
1.5   Discovering elements     12
1.6   Which are more intelligent, rats, mice or hamsters?     14
2.1   Exploring the nature of water through observing the behaviour of different liquids, including water, on a coin     21
2.2   Extinct *Archaeopteryx*     26
2.3   The theory of plate tectonics     28
3.1   Year 7 students using drawings to explain day and night     44
3.2   A digital simulation for natural selection     46
4.1   Learning mixtures and compounds from an epistemological perspective of conceptual change     54

| | | |
|---|---|---:|
| 4.2 | Learning about electric current from an ontological perspective of conceptual change | 55 |
| 4.3 | Learning about acids and bases from an affective perspective of conceptual change | 57 |
| 4.4 | Learning about genetics from a multidimensional perspective of conceptual change | 58 |
| 4.5 | Diagnosing pre-instructional conceptions in optics, and using them to plan teaching/learning | 60 |
| 6.1 | A section of a Year 8 whole-school curriculum plan | 86 |
| 6.2 | A contextualised approach to the Year 9 Science (ten-week) Environmental Unit Plan: monitoring the health of Spring Creek | 92 |
| 6.3 | Year 9 Environmental Science lesson plan on energy flow into and out of an ecosystem via the pathways of food chains and food webs | 98 |
| 8.1 | An inquiry astronomy program | 125 |
| 9.1 | An example of using slowmation for assessment | 150 |
| 9.2 | Quality test items | 151 |
| 9.3 | Assessment rubric for data-handling skills | 154 |
| 9.4 | Quality feedback | 155 |
| 10.1 | Tiering using the chilli method | 166 |
| 10.2 | A menu using formative assessment that caters for readiness and interest | 167 |
| 11.1 | Stargazing as an example of citizen science | 180 |
| 12.1 | A lesson outlining the use of an industry partnership in a secondary-school science class | 205 |
| 13.1 | Technology-supported science-learning procedures | 215 |
| 13.2 | Inquiry-based science learning | 216 |
| 13.3 | Digital explanation | 217 |
| 14.1 | Using an integrated approach to teaching STEM | 233 |

# CONTRIBUTORS

**Hye-Eun Chu** is a lecturer in science education at Macquarie University. Before joining Macquarie University, she was Assistant Professor in science education at Nanyang Technological University, Singapore. Her research interests include the investigation of students' conceptual development in science learning with a focus on the inclusion of the arts (STEAM), students' explanatory models, the influence of learner belief on science learning, and formative assessment in the context of inquiry-based teaching.

**John Cripps Clark** teaches science and technology education and science communication at Deakin University. He has taught science and mathematics in primary schools, secondary schools and universities in Victoria and New South Wales and has researched STEM education in schools across Australia and Vanuatu. John, with his Deakin colleagues, has delivered professional development to teachers through the Victorian government-funded Successful Students - STEM program and STEM Catalysts. He currently uses cultural–historical activity theory in research involving off-campus students, professional experience, school gardens and science games.

**Vaille Dawson** is Professor of Science Education in the Graduate School of Education at The University of Western Australia, where she teaches pre-service secondary-science education and conducts classroom-based research. She was previously a medical researcher and secondary-science teacher. Her research interests include scientific literacy, pre-service teacher education, argumentation and decision-making about socioscientific issues. In 2013, she was made

x

a Fellow of the Royal Society of Biology (United Kingdom) for her service to biology education.

**Jennifer Donovan** is a science educator with many years of experience teaching secondary-school science and a variety of tertiary science and science education courses. Jenny is now a lecturer in education at the University of Southern Queensland. Her research interests are now focused on improving primary science education in terms of what children learn about genes and DNA from the mass media and the surprising capacity of primary children to learn about atomic theory.

**Reinders Duit** is Professor Emeritus of Physics Education at the Leibniz Institute for Science and Mathematics Education in Kiel, the national institute for science education research in Germany. His research interests include the role of students' and teachers' conceptions of teaching and learning science with an emphasis on conceptual change perspectives. He is co-author of the Model of Educational Reconstruction as a way to conduct research on contextual learning considering students' and scientists' conceptions.

**Joseph Ferguson** is a science education research fellow at Deakin University. His research explores the ways in which students collaborate to reason their way to new science understandings through making use of different representational forms. His passion for film and video drives his current interest in reimagining the use of video-based educational research. Joseph is driven by a desire for education to provide opportunities for students and teachers to enact social, political and environmental change.

**Angela Fitzgerald** is Associate Professor of Science Curriculum and Pedagogy at the University of Southern Queensland. She has been involved in science education in primary and secondary settings as a teacher and teacher educator for 15 years. Her research focuses on supporting pre- and in-service teachers in developing their confidence and competence in the learning and teaching of primary-school science.

**Denis Goodrum** is an Emeritus Professor at the University of Canberra. He was the inaugural chair of the ACT Teacher Quality Institute and previously Executive Director for Science by Doing. During his career, he has been responsible for many national projects, including preparing the shaping paper for the Australian Curriculum: Science.

**Linda Hobbs** is Associate Professor of Education (Science Education) at Deakin University. She teaches primary-science education in the Bachelor of Education course and teaches in the Graduate Certificate of STEM Education. Her research interests include partnerships in primary-teacher education, out-of-field teaching in secondary schools and STEM education. She currently leads a multi-institutional Australian Research Council-funded project called Teaching Across Subject Boundaries (TASB).

**Matthew Kearney** is an Associate Professor in the Faculty of Arts and Social Sciences (FASS) at the University of Technology Sydney (UTS). His research interests are in the field of technology-enhanced learning and focus on how digital technologies can be used in pedagogically transformational ways in school education and teacher education. He is the deputy director of the STEM Education Futures Research Centre at UTS.

**Donna King** is an Associate Professor in science education. Her research spans three interconnecting fields: the emotional engagement of students in science in the middle years; using engineering contexts for teaching science; and context-based science education. An outcome of this work is the development and implementation of innovative context-based units where teachers have adopted new pedagogical approaches for teaching science. For the last sixteen years, Donna has taught science education to primary and secondary pre-service teachers.

**Reece Mills** is a researcher and science-teacher educator in the Faculty of Education at the Queensland University of Technology. His PhD research employed a cognitive-affective perspective of conceptual change to investigate the value of slowmation construction for students' learning in Earth science. Reece is now conducting research about earth- and environmental-science teachers' attitudes towards teaching sustainable development and how their attitudes mediate the intended and enacted curriculum.

**Catherine Milne** is a Professor in Science Education and Chair of the Department of Teaching and Learning at New York University. Her research interests include material culture in the teaching and learning of science, sociocultural elements of teaching and learning science, the role of the history of science in learning science, and models of teacher education. She is the author of *The Invention of Science: Why History of Science Matters for the Classroom* (2011). She is a co-editor-in-chief for the journal *Cultural Studies of Science Education* and co-editor of two book series, one for Springer Nature and the other for Brill Sense Publishers.

**Wendy Nielsen** is an Associate Professor at the University of Wollongong and a science educator with interests in teacher education and the nature and history of science and environmental education. Her research focuses on teaching and learning in science and technology, particularly in pre-service primary-teacher education. She is an alumnus of The University of British Columbia and currently leads an ARC Discovery Project examining university science-student learning through the creation of digital explanations. Other research interests include doctoral education and supervising teacher knowledge.

**Debra Panizzon** is an Adjunct Associate Professor at Monash University and a research analyst for the Teachers Registration Board of South Australia. Her research interests include STEM policy, assessment in science and mathematics education, conceptual development and growth, and rural education. As a highly experienced science-education academic she has worked with both primary and secondary pre-service teachers, with much of her research involving partnerships with science and mathematics teachers.

**Gemma Scarparolo** is an early-career researcher at The University of Western Australia in the Graduate School of Education. She teaches in the Master of Teaching degree in the Early Childhood, Primary and Secondary programs and runs professional-development workshops on differentiation in schools. Her research interests include differentiation, professional development and teacher education.

**David Treagust** is a John Curtin Distinguished Professor at Curtin University and a member of the STEM Education Research Group (formerly SMEC) in the School of Education. His research interests include understanding students' ideas about science concepts and how these ideas relate to conceptual change, the design of curricula and teachers' classroom practices. He is also interested in the challenges teachers face helping students learn chemistry, biology and physics using multiple representations.

**Russell Tytler** is an Alfred Deakin Professor and the Chair in Science Education at Deakin University. He has researched and written extensively on student learning and reasoning in science. His interest in the role of representation in reasoning and learning in science extends to pedagogy and teacher and school change. He researches and writes on student engagement with science and mathematics, school–community partnerships and STEM curriculum policy.

**Grady Venville** is Professor of Science Education and Pro Vice-Chancellor (Education) at the Australian National University. She is responsible for teaching- and learning-related strategy across the university. Grady's research focuses on conceptual development, curriculum integration and cognitive acceleration.

**Peta White** is a science and environmental education lecturer at Deakin University. Peta has worked in classrooms, as a curriculum consultant and manager, and as a teacher educator in several jurisdictions across Canada and Australia. Her passion for initial teacher education, activist environmental education and action-orientated methodologies drives her current teaching/research scholarship.

Peta's current research examines how to put contemporary science research and science practice into schools, foregrounding socio-scientific understandings.

**Siew Fong Yap** is the Head of Science at Perth's Kingsway Christian College and a sessional academic at Curtin University, Western Australia. She is the co-author of *Oxford Science Western Australian Curriculum* Years 7–10 textbooks (2016). Her research focus is on bioethics and values in science education. Her book publications include *Classroom Teaching Strategies in Bioethics Education* (2013), *Science at the Movies—Remediating the Misconceptions* (2016) and *A Teacher's Guide to Teaching Science and Religion in the Classroom* (2018).

# ABOUT THE EDITORS

We are passionate about science and science teaching. The common goals of our working lives are twofold: to improve the science literacy of the Australian population and to encourage those students who find the excitement in science that we have found to make it their careers. This book is one more step towards those goals, by encouraging and assisting you as teachers, at whatever stage of your career, to make science meaningful and memorable for your students.

We have known each other for many years and work well together as a team. That means we recognise each other's strengths but we also actively help each other out when we need it. We don't always agree; in fact, we are very comfortable about disagreeing and nutting out problems together in a respectful and collegial manner. We always listen to each other's views and we have found this approach to teamwork is great fun and always results in improvements.

Collectively, we spent many years teaching in schools so we have had lots of experience 'at the chalk face' . . . when we still used chalk! We have also used our fair share of whiteboards and embraced the move to digital technologies. At the right time for each of us, we moved on to complete PhDs in science education and transitioned to teaching at university. We continue to engage with science and the latest scientific issues on a daily basis, and we each still love teaching and actively contribute to education in different ways. Critically important to each of us is an evidence-based approach to the teaching of science. Our in-depth knowledge of educational research has provided the framework for our approach to this book. With the contributors, we have attempted to translate sometimes complex and decontextualised research outcomes into useful ideas contextualised in the secondary science classroom.

In writing and editing this book, we aspire to inspire you. We have collaborated with top educators to contribute chapters to cover as many aspects of teaching secondary science as possible. We aimed for this to be a comprehensive guide, so we hope you will not only use this book as a text for university courses but also will keep it in your professional library so you can return to it from time to time and find something new. If you would like to know more about us individually, you will find more information in the Contributors section.

*Vaille Dawson*
*Grady Venville*
*Jennifer Donovan*

# PREFACE

Science is not just for scientists or those who aspire to be scientists. Science is for everyone.

Science affects everyone. It is a huge part of everyday life. Because of science, we have drugs to treat diseases, telescopes finding planets in other solar systems, we can (mostly!) predict the weather, eat a wide range of foods and keep them safe to eat, and, of course, we have diverse materials with which to make all of the goods we use, including our digital technologies. This just scratches the surface of our daily involvement with science. Where would we be without science? That's a great question to pose to your class.

This is the reason for this book. If science is for everyone, then clearly it is essential that science in secondary school is taught in such a way as to make it accessible to everyone. The aim of 21st-century science education is to create scientifically literate citizens, so you will find scientific literacy is a theme that appears often in these chapters. However, it is all very well to say you should teach to foster scientific literacy—how can this be done? One of the strengths of this book is that it includes both theory and practice. It offers practical ways to achieve the desired goals.

Everyone really means EVERY one. With the breadth of approaches, strategies and procedures within these pages, there are ways of challenging the most gifted as well as assisting the less able by using an approach we call *differentiation*. Chapter 10 focuses on differentiation, but there are ideas to help you throughout the book. Many pre-service teachers (and some more experienced ones) tend to *teach to the middle* (in other words, they focus on the average learner). This can create behavioural management problems, as you risk having some bored more able students and some lost less able students, all of whom may tune out and seek alternative ways to amuse themselves. So you would be wise to take these ideas about differentiation on board, so all students can become engaged in their science learning.

Science as performed by scientists involves some routine, known procedures but it also involves the unknown and the excitement of discovery. It is impossible to teach all school science by discovery but that sense of finding out some things for themselves is very important to inculcate in your high-school scientists. This is best fostered by using approaches that actively engage them in observing interesting phenomena, thinking through problems, posing questions and working out ways to find the answers. One such well-researched approach is the inquiry approach, and while it is the focus of Chapter 8, different aspects of inquiry are discussed in several other chapters, particularly Chapter 7. Supporting strategies and procedures appear in several chapters, including Chapter 11, which offers a whole toolkit of them. Of course, we do not want our students injured while doing science, so Chapter 12 discusses how to conduct science safely. That is a must-read for all of you.

If you look carefully at this book, you will find it is divided into three parts. The first is called Understanding the Art of Teaching Science, with Chapters 1 and 2 explaining what is (and what is not) science and Chapters 3 and 4 exploring what is learning in science. Chapter 3 takes you on a clear journey from conceptions to conceptual change through a short history of research in science teaching and, along the way, it explodes the myth of 'I've taught it therefore they must have learned it!' Chapter 4 extends the discussion of conceptual change and teaching to stimulate this process.

The second part is Implementing the Art of Teaching Science, and this provides much of the practical 'how to' advice. Chapter 5 takes a look at curricula at different levels—exploring the Australian Curriculum: Science, but also the perceived, enacted, experiential and attained curricula. Chapter 6 brings us to a necessary, but sometimes perceived as boring and/or difficult, activity—planning. This chapter is very clear about different levels of planning, with examples of how to tackle each one. The focus of Chapters 7 and 8 is inquiry, and these chapters both lead into Chapter 9, assessment.

Critically, this chapter explains how assessment should be embedded in the whole process of teaching and learning, and not just tacked on the end. Authentic and diverse assessment that is fit for purpose is the focus, and this leads on to Chapter 10's discussion of differentiation for diversity.

The final part is titled Extending the Art of Teaching Science and it includes the toolkit in Chapter 11 and information about safety (and resources for science teaching) in Chapter 12. The last two chapters bring this book up to the cutting edge of science teaching, discussing digital technologies (Chapter 13) and integrating science, particularly as STEM (Chapter 14). Integration can allow students to explore authentic, real-world problems, which rarely have a solution found in only one discipline, and Chapter 14 provides practical solutions to issues that may arise, such as recruiting other teachers and designing integrated assessment. Note that all chapters in this book refer to the Australian Professional Standards for Teachers (reference below) to indicate how each chapter relates to the standards that you are required to achieve.

Science should be accessible to everyone—and so should information to guide science teachers. So, this book has been deliberately written in a more conversational tone than some other texts. Our guiding image was one of a more experienced teacher sitting down for a chat with a less experienced colleague. For that reason, we have kept references to a minimum and included lots of anecdotes (snapshots) from our wealth of experience gained over many years in this noble profession. We are speaking to you from our hearts—hearts that have experienced the many joys (and some tears) associated with teaching science in schools and remain passionate about science. Hearts that hope you will join us in experiencing those joys—those 'aha' moments when students 'get it'—without too many of the tears.

We hope you will keep this book and return to it many times for inspiration, for the details that you may forget over time and for your own 'aha' moments about teaching. We hope your fascination and curiosity about science itself have been piqued by what you have read and stay with you through lifelong learning. Collectively, we hope this new, refreshed and revised edition of this book has effectively shared with you the 'art' (as in creativity and imagination) and the 'science' (as in planning and analysis) involved in successfully teaching science.

*Jennifer Donovan*
*Vaille Dawson*
*Grady Venville*

Australian Institute for Teaching and School Leadership (AITSL), 2011, *Australian Professional Standards for Teachers*, <www.aitsl.edu.au/docs/default-source/apst-resources/australian_professional_standard_for_teachers_final.pdf>, accessed 24 January 2019.

# PART 1
# UNDERSTANDING THE ART OF TEACHING SCIENCE

# CHAPTER 1
# What is Science?

Catherine Milne, New York University

## GOALS

**The goals for this chapter are to support you to:**

- Develop a nuanced and rich understanding of the nature of science as a construct of human action
- Evaluate arguments about the structure of science as a discipline in education
- Start to develop your personal philosophy about the nature of science that will inform your practice as a teacher of science

**Australian Professional Standards for Teachers—Graduate Level:**

- Standard 2: Know the content and how to teach it (Focus areas 2.1, 2.2)

## WHAT CONSTITUTES SCIENCE?

I have always been concerned by the lack of conversation in science education about the nature of science and how teachers make decisions about what counts as science. Combined with this is my concern about how teachers interpret the claims of textbook authors or education-standards developers about what constitutes science. So, here is a little test. Read the following snapshots and decide whether or not they are examples of science. How did you make that decision? Also, note down any questions that come to mind as you read each snapshot.

> **SNAPSHOT 1.1:** MMR vaccine and autism
>
> In early January 2011, the popular news was awash with articles on the decision of the *British Medical Journal* (Godlee, Smith & Marcovitch, 2011) to accuse Andrew Wakefield, a medical doctor and researcher, of not just shoddy research, but fraud. He was the lead author of a famous study, published in 1998 in *The Lancet* and withdrawn in February 2010 (Wakefield et al. 1998), which identified a link between the measles, mumps and rubella (MMR) vaccine and autism. He was accused of changing children's medical records to support the argument he wanted to make. The science community was overwhelmingly critical of Wakefield, presenting him as a fraud.

> **SNAPSHOT 1.2:** Schoolgirl discovers supernova
>
> Kathryn Aurora Gray, a ten-year-old girl from New Brunswick in Canada, was in the news for discovering a supernova using software that allowed her to make time comparisons of a specific area of the night sky near Galaxy UGC3378, which is about 240 million light years away (Jackson 2011).

> **SNAPSHOT 1.3:** Yanyuwa and Garrwa people and cycads
>
> The Yanyuwa and Garrwa people of the south-west Gulf of Carpentaria in Australia use cycads (*Cycas angulata*) for food. In the Yanyuwa language, the cycad is classified as *wurrana* or *being of authority*, with economic and religious significance to the maritime environment. Use of the nut of the *wurrana* as a food

source constitutes a challenge because the nut, located inside the fruit, contains a neurotoxin. To remove the toxin, Aboriginal people treat the nuts by heating them and then pounding or grinding them into flour. Stones used to grind the nuts are often found in groves of cycads. The flour is strained using a tool made from fronds to leach out the toxin. From this flour, bread called *damper* can be made (Bradley 2005).

The fruits of *wurrana* (*Cycas angulata*) used to make flour

**SNAPSHOT 1.4:** Antibodies and water memory

In 1988, the science journal, *Nature*, published a paper of which the lead author was Jacques Benveniste, head of a biomedical laboratory run by the French National Institute of Health and Medical Research (INSERM). The research team was studying the antibody response in basophils, a type of white blood cell. They found that basophils showed an allergic response even when the antibody solutions used were so diluted that there was a *calculated absence* of any antibody at the highest dilutions (basically, no antibodies were left in the solution). Benveniste and his colleagues argued that since the effects were observed when the dilutions were accompanied with vigorous shaking, transfer of biological information was related to the molecular structure of water (Davenas et al. 1988). One of the challenges for this area of study is that liquid water at the molecular level behaves in a way that is still not fully understood. The press called this

> phenomenon *water memory*. Anyone familiar with homeopathy might see a relationship between this study and homeopathic remedies requiring high dilution. In an unprecedented step, the editor of *Nature* at the time led a team of *fraud busters* demanding the studies be repeated with external observers, which they were, but the results were inconclusive.

Which of these snapshots did you locate within science? In making that decision, did you focus on: whether the case described was a study of nature? Where the study was published? The procedures the researchers used to produce the knowledge? And whether the data produced had been confirmed by others? Did you focus on whether a scientific theory was central to each case? Or was there some other aspect of each case influencing your decision about whether or not it belonged to science?

Think about how your response to each snapshot is indicative of your understanding of what science is and what lies outside the boundaries of science, which might be called pseudoscience. You might also be asking: well, what is the right answer? Which of these snapshots are really science? Unfortunately, the answer to that question is not a simple one. Equally unfortunately, science textbooks often try to maintain the myth that there is a simplistic scientific method that, if followed, will allow you to say you are doing science. As these snapshots suggest, it is not that simple, because there are cultural and historical structures that support the discipline of science to decide what counts as science.

Complexity aside, I hope you will agree that each of these examples has some features that are important for identifying an endeavour as scientific. Each of the snapshots has something to say to us about the following statement: the practice of science involves working in a field of study with structures, values, and ways of doing things that are used by members of the field of science to decide what should count as science. These structures, values, and ways of doing things are referred to in this chapter as *norms*. *Norms* are human constructions, developed or *constructed* by people within the field, and are used to test knowledge claims. This process of

WHAT IS SCIENCE? 7

testing knowledge claims through the structures, values, and ways of doing things defines the field and boundaries of science.

An example of this testing process is evident in Snapshot 1.4: Antibodies and water memory. The demand by the editor of *Nature* that Benveniste and his colleagues *replicate* their experiments with witnesses and generate similar data to the study they submitted is an extreme example of some of the structures that the science community has in place to organise what counts as science. Other scientists were critical of the decision of the editor of *Nature* to publish this paper, suggesting that decisions about what counts as science is a communal process. Also, as *Nature*'s editor acknowledged, the results were startling and seemed inconsistent with longstanding *scientific laws*, such as the Law of Mass Action (a *mathematical model* of the constant relationship between the concentration of products and reactants in chemical reactions that reach dynamic equilibrium), and therefore needed to be explored further rather than dismissed.

In Snapshot 1.1: MMR vaccine and autism, retraction by *The Lancet* of Wakefield's autism–vaccination paper was initially based on the inability of other researchers to replicate the original results claimed by Wakefield's research team. Snapshot 1.2: Schoolgirl discovers supernova challenges us to ask whether there are *norms* in place that try to control the members who are identified as *scientists*.

How did you respond to Snapshot 1.3: Yanyuwa and Garrwa people and cycads, concerning the Aboriginal groups from Groote Eylandt who extract flour from a toxic nut? This case raises the question of the role of *Indigenous knowledge* in the science that students learn at school. As a form of systematic knowledge, how is Indigenous knowledge similar to, and different from, the science that typically informs curricula? I think of the science typically taught in schools as a local knowledge that has gone global. Historically, the dispersion of the systematic knowledge we call *science* was helped by its association with languages, such as Greek, Latin and Arabic, which were the lingua franca of large swathes of Africa, Asia and Europe. What role does language play in Indigenous knowledge? Consider the role that English now plays in the communication of scientific knowledge. If all forms of systematic knowledge about the natural world are called science, then the science typically taught in schools might more accurately be called *Eurocentric science*, which communicates the place from which this form of science emerged over time.

## WHAT DO NATIONAL DOCUMENTS SAY ABOUT SCIENCE?

Often, when science is offered as a subject at school, little thought is given to how we identify the borders of science that allow teachers and students to make the claim that they are teaching or learning science. Instead, students know they are doing science, or biology, or chemistry, or physics, or whatever, because of the context in which this activity takes place—a school classroom or laboratory—and/or the resources, such as textbooks and lab manuals, they use in this space.

If we look at national curriculum documents, we can get a sense of how specific groups of people frame their response to the question 'what is science?' For example, in the Australian Curriculum, science is presented in the following way:

> Science provides an *empirical way* of answering *interesting and important questions* about the *biological, physical and technological world*. The knowledge it produces has proved to be a reliable basis for action in our personal, social and economic lives. Science is a dynamic, collaborative and creative human endeavour arising from our desire to make sense of our world through exploring the unknown, investigating universal mysteries, making predictions and solving problems. Science aims to understand a large number of observations in terms of a much smaller number of broad principles. Science knowledge is contestable and is revised, refined and extended as new evidence arises. (ACARA 2018 Rationale)

Thoughtful scholars developed this description using available resources and their experiences in the field. This definition communicates a description of science that the authors expect educators building a curriculum to use. However, how this definition is enacted and enforced involves political, social and cultural decisions. The social and cultural decisions that structure science focus on knowledge (epistemology), how we come to know about what is reality (ontology) and the values that are key to science (axiology). In the following sections, we will examine some of the epistemological elements, beginning with the term *empirical,* which seems to be key since science is described as providing an empirical way of answering questions.

## EMPIRICISM

In contemporary usage, the word *empirical* is typically associated with the practice of observing. This can be direct, through the use of senses such as sight, smell and hearing, or indirect, using instruments that detect objects and changes that are not available to our senses. Made famous by seventeenth-century philosopher John Locke, empiricism as a theory of knowledge associates true knowledge with sense experiences. According to empiricism, our observations provide us with knowledge about something. For example, you walk outside on a summer's day. Applying your sense of touch, you feel warmth. You can claim to know that it is hot. An empiricist would accept your observation as truthful.

So what do we know about the term *empirical*? As a word and associated meaning, *empirical* comes from the Latin *empiricus* and Greek *empeirikos* and means experienced or skilled in trial or experiment. Empiricism was associated with an ancient school of physicians in Greek medicine called the empiricists (Lindberg 2007). Greek medical empiricists argued that, if the causes of diseases were the same in all places, then the same remedies should be used in these places. This approach to medicine suggests that there has always been a universal element to empiricism from its origins to modern science. Greek empiricists argued that experience was the most productive way of understanding how it was possible to find relief from sickness, and that actions or practices, not opinions, were the most important for developing knowledge (Milne 2011). Valuing what we do above what we say can be understood as having some connection to how we comprehend *empirical* today, even if the connection of *empirical* to the senses was not as highly emphasised then as it is now.

## ANSWERING INTERESTING AND IMPORTANT QUESTIONS

Think back over the snapshots you read that introduced this chapter. Did any questions come to you as you read each one? Did you ask any questions that required exploring the science context further? For example, one of the questions that came to me as I read about Wakefield in Snapshot 1.1 was: what do data from other studies have to say about the connection between immunisation and autism? After hearing about Kathryn Aurora Gray and her discovery of a supernova in Snapshot 1.2, I asked: are supernovas more likely to be observed in specific locations in the universe, or are they spread out equally all over the universe? How do people go about finding a supernova? Do some people have an issue with ten-year-olds making discoveries in science?

Note that the questions I asked, and perhaps the ones you asked, make some assumptions about the world. For example, the way I asked my questions assumes that I can investigate them using logical means and that the phenomenon being explained will respond to inquiry in ways that are predictable. The belief that nature behaves in predictable ways is a cornerstone of science. To answer these questions, I do not expect to have to invoke anything else, including supernatural beings or magic, for answers. Where in the definition for science from the Australian Curriculum is this notion of predictability captured?

The questions we both asked as we read Snapshots 1.1 to 1.4 raise the bigger question of how science decides if a question is important or interesting. In the case of Snapshots 1.1 and 1.4, publication in a significant journal such as *The Lancet* or *Nature* provided a discipline-based endorsement of the importance and interest of the questions being asked by the researcher. As you have probably experienced in your own education, questions are important to science. A justification for the existence of science as a discipline is that its basis is a series of questions put to nature as science seeks to understand and explain the world we experience. But if we think of science as questioning, then we also need to acknowledge that what we accept as the answer is partly determined by the question we ask. In other words, we ask questions to fill in the gaps that we know about.

Note that, in science, to ask questions that will support further construction of science knowledge, you first need to know something about that field; you need to have some understanding of what the gaps are. For me, this is a key element for understanding how to support science inquiry in schools. Questions that can be explored do not come from nothing, so students need some background to ask questions that they can explore through the processes associated with science. This background can come from their everyday experiences. For example, abrupt changes in weather might lead a student to ask whether such changes are due to global warming or just a cyclical process. Observing the amount of car traffic in Sydney, students might ask if the ozone level is worse there than at the site of a factory near their home. Of course, to ask about ozone, they would need to have some experience of ozone.

Within the cultural discipline of science, the types of questions that tend to be asked are *what*, *how* and *why* (Milne 2008). Think about the questions you asked as you read the snapshots. Do they fit into those categories of questions? For science, *what* questions—such as 'what is a supernova?', 'what type of reaction is that? or 'what gas is given off?'—can be thought of as definition questions. *How* questions—such as 'how is the reaction similar to the reaction in an instantaneous ice pack?' or 'if we add less or more water will the reaction still take place?'—can be thought of as pattern questions. Finally, *why* questions tend to be what we might call theory questions. These are the questions that require the use of ideas, such as atoms, molecules, energy and cells, which are not directly observable but can be used to explain observations. Each of these different types of questions initiates different research methods.

For scientists, and perhaps also for students working in science, questions often come from the unexpected results of experiments,

# THE ART OF TEACHING SCIENCE 3RD EDITION

results that do not conform to their expectations. There are lots of examples of this from the history of science, such as that presented in Snapshot 1.5, which describes how Marie and Pierre Curie discovered two new elements, polonium and radium. As you read through this example, think of what was known about this field before Marie Curie decided to become involved. What question did she decide to explore, and how did she make sense of the answer?

---

**SNAPSHOT 1.5:** Discovering elements

Antoine Henri Becquerel, a French physicist, discovered Becquerel rays in January 1896 when he began to explore the question of whether all phosphorescent material emitted rays similar to X-rays. Becquerel decided to study uranium salts because he knew they gave off very strong phosphorescence and absorption spectra. Phosphorescence is an effect of substances that are able to absorb light energy and release it back over time. However, Becquerel discovered that the uranium salts did not need to be in sunlight to emit rays. He observed that the rays seemed to be emitted all the time; this was different from X-rays, which needed an energy source. Becquerel noted that the rays he discovered seemed to have some effect on the electrical character of the surrounding environment.

Marie and Pierre Curie were intrigued by Becquerel's account of his discovery. Marie Curie wrote:

> Our attention was caught by a curious phenomenon discovered in 1896 by Henri Becquerel. The discovery of the X-ray by Roentgen had excited the imagination, and many physicians were trying to discover if similar rays were not emitted by fluorescent bodies under the action of light. With this question in mind, Henri Becquerel was studying uranium salts, and, as sometimes occurs, came upon a phenomenon different from what he was looking for: the spontaneous emission by uranium salts of rays of a peculiar character . . . The study of this phenomenon seemed to us very attractive and all the more so because the question was entirely new and nothing yet had been written upon it. I decided to undertake an investigation of it. (Curie 1929: 93–4)

WHAT IS SCIENCE? 13

Marie Curie decided to examine other minerals and elements by modifying an instrument developed by Pierre Curie to measure the ionisation of the air exposed to the sample and, from that, imputing the level of radiation. She expected to confirm Becquerel's earlier studies that the purer the sample of uranium, the more rays that were released. However, when she compared high-quality pitchblende (uraninite) against pure uranium metal, she found that the pitchblende was releasing more rays than the pure uranium. How could that be? As she records in her autobiographical notes, the pitchblende was four to five times more active than expected based on the amount of uranium present. She confirmed her finding was not due to experimental error. She suggested that there must be another more active material, perhaps a previously undiscovered element, existing with uranium in the mineral.

Note that Curie's finding of higher radioactivity, a term she proposed, from pitchblende than from uranium metal was unexpected. She asked a *how* question, 'how can that be?' Her first move was to check the instrument she used to detect the rays, to make sure that what she observed was not an artefact of instrument calibration but could be attributed to the material she was observing. Once she had established that the instrumentation was reliable and accurate, she had to find another possible answer to the question about the cause of the ray activity. She addressed this question by exploring patterns, looking for a new element using spectra. Using spectra in this way was innovative. This process was initially developed by Robert Bunsen and Gustav Kirchhoff; they identified that each element has a unique spectrum, which allowed them to discover caesium and rubidium in 1860 and 1861, respectively. Curie understood that a sample of a new element would be expected to emit a unique spectrum. Her explanation/hypothesis was that extra ray activity was due to a previously unidentified element or elements present in pitchblende, and once she had reached a certain level of purity, she used spectra to look for these new elements.

THE ART OF TEACHING SCIENCE 3RD EDITION

Let us compare Marie Curie's approach to addressing a question of interest with the activities of a group of students in Snapshot 1.6.

---

**SNAPSHOT 1.6:** Which are more intelligent, rats, mice or hamsters?

A biology teacher decided to adopt an inquiry-based biology curriculum. The students in the course were excited by the idea that they would be doing research in their biology class. They began by discussing with the teacher questions they could investigate. Understandably, the students' access to rats, mice and hamsters—which were living in the classroom—had some influence on the students' choice of question. They had observed these animals over a number of weeks and were interested in providing other environments in which to observe them completing various tasks. The students decided to investigate the question 'which are more intelligent, rats, mice or hamsters?' Is this question refined enough to allow students to conduct a scientific inquiry? If you were the teacher, what would you do to support students as they explored some aspect of this question?

Here are some general suggestions, by no means exhaustive, which might help these students to refine their question. They also might help any group of students to refine a question they have about phenomena, while concurrently suggesting subsequent investigations. How do these ideas compare with your thinking?

- What purpose is served by this question? In other words, why would anybody be interested in finding an answer to this question? In the case of the rodents, you might have asked the students why anyone would be interested in the comparative intelligence of hamsters, rats and mice. This means you need to have a rationale for the inquiry. A question of this nature introduces students to the cultural and social dimensions of question-asking. When conducting scientific inquiry, scientists support the relevance of their question by providing a review of current research and arguing that their research will build on the science knowledge that currently exists, like Marie Curie did.

WHAT IS SCIENCE? 15

- What can you find out about rodent (animal) intelligence that has already been published? This question reinforces the twin ideas that your investigation is located within a broader area of research, and that you should use the research outcomes or knowledge that already exists to inform your own study or studies. This step also reminds you that both knowledge and ignorance are necessary for inquiry. Sometimes in classroom settings this can be forgotten, but helping students to recognise what they do and do not know about the phenomenon they wish to study will help them to understand the value of searching to find out what is already known and how they could use this information to inform their own research. At this stage, students might also be encouraged to carry out some simple observations of the organism or phenomenon, and think about instruments that might help them develop the data needed to answer their questions.
- How will you define/operationalise *intelligence* for this study, so that intelligence can be empirically investigated? You need to decide how to define and model a term such as intelligence. This question might emerge in the planning of the inquiry, as students develop instruments to test the intelligence of animals. In the case described, the students wanted to build mazes to test the intelligence of these rodents; in the process of developing their mazes, they began to examine questions related to the challenges of developing useful instruments and how their instrumentation could affect their observations. This might lead to an examination of the question of how definitions and models can affect the design of investigations.

The case of the students exploring rodent intelligence suggests that only some questions can be explored using tools that are culturally and socially associated with science. Science also is a balancing act, because typically when you ask a question you anticipate the answer, so there is a challenge associated with not letting anticipation lead you to make claims that you cannot support with empirical evidence obtained from experimental investigations. In other words, you should not be seduced by what you think the answer should be. In *The Disappearing Spoon* (2010), Sam Kean describes how, in the search for new elements, many scientists were seduced by their expectations into making claims that they had discovered one of the elements, such as element 43, predicted by Dmitri Mendeleev when he proposed his version of the periodic table because there was a gap between element 42, molybdenum, and element 44, ruthenium.

Note the cultural elements in this story of discovery, identified also in the Australian Curriculum definition of science, *collaboration through the sharing of resources and the attribution of discovery*. For a scientist, there was capital associated with being identified as the discoverer of a new element. For example, Marie Curie was awarded the 1911 Nobel Prize in Chemistry for the discovery of radium. However, discovery of an element does not always presage a Nobel Prize. Ida Noddack and her husband, Walter, discovered element 75, rhenium. They also claimed to have discovered element 43, which they called masurium, although attempts to replicate their discovery of that element were unsuccessful. Noddack was nominated three times in the 1930s for the Nobel Prize in chemistry without success.

## SUMMARY OF KEY POINTS

Science is a global form of systematic knowledge. Central to science is a specific way of asking questions that assumes we can attain answers to those questions through specific practices. To answer the questions, we use our senses to observe the world naturally or through experiments in which we change the world in some way. We do this because we believe nature behaves in ways that are predictable and can be observed and measured. I always think of science as valuing purposeful observing, but observing can only be purposeful if we have some sense of what we need to observe. As a science educator, you have a responsibility to construct learning experiences in which the students in your care have opportunities to engage in purposeful observing and other practices that we have touched on in this chapter, including asking questions that science can seek to answer, using instruments, and reasoning from evidence. But it could be argued that these are also the practices valued in Indigenous knowledge. If that is the case, then what makes science different, or is it the same?

## DISCUSSION QUESTION

In 2015, Tu Youyou was the first Chinese scientist to be awarded a Nobel Prize when she shared the Nobel Prize in Physiology or Medicine for her role in the development of the antimalarial drug, artemisinin (Jia 2015). She had retired from the China Academy of Traditional Chinese Medicine. In 1967, Tu was one of the scientists assigned to the highly secret Project 523, which brought many Chinese scientists together to develop an antimalarial drug. The teams working on the project decided to look for a drug in traditional Chinese medicine. Tu developed a low-temperature technique for extracting artemisinin from the biologically active component of wormwood that preserved the active ingredients. There were a few issues associated with her award of a Nobel Prize by the Nobel committee, including the question of assigning authorship for the development of artemisinin as a pure drug to control malaria, but my question to you is somewhat different. The World Health Organization discourages people in countries such as Uganda from drinking wormwood tea, the source of the raw ingredient for artemisinin. Can you think why that might be, and how would you respond? How might you use this example in a science class?

## REFERENCES

Australian Curriculum, Assessment and Reporting Authority (ACARA), 2018, *Rationale*, <www.australiancurriculum.edu.au/f-10-curriculum/science/rationale/>, accessed 5 April 2018.

Bradley, J.J., 2005, '"Same time poison, same time good tucker": The cycad palm in the south west gulf of Carpentaria', *Journal of Australian Studies*, vol. 29, no. 86, pp. 119–33.

Curie, M., 1929, *Pierre Curie*, C. & V. Kellogg trans., New York, NY: Macmillan.

Davenas, E., Beauvais, F., Amara, J., Oberbaum, M., Robinzon, B., Miadonna, A., Tedeschi, A., Pomeranz, B., Fortner, P., Belon, P., Sainte-Laudy, J., Poitevin, B. & Benveniste, J., 1988, 'Human basophil degranulation triggered by very dilute antiserum against IgE', *Nature*, vol. 333, no. 6176, pp. 816–18.

Godlee, F., Smith, J. & Marcovitch, H., 2011, 'Wakefield's article linking MMR vaccine and autism was fraudulent', *British Medical Journal*, vol. 342, no. 7788, pp. 64–5.

Jackson, N., 2011, 'Ten-year-old girl becomes youngest person to discover a supernova', *The Atlantic*, 5 January, <www.theatlantic.com/technology/archive/2011/01/10-year-old-girl-becomes-youngest-person-to-discover-a-supernova/68911/>, accessed 13 January 2019.

Jia, H., 2015, 'China's first science Nobel Prize exposes anxiety on research', *Chemistry World*, 10 November, <www.chemistryworld.com/news/chinas-first-science-nobel-prize-exposes-anxiety-on-research/9139.article/>, accessed 13 January 2019.

Kean, S., 2010, *The Disappearing Spoon: And Other True Tales of Madness, Love, and the History of the World From the Periodic Table of the Elements*, New York, NY: Little, Brown and Company.

Lindberg, D., 2007, *The Beginnings of Western Science*, 2nd ed., Chicago, IL: The University of Chicago Press.

Milne, C., 2008, 'In praise of questions: Elevating the role of questions for inquiry in secondary school science', in J. Luft, R.L. Bell & J. Gess-Newsome (eds), *Science as Inquiry in the Secondary Setting*, Washington, DC: National Science Teachers' Association, pp. 99–106.

Milne, C., 2011, *The Invention of Science: Why History of Science Matters for the Classroom*, Rotterdam: Sense.

Wakefield, A.J., Murch, S.H., Anthony, A., Linnell, J., Casson, D.M., Malik, M., Berelowitz, M., Dhillon, D.H., Thompson, M.A., Harvey, P., Valentine, A., Davies, S.E. & Walker-Smith, J.A., 1998, 'Ileal-lymphoid-nodular hyperplasia, non-specific colitis, and pervasive developmental disorder in children', *The Lancet*, vol. 351, no. 9103, pp. 637–41.

CHAPTER 2

# Facts, Laws and Theories: The Three Dimensions of Science?

Catherine Milne, New York University

## GOALS

**The goals for this chapter are to support you to:**

- Understand that theories and laws are creative constructions that are always limited by data and form the basis of scientific explanations
- Enrich your understanding of the nature of science

**Australian Professional Standards for Teachers—Graduate Level:**

- Standard 2: Know the content and how to teach it (Focus areas 2.1, 2.2)

## INTRODUCTION

In this chapter, I want to take you on a journey through an exploration of facts, laws and theories in science. Sometimes these elements are conflated, especially laws and theories. I hope to convince you in this chapter that, as a discipline, science treats laws and theories as very different elements. Indeed, laws are creative human constructions of observations or facts that are valued in a specific phenomenological (related to phenomena) or empirical context.

## A LARGE NUMBER OF OBSERVATIONS AND THE NATURE OF A FACT

Reflect back on Marie Curie's experience of discovering polonium and radium (Curie 1929) in Snapshot 1.5, and think how that experience compares with the way science is typically taught in science classrooms. As Curie explored the rays released by various substances, she had to verify that the observations of phenomena she noticed were truthful and reliable, that is, that they had the character of a *fact*. As I mentioned in Chapter 1, we can understand an *observation* as using our senses, or instruments that extend our senses, to make statements about what seems real. We can think of a scientific fact as an idea that is developed or *constructed* by scientists. Critically, facts are based on observations that have been confirmed through processes involving multiple cases and multiple witnesses. Lurking in the background, often unacknowledged, is a theory that gives significance to the facts that are being constructed. In Marie Curie's case, what counted as a fact was based on both the phenomenon she was observing and personal and public theories associated with understanding ionising rays. If she had no knowledge of this area of science, she would not have thought to ask questions about rays, and she would not have thought to record the level of radiation.

Facts are constructed from observations, which can be thought of as systematic perceptions, that is, how we use our senses to understand the natural world (Milne 2011). Think about how that definition for observations applies to Snapshot 1.3 about the Yanyuwa and Garrwa people, who removed the toxins from cycads. In your practice of teaching science, you will have a responsibility to provide experiences that support learners to observe and to value the observations they make. I describe science as valuing *purposeful observing*. We do lots of observing in our everyday lives, but science creates a context for valuing specific observations. For example, in exploring the chemistry of water and sustainability, I begin by asking students to investigate how many drops of liquid they can put on a coin, and I ask them to observe what the liquid looks like on the coin. See Snapshot 2.1 for a student's result.

**SNAPSHOT 2.1:** Exploring the nature of water through observing the behaviour of different liquids, including water, on a coin

| | Drops on a Penny (Round 1) | Drops on a Penny (Round 2) |
|---|---|---|
| Water | 48 | 52 |
| Vinegar | 40 | 43 |
| Butanol | 19 | 18 |

How many different types of observations did the student make? Because we are seeking to understand the chemistry of water, these observations lead us to try to explain why water behaves the way we observe (in other words, to explain its apparent *stickiness*). This is where scientific theories are key; in this case, the important explanatory theory is atomic theory.

# THE ROLE OF THEORY IN OBSERVING

My own experience of teaching a Year 8 unit on cells emphasised for me the role of theory in observing. I had taught a four-week unit that involved students observing many different cell types and cell structures. I was feeling pretty proud of myself. The students seemed to be enjoying themselves and were very actively engaged in the activities. Towards the end of the unit, I asked one of the students if he was getting good cells from his sample. 'Yes, Miss,' he replied. 'I can see lots of round cells with dark walls.' I realised right away, much to my dismay, that he was describing air bubbles, not cells.

How difficult it is to *see* cells was captured well by Robert Hooke in his most famous book, *Micrographia* (1665/2003). He struggled to describe to his readers what he saw when he looked down his new tool, a microscope, at a small sample of cork. He used a simile, describing the shapes he observed as 'perforated and porous, much like a honeycomb', and added that 'these pores or cells were not very deep' (p. 113). He was, of course, describing what came to be called *cells*, but often in the telling of this story in science textbooks, his struggles are not presented. Would it not be better for learners if they were? The experience of observing my students observe cells under the microscope was an *aha moment* for me. It brought together a number of previous experiences, which left me with an awareness that I subsequently applied to my teaching practice. The awareness was that unless a student has some knowledge of what something is like (their personal theory), their chance of observing that phenomenon is much reduced.

From the cell-observing activity and other experiences, I took away the understanding that observations cannot be theory-free. Your construction of a phenomenon through the practice of observation is shaped by your experience of that phenomenon. In the sciences, the increasing experience of scientists allows them to construct phenomena as specialists rather than as novices. In a way, this is part of the mission of science educators to support students to *see* the world in ways with which they have had little previous experience.

## UNDERSTANDING AND EXPLANATION

Within the culture of science, there is an expectation that if another researcher wants to replicate Curie's study and obtain the same results, they should be able to do so. Remember from Snapshot 1.4 the challenges Benveniste and his colleagues faced trying to replicate their results for water memory. However, if you think about the manner in which science is taught in schools, the phenomena presented to students are not presented as observations open to interpretation but as secure and true facts. The explanations presented in school science are based on phenomena that, for the students, are not contested or available to be contested. This means that often the laboratory work students do is based on verifying facts that are already known. For example, you might have a learning outcome such as *Students understand that the Earth is composed of materials that are altered by forces within it and on its surface*. The idea of *understanding* and the idea of *explanation* are interdependent. In order *to explain* you need *to understand,* and to show you understand you need to be able to explain. Note also that in this statement, the phenomenon—*the Earth is composed of materials that are altered by forces within it and on its surface*—is accepted as permanently true, so understanding in this case is based on a phenomenon that is not open to question. What seems to be missing from this statement is any consideration of a way to explain how and why these Earth forces are present.

For me, the search for *mechanisms*, usually presented in scientific theories, to explain why specific phenomena or facts make sense, is a fundamental element of the field of Eurocentric science. For example, DNA and genes are mechanisms that explain the observed phenomenon of inheritance; atoms and molecules are mechanisms that explain the observed phenomenon of chemical reactions such as rusting. This search for mechanisms owes much to the seventeenth-century notion promoted by philosopher René Descartes that 'Accordingly, just as when those who are accustomed to considering automata know the use of some machine and see some of its parts, they easily conjecture from this how the other parts which they do not see are made: so, from the perceptible effects and parts of natural bodies, I have attempted to investigate the nature of their causes and their imperceptible parts' (Descartes, 1644/1983, p. 286). While science may no longer completely endorse the idea of the mechanical universe, mechanisms remain a fundamental principle of a scientific worldview. Hence, I am of the view that an understanding of the role of mechanisms should be a focus of science taught in school. Mechanisms can be described as fundamental processes associated with, perhaps even responsible for, natural phenomena. The idea of a mechanism is central to the development of scientific explanations and is associated with cause-and-effect reasoning. Mechanisms also have their limitations, because they are associated with the idea that we can understand natural processes because they are like machines. Although this model of the Earth as a machine has been very productive for science, it is still a model and can limit our understanding of the world if it is the only model used.

Explanations are also central to answers. Once you get an answer to your question, you are left to decide how you can make the claim that Answer A is a real answer to Question 1. Typically, in science it is considered important to not only generate observations associated with a specific question but also to associate these observations with a pre-existing theory or model that helps us to *explain* why those observations were made and how they answer the question appropriately. To explain is not to answer a question but to supply the missing extra information that makes the conditions for a convincing answer to a question possible. In general, a scientific explanation is composed of an observation or observations, which are used as evidence, and warrants—usually theories, models or laws—that support the use of these observations to make this explanation. This is what constitutes a *scientific worldview*, a culturally dependent belief that explanations exist to help us better understand and explain the natural world. You might notice some similarities between what I have labelled an explanation and how you might think of an argument. I believe an explanation and an argument in science share characteristics, but I think the emphasis for each is somewhat different. In an explanation, the emphasis is on *making data comprehensible* with *reference to a specific accepted model/theory*. In an argument, the focus is on *using evidence from data/observations/ facts* to *make a claim* that is *warranted by a specific model/theory*.

## DATA, FACTS, PATTERNS, AND LAWS

Data become facts when they are associated with a specific theory or model. Typically, science seeks to organise data into patterns, with the expectation that such order is part of nature. By revealing the patterns, science is providing humans with greater insight into how the Earth and universe work. Can you think how science is able to do this? Read through Snapshot 2.2, and answer the question before reading on.

Did you select C as your answer? Well done! The researchers also produced scatter plots of the length of other bones (such as the ulna and tibia) and teeth against femur length and obtained similar relationships. These results led them to conclude that the fossils were consistent with a single species of different sizes, none of which were full-grown. To have a sense of how robust this apparent relationship might be, what other questions would you think to ask?

Another strategy for making facts more compelling is to look for patterns in the facts that can be represented as a scientific *law*. Finding patterns in data is a creative act. If these patterns are found in other places and at other times, and it seems that the patterns are consistent through time and space, then other scientists are more likely to accept that the patterns described exist in nature. The identification of a pattern is an initial criterion needed for the formulation of a law from observations of phenomena. Intuition and creativity are needed for someone to make a claim for a relationship or pattern in data that can be framed as a law. For me, this creativity is one aspect of science that is neglected in typical representations of laws in science education. A law represents a statement, often mathematical, describing a phenomenon that does not vary through space or time.

An example of a law is Boyle's Law. The discovery of this law was associated with a number of experimental philosophers in seventeenth-century Europe, but the paper outlining the law was published by Robert Boyle in 1662 as an appendix to his famous publication, *New Experiments Physico-Mechanicall, Touching The Spring of the Air, and its Effects* (1660). The phenomenon Boyle explored and reported was the relationship between pressure and

## SNAPSHOT 2.2: Extinct *Archaeopteryx*

*Archaeopteryx* is an extinct animal that possesses both scales and feathers, and at one stage it was thought to be the *missing link* between lizards and birds. Only six fossil specimens exist, and they vary greatly in size. As a result, there has been a lot of discussion about whether the fossils all belong to one species or to different species. To help answer this question, data from the length of the femur (a leg bone) was plotted against the length of the humerus (a bone in the arm) on a scatter plot (Houck, Gauthier & Strauss, 1990). These data were available for five of the specimens. If the specimens belong to the same species, and the differences in size are due to varying ages, then the points should show a linear positive relationship. If all of the fossils belong to different species, then there should be no association. Finally, if one of the specimens belongs to a different species from the others, then you should be able to observe an outlier.

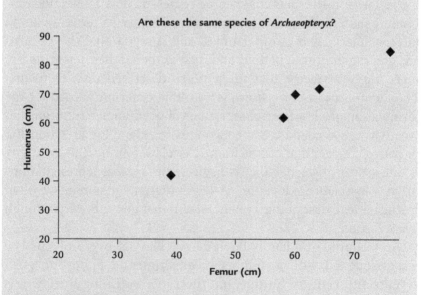

What does the scatter plot indicate?
A) No association, indicating that five separate species are present.

> B) An outlier can be observed, indicating the presence of two separate species.
> C) There is a strong positive association, indicating that the specimens belong to one species.
> D) It is not possible to make any statement about the possible number of species present from the data provided.

volume. Boyle wrote about this law before decimals and coordinate geometry—used to show relationships between variables—were generally accepted. This relationship can be represented mathematically as: $pV = k$ *(constant) at constant temperature.* When presented in the form $P_1V_1 = P_2V_2$, this law can be used to make predictions.

Physicist Richard Feynman recognised the constructed and creative nature of scientific laws in his comment, 'Nature obeys an elegant law. How clever she is to pay attention to it.' (1964, n.p.). The power of laws lies in their utility. They allow scientists to make predictions. Feynman claimed that laws were simple and beautiful in pattern, but not in action. By this he meant that a law could look simple and be represented by a simple mathematical formula, but have implications far beyond the specific context in which it was initially proposed.

## SCIENTIFIC LAWS AND THEORIES

Boyle's Law works under most conditions that we experience, but not at extremes of pressure and temperature. Boyle proposed this law based on observations of the effect of mercury on the volume of air trapped at the end of the mercury in a glass tube. He was able to support the law by showing how his observations were consistent with his prediction of an inverse relationship between pressure and volume. The law can also be derived theoretically from the motion of particles, which Daniel Bernoulli did in his book *Hydrodynamica* in 1738, although his work was virtually ignored at the time because his scientific colleagues had other questions they found more compelling (Brush 1965). Even Robert Boyle used the particle theory, in the form of corpuscles, to explain his observations about air. He argued that the concept of particles in motion could be used to explain many natural phenomena observed by experimental and natural philosophers. The corpuscular theory of matter was a theory that was part of the experimental conversation in the seventeenth century, so it is understandable that Boyle creatively applied his understanding of the theory, a conceptual framework, to explain the behaviour of the air he observed. I make him sound very modern, but by the eighteenth century, theories such as the caloric theory of heat provided far more powerful explanatory frameworks and were in use until the middle of the nineteenth century.

So, scientific laws exist between facts and theories. We can come at them from either direction, but typically they are associated with data. If data do not support a law in its current form, then the law can be modified to accommodate new data. It takes creativity to infer a law from observed phenomena, and it takes more creativity to propose a theoretical explanation for the phenomena and the patterns constructed from observations of phenomena. I think of scientific theories, and their associated models, as the explanatory frameworks for science, providing the needed mechanisms to explain phenomena. In particular, I have in mind theories such as atomic theory, kinetic molecular theory, evolution, plate tectonics, cell theory and special relativity. All theories in science have the potential to be transformative, because they support scientists to ask different questions. A case in point is plate tectonics, which is the focus of Snapshot 2.3.

**SNAPSHOT 2.3:** The theory of plate tectonics

Plate tectonics explains large motions of the Earth's crust and upper mantle based on the idea that the Earth's surface is broken into tectonic (built) plates that float on the upper mantle. For me, plate tectonics is interesting because I have worked with a geologist who began to learn geology before the theory of plate tectonics was generally accepted. He remembers being expected to learn the geology of specific regions, and each region was different because there was no underlying explanatory framework for geology.

The theory of continental drift, proposed by Alfred Wegener in 1912, was around, but there was no compelling evidence that could be used with this theory to explain how continents drifted. Fossil evidence, such as the discovery of fossil seed ferns, *Glossopteris*, over South Africa and India, had been used to support the argument for continental drift, but the geological community in the early twentieth century did not consider that this evidence was compelling enough to support this theory. In the first half of the twentieth century, the accepted model of the Earth's interior consisted of a liquid core and a solid mantle, and such a model made it difficult to explain how continents could drift when the mantle was solid. Applying geologic and tectonic observations, in 1954 S. Warren Carey (1961)—an Australian geologist and advocate of continental drift—proposed an expanding Earth hypothesis to provide a mechanism to explain how continents could drift to form the continental organisation we observe today. He had earlier proposed subduction as the driving mechanism but was unable to get his paper published. The discovery in the upper mantle of metamorphic rocks (serpentinised peridotite) formed from low pressure and temperature supported American Harry Hess's (1954) argument that convection in the Earth's mantle was the driving force behind island arcs, such as Hawaii, and for a phenomenon he called sea floor spreading. The geological community found the evidence for subduction and sea floor spreading more compelling than the evidence presented for the expanding Earth hypothesis. The ability to measure the age of the ocean floor using magnetic reversals (Vine & Matthews 1963) confirmed a prediction made by the sea floor spreading hypothesis and did not require an expanding Earth. Carey continued to be a supporter of the expanding Earth hypothesis, but he was definitely in the minority.

What does Snapshot 2.3 tell you about scientific theories? Studies of scientists in action (Gilbert & Mulkay 1984) have shown that a scientist's commitment to one of the competing hypotheses for experimental data was not wholly dependent on their rational interpretation of data. Generally, individual scientists presented themselves as holding the interpretation that was the true representation of reality, having correctly and rationally interpreted the data. They represented members of the other competing theoretical camp, which failed to acknowledge and accept their view of the physical world, as typically misled by non-cognitive factors beyond the empirical and technical, including emotional commitment and personal influence. However, there is no doubt that the theory of plate tectonics transformed scientific understanding of the geology and palaeoecology of the Earth.

In the Snapshot 2.3 example of a scientific theory and its mechanisms, we focused on plate tectonics, but I would like you to think about some other important scientific theories and the mechanisms that are core elements of those theories. Consider evolution. What is a mechanism that is part of evolution? Consider kinetic molecular theory. What is a mechanism for that theory? The disciplinary power of scientific theories and their internal mechanisms is that they have both explanatory and predictive power. Theories are so important that they become embedded in the language of science.

What is interesting to me is how, over time, these theories evolve from local knowledge to general knowledge and, in science's case, become a form of global knowledge. Scientific inquiry is a kind of purposeful and directed curiosity that brings together questions, data and theory to generate arguments or explanations. Scientific inquiry is also a peculiar way of letting the world be encountered by us in perception. If you think about scientific theories in history, you might note that theories change while questions can remain unchanged. For example, in the late eighteenth century, Antoine Lavoisier asked, 'Why did the candle wax burn my hand?' and creatively reasoned from this experience the caloric theory of heat. This theory was based on a mechanism for heat that required heat to have mass that could be transferred (Milne 2011). Today, we still have the same question, albeit in a slightly different form. Why does

FACTS, LAWS AND THEORIES: THE THREE DIMENSIONS OF SCIENCE?

heat transfer from one object to another? The theory that we use to explain this phenomenon is now a variant of kinetic molecular theory.

What can science tell us? How is science limited? Typically, you might argue that science can only explore knowledge that is available for investigation—in other words, knowledge that is associated with the natural, physical world. You might also argue that science can only tell us about the universe as it is, not the universe as it ought to be. Such an argument might then lead us to accept that while science can help us understand the world, it cannot tell us how we ought to lead our lives in that world. Such an argument challenges us, because some people might use it to claim that there is no place for values in science. As we have seen throughout this chapter, however, there are some values that are absolutely central to the practice of science. For example, science made it okay to be curious, found a place for quantification and accepted that nature is real, knowable and follows rules that can be discovered. How science makes sense of the world, through the use of questions, facts, laws, hypotheses and theories, is a strategy that can be used to distinguish between understandings and beliefs that are accepted as scientific, and understandings and beliefs that exist outside of science. We also should acknowledge that science is only one form of systematic knowledge and not the form.

## SUMMARY OF KEY POINTS

Science is based on the idea that, through observations, we can generate patterns that tell us more about the organisation of nature. For example, Boyle was able to claim an inverse relationship between pressure and volume in a gas. This relationship has been supported by experiments conducted in other places and times, and so it has become a law. You might even have carried out an experiment to confirm this relationship. Even though laws allow us to make predictions, as Boyle was able to do, they do not help us to understand why this relationship can be observed. For that we need a theory.

THE ART OF TEACHING SCIENCE 3RD EDITION

Science is a field of endeavour constructed by humans and, in the end, it is the science community that decides what counts as science. It is the community that judges whether claims for new knowledge, such as those presented in the Chapter 1 snapshots involving Andrew Wakefield, Kathryn Aurora Gray, Jacques Benveniste and Marie Curie, are convincing. In summary, Eurocentric science, the science represented in science classrooms all over the globe, is one community's attempt to explain the world in ways that influence every living thing on this planet. As an educator, your goal should be to engage your students in a science that captures aspects of the communal and knowledge processes that are involved.

## DISCUSSION QUESTIONS

I have presented you with a lot of information about how you might think about, and respond to, the question 'what is science?' Read each example presented below, and answer two questions.

2.1 Is this science, and what evidence allows me to say whether it is or not?

2.2 How would you use these examples in your teaching practice?

### Example 1

A good friend of mine has just had a tooth extraction, and she is given an instantaneous icepack to use as a compress to help reduce swelling. The instructions on the pack tell her to squeeze the pack to break the inner liquid bubble and then to shake the contents well, and they will turn cold immediately! Intrigued, I look at the contents: ammonium nitrate and water. I ask myself: what other examples are there of this type of reaction that use everyday chemicals?

### Example 2

In 2004, Ann Gibbons wrote of a *warrior* gene (Gibbons 2004). This gene, found on the X chromosome, codes for an enzyme called monoamine oxidase A (MAOA), which works like a molecular cleaver. In the brain, it breaks down neurotransmitters such as dopamine and serotonin. If it does not do its job, these neurotransmitters can build up, which could interfere with neuron communication. There was speculation that the shorter version of the gene (MAOA-L) would code for less enzyme and therefore be less effective as a cleaver. An initial understanding of MAOA was based on a 1993 study by Han Brunner and colleagues, who studied the pedigree of a Dutch family. In this study, 14 out of 34 men in the family were shown to have been highly aggressive with slightly low IQs of about 85, but none of the women showed these symptoms (what does that suggest?). Urine analysis showed that a lack of MAOA might be the cause. The researchers suggested a link between MAOA deficiency, caused by a mutation in the gene for MAOA, and this aggression in men. In 2006, Rod Lea—presenting at the eleventh International Congress of Human Genetics held in Brisbane—claimed that in a study of 46 Maori men, 56 per cent carried the gene for the shortened form of MAOA (about twice as many as in the white population). Analysing a smaller sample of 17 men (from the 46), Lea and Chambers (2007) claimed that MAOA-L might have given Maori men an advantage when they were colonising parts of the Pacific. This study was highly contentious (why might that be?). Other researchers noted the link between MAOA-L and aggression had been established in white males.

## REFERENCES

Bernoulli, D., 1738, *Hydrodynamica, sive de viribus et motibus fluidorum commentarii* (in Latin, source ETH-Bibliothek Zürich, Rar 5503).

Boyle, R., 1660, *New Experiments Physico-Mechanicall, Touching the Spring of the Air, and Its Effects*, Oxford: H. Hall.

Brunner, H.G., Nelen, M.R., Breakefield, X.O., Ropers, H.H. & van Oost, B.A., 1993, 'Abnormal behavior associated with a point mutation in the structural gene for monoamine oxidase A', *Science*, vol. 262, no. 5133, pp. 578–80.

Brush, S.G., 1965, *Kinetic Theory, Vol. 1, The Nature of Gases and of Heat*, Oxford: Pergamon Press.

Carey, S.W., 1961, 'Palaeomagnetic evidence relevant to a change in the Earth's radius', *Nature,* vol. 190, p. 36.

Curie, M., 1929, *Pierre Curie,* C. & V. Kellogg trans., New York, NY: Macmillan.

Descartes, R., (1644/1983), *Principles of Philosophy.* V. R. Miller and R. P. Miller (trans.), Dordrecht: The Netherlands: D. Reidel Publishing Company.

Feynman, R., 1964, *The Character of Physical Law,* BBC Video, http://research.microsoft.com/apps/tools/tuva/#data=3>, accessed 13 January 2019.

Gibbons, A., 2004, 'Tracking the evolutionary history of a "warrior" gene', *Science,* vol. 304, no. 5672, pp. 818–19.

Gilbert, G.N. & Mulkay, M., 1984, *Opening Pandora's Box: A Sociological Analysis of Scientists' Discourse,* Cambridge: Cambridge University Press.

Hess, H.H., 1954, 'Geological hypotheses and the Earth's crust under the oceans', *Proceedings of the Royal Society of London,* vol. 222, no. 1150, pp. 341–8.

Hooke, R., 1665/2003, *Micrographia,* Mineola, NY: Dover.

Houck, M.A., Gauthier, J.A. & Strauss, R.E., 1990, 'Allometric scaling in the earliest fossil bird, *Archaeopteryx lithographica',* *Science,* vol. 247, no. 4939, pp. 195–8.

Lea, R. & Chambers, G., 2007. 'Monoamine oxidase, addiction, and the "Warrior" gene hypothesis', *The New Zealand Medical Journal,* vol. 120, no. 1250, pp. 1–6, <www.researchgate.net/publication/6466626_Monoamine_Oxidase_Addiction_and_the_Warrior_Gene_Hypothesis>, accessed 24 January 2019.

Milne, C., 2011, *The Invention of Science: Why History of Science Matters for the Classroom,* Rotterdam: Sense.

Vine, F.J. & Matthews, D.H., 1963, 'Magnetic anomalies over oceanic ridges', *Nature,* vol. 199, pp. 947–9.

CHAPTER 3

# Constructivist and Sociocultural Theories of Learning

Russell Tytler, Joseph Ferguson, and Peta White,
Deakin University

## GOALS

**The goals for this chapter are to support you to:**

- Describe and give examples of students' conceptions in science, including alternative conceptions
- Distinguish between different theories of learning, including constructivist, social constructivist, sociocultural and representational perspectives
- Describe the main features of a multimodal literacy perspective on science learning and teaching
- Describe learning experiences that are emphasised in these different perspectives

**Australian Professional Standards for Teachers—Graduate Level:**

- Standard 1: Know students and how they learn (Focus areas 1.1, 1.2)
- Standard 2: Know the content and how to teach it (Focus areas 2.1, 2.2)

# INTRODUCTION

The purpose of this chapter is to connect theories and perspectives of learning with classroom practices that support learning. We take a historical journey through the past 50 or so years of research in science education and explain how some theories of learning have changed and developed. In particular, constructivist and sociocultural perspectives of teaching and learning are described and critiqued. We begin in the first section by exploring students' conceptions in science.

# STUDENT CONCEPTIONS IN SCIENCE

It is by no means easy for students to come to grips with significant scientific concepts such as energy, adaptation or chemical change. All teachers will have experienced the frustration of explaining a concept, in what they thought was the clearest possible way, only to be faced with expressions of mute incomprehension (or worse). They will also have experienced interesting and seemingly productive conversations in class, only to find on testing that their students didn't seem to have learned what was taught. How can learning scientific concepts be so difficult? How can we teach them in a better way?

Since the mid-1980s, a substantial body of research on learning in science has focused on the knowledge and ideas students bring with them to the classroom and how these affect what and how they learn. In this chapter, we refer to the knowledge and ideas that students have as *conceptions*. If students' conceptions are not consistent with the prevailing scientific view, we refer to them as *alternative conceptions*. The research on students' conceptions and alternative conceptions has helped us understand the problem that children can often emerge from a science course with very different understandings from those intended by the teacher. Further, even when students perform at a high standard on classroom tests, it has been found that they may display a range of very different understandings when asked to apply these ideas to other problems and contexts, especially out of school.

The research on conceptions (Duit 2009) has demonstrated how students come to our classrooms not as *empty vessels* waiting to be filled with information but with conceptions that can differ in important ways from those constructed by scientists. Many of these conceptions are based in everyday language that is at odds with the specialised language and ideas of science. For example, in everyday language we say that when the sun sets, it goes *down* below the horizon. From a scientific point of view, however, we know that the sun setting is a result of the *daily rotation of the Earth*. In some cases, alternative conceptions form useful prior knowledge that a teacher can build on with students. In other cases, students' alternative conceptions have proved surprisingly difficult to shift and can offer serious barriers to effective learning. A large number of alternative conceptions that interfere with intended learning have been identified across a range of science topics. We discuss some examples of these alternative conceptions below.

The first example is from physics. Students and many adults have conceptions of motion where force is thought to be a property of an object associated with motion (its *impetus*), rather than something that acts on an object externally to influence motion. Thus, when asked if there is a force on a golf ball flying through the air, an adult may answer: 'Well, as it's still going forward, I would have thought yes, the force of the hit is still with it. If there were no force, it would drop straight down.' Intuitively, it is quite understandable why many adults and children hold this view. However, from a scientific perspective, objects don't retain forces. The force from the club on the ball only lasts while the ball is in contact with the club.

The second example is from biology. A common alternative conception is that young children interpret animal behaviour in terms of the animal's wishes (a psychological view) and find it difficult to think of behaviour as having an adaptive function. Thus, a Year 3/4 child may say, in response to an observation that worms congregate in moist soil when given a choice: 'Because they might be dry, and they wanted to be wet'. When asked why Himalayan rabbits' fur turns white in winter, they may say: 'They want to turn white . . . so they can be different from other rabbits'. In response to the question 'why do plants have flowers?', the main responses selected by 7–8-year-old children are 'to make them look nice' or 'because bees need the pollen and nectar', whereas older children look for explanations focusing on how flowers form part of plants' survival adaptations that are intimately linked with the survival of pollinators.

The third example involves a frequently occurring alternative conception that heat is a substance rather than a form of energy, as scientifically understood. This can result in students running the concepts of temperature and heat together. Younger children with this alternative conception may think that if a cup of hot chocolate is divided, the temperature is halved. Secondary-school students may find it difficult to understand heat as thermal energy transferred between two systems at different temperatures. The scientific concepts of thermal energy, heat, and temperature are at odds with everyday usage of these terms.

Significant alternative conceptions often centre on concepts for which the common use of language differs from the scientific use, for example, *animal*, *energy*, *adaptation*, *living* and *heat*. This helps to explain why such conceptions can be extremely difficult to shift. In everyday life, a human being is not thought to be an animal but, from a scientific point of view, human beings are classified in the animal kingdom. There have been many studies that show alternative conceptions can persist despite carefully planned teaching, and often despite students being able to gain high scores on science tests. When a student is presented with a scientific idea that differs from previously held conceptions, they may accept it, reject it or accept it for the science class but continue to use their prior conceptions in their daily lives. Sometimes they will form a hybrid conception combining the two ideas. For example, some students may have the alternative conception that electricity is *used up* by a light globe when it is switched on. These students may find it difficult to understand the concept of electric current when they are learning about electricity in their science course. Thus, alternative conceptions have the capacity to interfere with intended learning in science and need to be acknowledged when planning teaching sequences. Chapter 4 in this book provides you with ideas about how you can do this when you are teaching science.

There has been ongoing debate concerning the nature and status of alternative conceptions. Are they coherent belief systems, mistakes of fact or judgement, or useful entry points into more powerful scientific conceptions? There are many terms used by researchers in this area that reflect different views, including misconceptions (mistaken beliefs), intuitive or naive ideas (unformed ideas) or alternative conceptions (different but valid ways of looking at the world).

# CONCEPTUAL CHANGE VIEWS OF LEARNING

Conceptual change views of learning are underpinned by the idea that learning involves complex changes to students' knowledge from alternative conceptions to scientific conceptions. From this perspective, the task of science teachers is not to simply insert new ideas into students' minds but to find ways of enabling them to undergo major shifts, or conceptual changes, in their knowledge structures. The conceptual change idea received a lot of support from researchers throughout the 1980s and 1990s (Posner, Strike, Hewson & Gertzog 1982).

Why should this issue matter for us as teachers? If we consider that teaching science concepts is a process of fundamental change, then it helps to explain why learning about animal behaviour or Newtonian physics is so difficult. We are managers of personal scientific revolutions in the minds of our students! It follows that we can't consider teaching as simply involving the clear explanation and demonstration of new ideas, but rather need to recognise students' alternative conceptions and be strategic in challenging them.

Should we view alternative conceptions as unhelpful, childish, and in need of eradication? A number of writers (for example, Treagust & Duit 2008) have argued that non-scientific conceptions can be useful as platforms from which more sophisticated ideas can spring, and they may persist to support the scientific view. Other writers have questioned whether students really are consistent in the way they use either alternative or scientific conceptions. Further, there is evidence to suggest that students do not abandon their alternative conceptions once they learn to operate with a scientific conception, but carry them alongside, to be used in situations where the scientific conception is difficult to apply. They can even use a number of conceptions together to provide different perspectives on the same event! Often, adult scientists will carry a range of views about animals or energy alongside their more sophisticated understandings.

## PERSONAL CONSTRUCTIVIST PERSPECTIVES

The research into children's conceptions raised questions about the nature of student learning. An individual, conceptual view of learning owed much to the child development theories of twentieth-century Swiss developmental psychologist Jean Piaget (1936), who viewed learning as arising from children's acting within their world. From this perspective, learning is viewed as the construction of personal meaning, and learning in the classroom is simply an extension of the same process. During the late 1980s and 1990s, these views were gathered under the more general label of *constructivism* or a *constructivist theory of knowledge*. In terms of education, a key insight of personal constructivist perspectives is that learners have the final responsibility for their own learning. Thus, a teacher can never learn for a student, and teaching is never more than the promotion of opportunities and support for learning. Constructivist teaching approaches from this period paid particular attention to students exploring phenomena and openly discussing their developing ideas, guided by the teacher, so that alternative conceptions were acknowledged and worked with.

Constructivism has had some vociferous critics. For example, some critics have argued that the view that students construct coherent *alternative frameworks* gives too much credence to students' ideas and leads to a downgrading of science understandings as *just another viewpoint* (Matthews 2002). Others question the effectiveness of constructivist teaching strategies given their time-consuming nature. Indeed, those advocating for constructivist approaches vary considerably in regard to the time they recommend that teachers spend exploring and negotiating understandings with students, as against directly representing the view of science.

The ground has shifted within the constructivist perspective. There is substantial critique of the earlier constructivist and conceptual change literature, pointing out the narrowness of this purely conceptual view of learning and the excessive focus on the learner at the expense of the teacher and classroom. Treagust and Duit (2008) reviewed the many changes that are now accommodated within conceptual change perspectives as a result of new research findings on learning, and propose a multiperspective view of conceptual change. This includes affective dimensions; views on the nature of science, including the role of modelling; and recognition of both evolutionary and revolutionary change processes, as well as of the role of multimodal representations in learning (Lemke 2004).

## SOCIAL CONSTRUCTIVIST PERSPECTIVES

Since the mid-1990s, there has been much greater interest in exploring learning as a social phenomenon, with a shift in focus from individual students' understandings to the way classroom environments support effective learning. A *social constructivist* position focuses our attention on the social processes operating in the classroom, by which a teacher promotes a community in which they *co-construct* knowledge with students. The aim of science education then becomes the establishment within the class of shared meanings. In a sense, social constructivist perspectives put the teacher back in the picture, compared with what many felt was a tendency within personal constructivist positions to write the teacher out of the learning process.

Consistent with this perspective, researchers such as Mortimer and Scott (2003) argue that the key to understanding effective science teaching and learning is classroom discourse: the pattern of teacher and student talk during science lessons. One such instance (Scott 1998) is a lesson in which Year 9 students were each given a nail and challenged to put it somewhere to rust. When students brought the nails back for display, the classroom discussion included a mix of open and exploratory sequences during which students contributed lots of ideas, and sequences where the teacher controlled the conversation more strongly. The ability to shift between these different discourse modes is an important aspect of effective teaching and learning.

## SOCIOCULTURAL PERSPECTIVES

Corresponding to social constructivist perspectives, there has been growing interest in theories of learning that give a more fundamental role to language and culture in the construction of knowledge—the way we think about the world. The ideas of twentieth-century Russian psychologist Lev Vygotsky (1962) have provided a framework to argue for the central role of discourses and communities in knowledge production. From a Vygotskian perspective, thinking and learning are *mediated* by language—that is, language is the tool through which we think.

The theoretical perspectives built around this idea of mediation are more broadly known as *sociocultural*. This term can be understood to correspond to *social constructivism* but does not limit its focus to classroom interactions. A sociocultural perspective takes the more fundamental position that knowledge and learning should be seen in terms of increasing access to, and competence with, the wider community of science. Learning is seen as a process of *enculturation*, involving increasing capacity to *participate* in scientific ways of talking and acting, rather than as the *acquisition* of mental structures that reside in our minds (Sfard 1998).

Learning about chemical reactions, for example, involves students learning about concepts such as bonding, equations and electron transfer using many different types of scientific languages, including text, models, diagrams and symbols. We refer to this bundle of different types of languages as *multimodal languages*. Moreover, students learn the experimental practices of chemistry, the history of the development of ideas related to chemical reactions, and the ways chemical reactions are applied in industry and the home.

These specialised multimodal languages of science act as *mediators* in conceptual learning—the specialised vocabulary, images, equations and grammars of description and explanation that are both the pathway to conceptual understanding and the way we express this understanding.

## SCIENTIFIC LITERACY AND REPRESENTATIONAL PERSPECTIVES

There is growing acceptance of scientific literacy as a fundamental aim of school science in preparing students for a future in which they can interpret and reason with the ideas of science (Roberts & Bybee 2014). Thus, learning science involves students gaining access to a range of subject-specific and general representational tools used by the scientific community to construct knowledge about the natural world. Doing science involves working with rich and multimodal representations, such as diagrams, models, simulations, graphs, tables and animations. These are powerful resources for speculating, reasoning, developing explanations, theory-building and communicating within the science community and beyond (Tytler, Prain, Hubber & Waldrip 2013). Becoming *literate* in science therefore involves being able to generate and coordinate a range of representational resources to work and think scientifically. For example, ideas such as *diversity* are understood through a range of representational practices, including drawings, food webs, dichotomous keys, naming conventions etc. (Tytler, Haslam, Prain & Hubber 2009). In the next sections, we describe two examples of types of activities where students are challenged to generate, coordinate and transform across representational modes to develop fluency in these literacy practices. These relate to drawing and simulations.

### Drawing

Drawing has always had a place of significance in the science classroom. Indeed, drawing is one of science's key modes of representation, such that generating and interpreting drawings is an

# THE ART OF TEACHING SCIENCE 3RD EDITION

important literacy. Recent research into the important role of visualisation in science (Gilbert 2005) has clarified the importance of drawing for the visual/spatial aspects of phenomena that are difficult to render in text.

Drawing has educational value as a means for students to *communicate* their pre-existing ideas to teachers and peers. By drawing their ideas, students can share their understandings with others and start to play with and refine these ideas. Teachers can make use of such drawings to get an understanding of the prior and developing knowledge of students and, in particular, to identify students' alternative conceptions that they may then need to work with to develop into ideas aligned with the accepted ideas of the discipline.

Drawing can also help students to *generate* new understandings. Through drawing, students can create new ideas by making visual and spatial claims about the phenomena of interest. Drawing should always be conducted in conjunction with other modes of meaning-making, such as discussion, and it is the translation between these different modes that can be particularly valuable for student learning. For example, Snapshot 3.1 shows drawings by two Year 7 students of the rotation of the Earth to explain why it is day in Melbourne when it is night in London.

## SNAPSHOT 3.1: Year 7 students using drawings to explain day and night

Ms Thornly noticed that some of her Year 7 students struggled to explain why it was night in Melbourne when there was a direct telecast of a Wimbledon tennis match held in London during the day. She set up an activity for the students where they used drawings, a torch, and a globe to help them develop a coherent explanation. The two pictures below show some of Ms Thornly's students' drawings on the left, and coordinating between the drawing and their torch and globe model on the right. Part of the value of drawing is that students are required to be selective in what they pay attention to, and represent, as they strive to ensure their drawings are visually and spatially representative.

Through a process of selection and abstraction, they are guided towards greater clarity and refinement of their ideas.

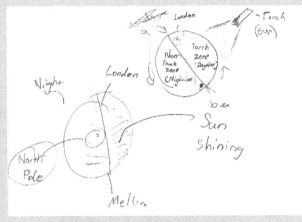

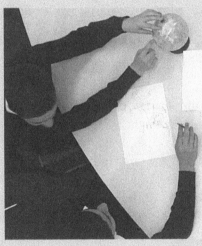

In serving an important role in reasoning, as illustrated by Snapshot 3.1, drawing can also facilitate both self-checking of ideas and collaborative learning among students (Ainsworth, Prain & Tytler 2011). By jointly constructing drawings, students can explore each other's ideas and coordinate these through their shared engagement with the drawings. Drawing in pairs is particularly effective when students are working with whiteboards and markers, where they are able to rapidly propose, share, and refine their developing ideas about, for example, the astronomical causes of the day/night cycle.

## Simulations

In considering multimodal literacy, it is hard to ignore the rapid development in the availability (often free and in open-source format) of digital simulations. The variety of software available is vast, and each offers something different when it comes to teaching and learning about scientific phenomena. The power of such simulations is that they are dynamic and interactive, and offer time sequencing to the visual/spatial affordance of diagrams and photographs. Snapshot 3.2 provides an example of a digital simulation for natural selection, a particularly difficult phenomenon for students to understand as they enter the classroom with many hard-to-shift alternative conceptions.

---

**SNAPSHOT 3.2:** A digital simulation for natural selection

Mr Franklin provided Year 10 students with a digital model that simulated the relationship between humans (and their genes), mosquitos and the malaria parasite, to assist their understanding of sickle cell anaemia. By interacting with this simulation, students were able to not only improve their understanding of the key natural selection concepts that determine the impact of sickle cell anaemia and malaria on different genetic populations, but also develop their ability to predict, observe and explain processes that underpin inquiry and discovery in science.

Through the use of such a simulation, students were able to see and sometimes hear the organisms—and even their genes—as they interacted with each other and changed over time. Further, the students could adjust the variables in the simulation—for example, speeding up and slowing down time, or introducing a new genetic mutation into the gene pool—and observe what resulted. Students could experiment in ways that would not be possible in the real world. They used the simulation to reason, work things out, and potentially develop their own, new ideas.

Simulations, such as the one described in Snapshot 3.2, enable students to interpret the output of models that come in various representational forms—such as graphs or frequency counts—and to understand the link between this output and the variables they are adjusting. Students need to be able to coordinate between these different forms of input and output if they are to utilise the simulation to creatively reason and develop a comprehensive understanding of the phenomenon. Again, the development of such a scientific literacy involves the active engagement of student reasoning across a variety of representational modes.

## SUMMARY OF KEY POINTS

So, where are we with our quest for a meaningful understanding of the learning of science? It seems clear that it involves students in some sort of shift in perspective from their existing understanding to a scientific understanding, and this can involve challenging their existing ideas. It also seems clear that this process is gradual and involves students learning to use both scientific and everyday ideas in a range of situations. Learning also involves the engagement of students in a process of shared meaning-making, guided by the teacher. Students need to move towards mastery of the discourses of science, including using language; developing ways of questioning and arguing, and linking ideas with evidence; and coordinating across multimodal representations and artefacts.

## DISCUSSION QUESTIONS

3.1 'They must have learned this! I distinctly remember teaching it to them!' How would you respond to such a statement?

3.2 Constructivist perspectives emphasise that responsibility for learning resides with the learner. What, therefore, is the role of the teacher? To what extent might it be appropriate or effective to *tell* students about science concepts?

3.3 There have been debates in the research community about

whether learning science is better viewed as *acquisition* or *participation*. Are these metaphors for learning necessarily opposed? In what senses might both have something to offer?

3.4 Students in secondary-school science need to become *literate* in reading texts that are complex, technical and have specialised grammars for describing scientific objects and time-sequenced processes. What do you think is involved as students translate such text into visual and time-sequenced modes, such as the drawing and simulation examples?

## REFERENCES

Ainsworth, S., Prain, V. & Tytler, R., 2011, 'Drawing to learn in science', *Science,* vol. 333, no. 6046, pp. 1096–7.

Duit, R., 2009, 'Bibliography–STCSE', *Students' and Teachers' Conceptions and Science Education,* <http://archiv.ipn.uni-kiel.de/stcse/>, accessed 13 January 2019.

Gilbert, J.K., 2005, 'Visualization: A metacognitive skill in science and science education', in J.K. Gilbert (ed.), *Visualization in Science Education,* Dordrecht: Springer, pp. 9–27.

Lemke, J.L., 2004, 'The literacies of science', in E.W. Saul (ed.), *Crossing Borders in Literacy and Science Instruction: Perspectives on Theory and Practice,* Newark, DE: International Literacy Association; Arlington, VA: NSTA Press, pp. 33–47.

Matthews, M.R., 2002, 'Constructivism and science education: A further appraisal', *Journal of Science Education and Technology,* vol. 11, no. 2, pp. 121–34.

Mortimer, E.F. & Scott, P.H., 2003, *Making Meaning in Secondary Science Classrooms,* Maidenhead: Open University Press.

Piaget, J., 1936. *Origins of Intelligence in the Child,* London: Routledge & Kegan Paul.

Posner, G.J., Strike, K.A., Hewson, P.W. & Gertzog, W.A., 1982, 'Accommodation of a scientific conception: Toward a theory of conceptual change', *Science Education,* vol. 66, no. 2, pp. 211–27.

Roberts, D.A. & Bybee, R.W., 2014, 'Scientific literacy, science literacy, and science education', in N.G. Lederman & S.K. Abell (eds), *Handbook of Research on Science Education, Vol. 2*, New York, NY: Routledge/Taylor & Francis Group, pp. 545–58.

Scott, P., 1998, 'Teacher talk and meaning making in science classrooms: A Vygotskian analysis and review', *Studies in Science Education*, vol. 32, no. 1, pp. 45–80.

Sfard, A., 1998, 'On two metaphors for learning and the dangers of choosing just one', *Educational Researcher*, vol. 27, no. 2, pp. 4–13.

Treagust, D. & Duit, R., 2008, 'Conceptual change: A discussion of theoretical, methodological and practical challenges for science education', *Cultural Studies of Science Education*, vol. 3, no. 2, pp. 297–328.

Tytler, R., Haslam, F., Prain, V. & Hubber, P., 2009, 'An explicit representational focus for teaching and learning about animals in the environment', *Teaching Science*, vol. 55, no. 4, pp. 21–7.

Tytler, R., Prain, V., Hubber, P. & Waldrip, B., (eds), 2013, *Constructing Representations to Learn in Science*, Rotterdam: Sense.

Vygotsky, L.S., 1962, *Thought and Language*, Cambridge, MA: MIT Press.

# CHAPTER 4

# Conceptual Change Teaching and Learning

David Treagust, Curtin University, Reinders Duit, Leibniz Institute for Science and Mathematics Education (IPN), and Hye-Eun Chu, Macquarie University

## GOALS

**The goals for this chapter are to support you to:**

- Distinguish between different types of conceptual change
- Describe and illustrate different approaches for teaching for conceptual change
- Describe and illustrate how you can know that student learning undergoes conceptual change

**Australian Professional Standards for Teachers—Graduate Level:**

- Standard 1: Know students and how they learn (Focus areas 1.1, 1.2)
- Standard 2: Know the content and how to teach it (Focus areas 2.1, 2.2)
- Standard 3: Plan for and implement effective teaching and learning (Focus areas 3.2, 3.3)

# INTRODUCTION

Research on teachers' and students' conceptions of science, and their roles in teaching and learning science, has become one of the most important research domains in education and has a strong history in Australia and New Zealand. As explained in the previous chapter, students come to secondary-school classrooms with varied life experiences that have allowed them to develop ideas and understandings that are often different from those of contemporary science. We refer to these ideas in this chapter as *pre-instructional conceptions*. A conceptual change approach involves the teacher taking students' pre-instructional conceptions into consideration and designing learning experiences that enable students to learn the new, scientific understandings. For science teachers, the findings from conceptual change research are important because school students have been shown to have many pre-instructional conceptions in the various disciplines of science. The research not only provides a rich resource about what those pre-instructional conceptions are, but also how instruction can be designed to maximise learning.

This chapter is divided into four parts. The first describes the main issues behind the notion of conceptual change; the second describes three different theoretical perspectives of conceptual change, with examples drawn from science-classroom research; the third provides a discussion of how teachers can engage students in science so that they may experience conceptual change; and the fourth and final part provides a summary of the key points.

# THE MAIN ISSUES BEHIND CONCEPTUAL CHANGE

There are eight main issues behind the notion of conceptual change:

1. Students are not simply passive learners but make sense of new information in terms of their previous ideas and experiences. This is the essential feature of the theory of constructivism (see Chapter 3).

THE ART OF TEACHING SCIENCE 3RD EDITION

2. Consequently, students attend science classes with pre-instructional knowledge or beliefs about the phenomena and concepts to be taught that are frequently not in harmony with science views and the teacher's intended instruction.
3. Students' knowledge is often fragmented. If this knowledge is to be built coherently, then students need to be intellectually engaged.
4. Students build their own knowledge. Recent studies on conceptual change emphasise the importance of the role of the learner, suggesting that the learner can play an active, intentional role in the process of knowledge restructuring.
5. In a general sense, conceptual change indicates learning pathways from students' pre-instructional conceptions to the science concepts to be learned.
6. Changes that lead to learning can be minor or major. There are two types of conceptual change, variously called weak knowledge restructuring—assimilation or conceptual capture—and strong/radical knowledge restructuring—accommodation or conceptual exchange.
7. The term conceptual change is used for learning when the pre-instructional conceptual structures of the learners are fundamentally restructured to allow a deeper understanding of the intended science concepts under consideration.
8. The term conceptual change has been given various meanings; change often has been misunderstood as being a simple exchange of pre-instructional conceptions for science concepts.

## DIFFERENT THEORETICAL PERSPECTIVES OF CONCEPTUAL CHANGE

For more than three decades, researchers have investigated students' pre-instructional conceptions and conceptual change in various science content areas, such as the electric circuit, force, refraction, energy, combustion, photosynthesis and respiration, chemical equilibrium and evolution (Duit & Treagust 2003). Through this research, it has become evident that to understand learning better we need to think about conceptual change from various theoretical perspectives. This chapter considers three of these theoretical perspectives: (1) an *epistemological* perspective, when students think about the status of their knowledge; (2) an *ontological* perspective, when students think about the nature of things in the world around them; and (3) an *affective* perspective, which considers how students feel about the knowledge and the learning process. In the following sections, we elaborate on and provide classroom snapshots to illustrate these three perspectives.

## An Epistemological Perspective

The best-known conceptual change model in science education is based on examining how students consider the status of their conceptual knowledge—that is, an epistemological perspective (Posner, Strike, Hewson & Gertzog 1982). In this conceptual change model, student dissatisfaction with a pre-instructional conception indicates it has *low status*—that is, the student doesn't think it is a helpful idea anymore. If a conception has low status, it then becomes possible for the teacher to introduce and increase the status of the scientific conception in the student's mind. We use the words *intelligible, plausible* and *fruitful* to describe the increasing levels of status of a conception. An intelligible conception is sensible if it is non-contradictory and its meaning is understood by the student; plausible means that, in addition to the student knowing what the conception means, the student finds the conception believable; and the conception is fruitful if it helps the learner solve problems related to the conception and answer new questions about the conception that the student might develop. The extent to which the conception meets these conditions is termed the status of a learner's conception. Ideally, teachers should aim for scientific conceptions to become intelligible, plausible and fruitful for their students. Conceptual changes may be permanent or temporary, and the higher the status of the conception, the more likely it is that conceptual change has taken place.

Sometimes, students can hold two or more conceptions at the same time. When competing conceptions are incompatible, two

THE ART OF TEACHING SCIENCE 3RD EDITION

things may happen. If the new conception achieves higher status than the pre-instructional conception, conceptual change may occur. If the pre-instructional conception retains higher status, conceptual change will not proceed for the time being. It should be remembered that a replaced conception is not forgotten, and the learner may wholly or partly reinstate it at a later date. Snapshot 4.1 provides an example of where an analogy used by the teacher of a Year 7 class helped to improve the conceptual status of a scientific explanation of mixtures and compounds.

**SNAPSHOT 4.1:** Learning mixtures and compounds from an epistemological perspective of conceptual change

Students have a conception of mixtures such as air, honey and yoghurt as being *pure substances* because in everyday language they are often labelled *pure* (Coştu, Ünal & Ayas 2007). To understand the meaning of pure, teachers can incorporate a hands-on activity involving two different coloured clay balls to help students distinguish essential differences between mixtures and chemical compounds. During the lesson, students are instructed to use yellow and blue modelling clay to make some yellow-coloured and blue-coloured balls to illustrate the conception of a mixture (sulphur powder and iron powder). In addition, students combine a yellow-coloured ball and a blue-coloured ball to form a *green* ball to illustrate the conception of a chemical compound (iron sulphide) (i.e. the conception is *intelligible*).

Next, students carry out laboratory experiments on mixtures and chemical compounds (e.g. actually using iron powder and sulphur powder) to compare the conceptions derived during the clay activity with the observations made in the real experiments (i.e. the new conception is *plausible*). Lastly, students may carry out further research using the internet and give a presentation about the conceptions in class (i.e. the new conception is *fruitful*).

## An Ontological Perspective

How a learner views the material world can have an impact on learning; such views of the material world are referred to as *ontology*—the ways in which different entities exist and how they are grouped depending on their behaviour (Chi, Slotta & de Leeuw, 1994). We can think about and ask ontological questions about scientific entities, such as: is it matter or is it a process? Is it concrete or abstract? Is it local or global? Scientists often understand scientific phenomena to be in different ontological categories when compared with many students' pre-instructional conceptions. Heat, for example, has various meanings in colloquial language. It may denote comparably high temperatures (for example, when it is claimed that the heat today is hard to bear) or something material stored in hot objects. In physics, heat is conceptualised as a flow of energy in transit from a hot object to a colder one due to the temperature differences—a process, not a material. Research has shown that conceptual change often involves a student rethinking the ontology of a scientific idea. For example, they might have to stop thinking of heat as a substance and start thinking of it as a process. Snapshot 4.2 provides an example of how an ontological perspective can help us understand conceptual change when secondary students learn about electric current.

---

**SNAPSHOT 4.2:** Learning about electric current from an ontological perspective of conceptual change

Students often have difficulty understanding the abstract nature of electric current and the concept of current conservation. Students should be informed that the concept of electric current is an abstract concept that is dependent on convection—that the flow of positive charge-carriers (instead of electrons) in a metallic wire is an idealisation and does not represent what happens in the real world (Wong & Chu 2017).

Lee and Law (2001) reported the usefulness of an ontological categorisation framework to promote conceptual change in the learning of basic electrical concepts with secondary-school students. Essentially, they found that students' conceptions of electric current often belong to the *matter* category. For example, some of the students in the Lee and Law study described electric current as being like a truck taking goods (energy) to customers (a light globe in a circuit). In this way of thinking, both the current (the truck) and the energy (the goods) are conceptualised as *matter* (a truck and goods are *things*). For a deeper understanding, teachers need to help students change the ontological status of their conception of electric current from *matter* to a *process*. For example, in the study by Lee and Law, students then did further experiments and participated in discussions in small groups until they came to explaining electric current as being like the *speed* of the truck, rather than the truck itself. While no analogy is perfect, this way of thinking helped the students to explain why a circuit with two globes has lower current that a similar circuit with only one globe. The current, like the speed of a truck, is slowed down more by two globes (the resistors) than one. This analogy has the potential to move students from thinking of electric current as matter (the truck) to something more akin to a process (speed).

## An Affective Perspective

Learning is never solely a cognitive concern; *affective* issues always play a significant role. Science teachers know very well that students' interests, enjoyment, willingness, intentions, needs and motivation for learning science are important issues to consider in the classroom, because they are indications of how students perceive the lesson being taught. These affective aspects of learning are the third perspective of conceptual change considered in this chapter. Some researchers argue that it is necessary to develop a unity between the cognitive and emotional dimensions so that emotions and cognitive outcomes have equal status in the lessons. This means that instruction should not only focus on developing cognitive issues (such as understanding concepts, principles and views of the nature of science) but also include affective variables, such as enhancing students' interests and motivation. Snapshot 4.3 illustrates the importance of students' mental state when learning about acids and bases.

> **SNAPSHOT 4.3: Learning about acids and bases from an affective perspective of conceptual change**
>
> Exploring students' mental states during the teaching and learning of acids and bases is important to facilitate conceptual change. Liu, Hou, Chiu and Treagust (2014) designed an instrument to measure Year 9 students' mental states, which consist of four categories: emotion (e.g. like or fear), intention (e.g. desire or want), internal mental representation (e.g. imagine or believe), and external mental representation (e.g. apply or express). Developing a student's internal mental representation may include using pictures to demonstrate the process of acid–base neutralisation. Developing an external mental representation may involve using the concepts of acid–base neutralisation to solve problems related to acids and bases.
>
> The findings from this study indicated that students' mental states are highly correlated with their achievement—high-achieving students had more positive emotions and intentions, and were good at internal visualisation and interpreting pictures. Lower-achieving students were not good at internal visualisation and were unable to interpret graphics and draw pictures. In short, students' mental states (emotion and intention) as well as students' mental representations of scientific conceptions do influence conceptual change.

## Multidimensional Perspectives on Conceptual Change

It seems obvious that taking into account only one of the three approaches to conceptual change may provide a limited understanding of student learning. Consequently, there are a growing number of multidimensional approaches to conceptual change that have promise for improving science teaching and learning. In brief, multidimensional perspectives on conceptual change that consider epistemological, ontological, and affective domains need to be employed to adequately address the complexity of the teaching and learning processes. Only such frameworks can sufficiently model the teaching and learning processes that exist in the classroom. Snapshot 4.4 provides an example of where a multidimensional perspective helped us to understand conceptual change learning in genetics.

---

**SNAPSHOT 4.4:** Learning about genetics from a multidimensional perspective of conceptual change

Venville and Treagust (1998) examined changes in Year 10 students' conceptions of genes during a ten-week genetics course. Data collected from student worksheets given before and after the course, lesson observations, recordings of classroom discourse and student interviews at the end of the course were interpreted using a multidimensional framework of conceptual change from epistemological, ontological and affective perspectives. From an epistemological perspective, students' conceptions were classified as being intelligible, plausible and/or fruitful. Students' ontological conceptions of genes developed from the idea that a gene is a passive particle passed from parents to offspring (a material), to being a more active particle that controls characteristics. However, the desired idea that a gene is a section of DNA that is a code for the transcription and translation of an amino acid (a process) did not become plausible for the majority of students. From an affective perspective, it was evident that even though the students stated that they enjoyed the genetics course and were observed to participate in classroom activities, they had less interest in the sub-microscopic explanatory mechanisms of genetics. They were not very interested in topics such as DNA structure, replication, transcription and translation, preferring to use simple Mendelian genetics to try to answer questions about their own physical characteristics. Overall, despite the intent of the teacher, the teaching approaches did not encourage a sophisticated conception of a gene in the minds of the majority of students.

# TEACHING FOR CONCEPTUAL CHANGE

In this section, we describe four ways in which teachers can enhance the opportunities for students to experience conceptual change: (1) being aware of students' conceptual frameworks; (2) using cognitive conflict, such as the Predict–Observe–Explain sequence; (3) using analogies; and (4) focusing on modelling and linking explanations at different levels.

## Students' Pre-instructional Conceptions

Many teachers are intuitively constructivist in their approach to teaching—for example, they want to be able to assist students in their learning, and they are aware of the importance of students' cognitive activity and observations. Being aware of students' pre-instructional understandings and how they impact on learning is an important first step to becoming an exemplary science teacher. This awareness opens teachers' minds; it helps them listen to their students, and it helps them to start thinking about ways that they can take their students' pre-instructional conceptions into consideration when planning and teaching.

## Using Cognitive Conflict

One way in which teachers can teach for conceptual change is to incorporate strategies into their teaching repertoires that overtly provide insights into students' pre-instructional understanding of the scientific phenomenon being examined. One such strategy is the

# THE ART OF TEACHING SCIENCE 3RD EDITION

> **SNAPSHOT 4.5:** Diagnosing pre-instructional conceptions in optics, and using them to plan teaching/learning
>
> Students can have unstable conceptions about how light travels in different contexts. As a result, they apply consistent alternative conceptions in one context (e.g. light propagation during night and day) but inconsistent alternative conceptions in a different context (visibility of luminous objects and non-luminous objects). The awareness that students' pre-instructional alternative conceptions may vary according to the nature of the topic in optics can help teachers plan which possible alternative conceptions to address in a particular lesson.
>
> To address context-dependent alternative conceptions, Chu and Treagust (2014) suggest providing students with a range of different optics situations with light rays to enable students to reflect on and apply the correct science concept in a variety of situations until their conceptual understanding becomes scientifically acceptable and context-independent. Solving problems in different situations by applying the same scientific concept helps students to generalise their understanding of the concept across the different situations.

Predict–Observe–Explain sequence, which is both a probe to expose students' pre-instructional knowledge and a teaching strategy. In this teaching strategy, students are presented with an event that may be an experiment or a demonstration and are asked to predict the outcome. They then conduct the experiment or observe the demonstration and make observations. Finally, students explain their observations in relation to their predictions. Sometimes the prediction and observation will be consistent, and other times they will not. When they are not consistent, we can say cognitive conflict has occurred because the students' predictions, based on their pre-instructional understanding, conflict with their observations. This is a very powerful strategy because it can make students become dissatisfied with their pre-instructional conceptions and lower their conceptual status, making the students more receptive to scientific explanations.

## Using Analogies

Science teachers use analogies to explain things to students; an example is when we say that a *lock and key* is an analogy for enzyme action. The target is the science concept—enzyme action; the analogy is the everyday objects of a lock and a key. There are different types of analogy, including verbal, pictorial, personal, bridging and multiple analogies. When the teacher provides verbal analogies in class, the students are left to work out the comparisons and conclusions about the target (in other words, the science concept) from the description of the analogy (Treagust, Harrison & Venville 1998).

From a teaching perspective, the use of analogies can enhance conceptual change learning since they open new perspectives and can be motivational in that, as the teacher uses ideas from the students' real-world experience, a sense of intrinsic interest is generated. The presentation of a concrete analogy facilitates understanding of abstract concepts by pointing to the similarities between objects or events in the students' world and the phenomenon under discussion. In addition, when teachers use analogies, this creates an increased awareness on the part of the teacher that they need to take students' pre-instructional conceptions into consideration when teaching. Despite the advantages and usefulness of analogies, using this teaching tool can cause incorrect or impaired learning. For example, the analogy may be unfamiliar to the learner. Moreover, if the students lack visual imagery, analogical reasoning or correlational reasoning, then the value of analogies may be limited.

## Using Models

While the macroscopic, observable chemical phenomena are the basis of chemistry, explanations usually rely on models of the submicroscopic behaviour of particles (Coll, France & Taylor 2005).

Indeed, the use of computer modelling programs or ball-and-stick models that students can handle and visualise has been shown to develop students' understanding of chemical compounds at the sub-microscopic level, and hence result in conceptual change. Like analogies, it is important that students are made aware of the limitations of models and the differences between the representations and reality.

The extensive and accepted process of using models for explanations has made the models appear as fact to many teachers and students. Research has shown that students often are unable to differentiate models from the scientific phenomenon that the model is being used to explain. Indeed, teachers and textbooks often provide students with representations of atoms and molecules as though they were real and factual. Research has shown that it is important for teachers to link different types of models, including symbolic representations such as chemical formulae and equations, with sub-microscopic representations such as ball-and-stick models (Gilbert & Treagust 2009).

It is important for science students to have a comprehensive understanding of the nature and role of models in science so that they can create models to express their own understanding of a science concept. Treagust, Chittleborough and Mamila (2002) investigated secondary-school students' understanding of the nature, role and purpose of models in science. Their data-collection instrument consisted of a scale with five factors: models as multiple representations, models as exact replicas, models as explanatory tools, uses of scientific models and the changing nature of models.

Most students recognised the usefulness of models as multiple representations and appreciated the changing nature of scientific models due to the changing nature of scientific knowledge. However, some students had conflicting ideas about scientific models due to holding the idea of a model as an exact replica of a scientific phenomenon. The findings suggest that if teachers guide students to develop an understanding of the role of models in making predictions, testing ideas, and other scientific ways of thinking, students will be able to use models as a tool of inquiry and enhance their learning of science.

## SUMMARY OF KEY POINTS

Teaching for conceptual change can be considered from an epistemological perspective (which indicates the status of students' conceptions), an ontological perspective (how students perceive the nature of scientific entities) and students' affective responses to learning (related to their interests, motivation, and attitudes to school and to science). Each of these vantage points is supported by a particular theoretical position. Teachers intend for students to learn the planned curriculum, but this does not always occur. With a focus on challenging students as they learn a new topic, conceptual change can take place by teachers: (1) being aware of students' conceptual frameworks; (2) using cognitive conflict, such as the Predict–Observe–Explain sequence; (3) using analogies; and (4) focusing on modelling and explicitly connecting different levels of representation.

## DISCUSSION QUESTIONS

4.1 Describe the three types of conceptual change and the ways you can identify them, based on students' responses to the teacher's questions or answers to questions in the textbook.

4.2 Describe at least three approaches to science lessons where you can teach to bring about conceptual change.

4.3 Why does a focus only on test scores not provide a complete picture of learning?

## REFERENCES

Chi, M.T.H., Slotta, J.D. & De Leeuw, N., 1994, 'From things to processes: A theory of conceptual change for learning science concepts', *Learning and Instruction*, vol. 4, no. 1, pp. 27–43.

Chu, H.-E. & Treagust, D.F., 2014, 'Secondary students' stable and unstable optics conceptions using contextualized questions', *Journal of Science Education and Technology*, vol. 23, no. 2, pp. 238–51.

Coll, R.K., France, B. & Taylor, I., 2005, 'The role of models and analogies in science education: Implications from research', *International Journal of Science Education,* vol. 27, no. 2, pp. 183–98.

Coştu, B., Ünal, S. & Ayas, A., 2007, 'A hands-on activity to promote conceptual change about mixtures and chemical compounds', *Journal of Baltic Science Education,* vol. 6, no. 1, pp. 35–46.

Duit, R. & Treagust, D.F., 2003, 'Conceptual change: A powerful framework for improving science teaching and learning', *International Journal of Science Education,* vol. 25, no. 6, pp. 671–88.

Gilbert, J.K. & Treagust, D. (eds), 2009, *Multiple Representations in Chemical Education,* New York, NY: Springer.

Lee, Y. & Law, N., 2001, 'Explorations in promoting conceptual change in electrical concepts via ontological category shift', *International Journal of Science Education,* vol. 23, no. 2, pp. 111–49.

Liu, C.-J., Hou, I.-L., Chiu, H.-L. & Treagust, D.F., 2014, 'An exploration of secondary students' mental states when learning about acids and bases', *Research in Science Education,* vol. 44, no. 1, pp. 133–54.

Posner, G.J., Strike, K.A., Hewson, P.W. & Gertzog, W.A., 1982, 'Accommodation of a scientific conception: Toward a theory of conceptual change', *Science Education,* vol. 66, no. 2, pp. 211–27.

Treagust, D.F., Chittleborough, G. & Mamiala, T.L., 2002, 'Students' understanding of the role of scientific models in learning science', *International Journal of Science Education,* vol. 24, no. 4, pp. 357–68.

Treagust, D.F., Harrison, A.G. & Venville, G.J., 1998, 'Teaching science effectively with analogies: An approach for preservice and inservice teacher education', *Journal of Science Teacher Education,* vol. 9, no. 2, pp. 85–101.

Venville, G.J. & Treagust, D.F., 1998, 'Exploring conceptual change in genetics using a multidimensional interpretive framework', *Journal of Research in Science Teaching,* vol. 35, no. 9, pp. 1031–55.

Wong C.L. & Chu, H.-E., 2017, 'The conceptual elements of

multiple representations: A study of textbooks' representations of electric current', in D.F. Treagust, R. Duit & H. Fischer (eds), *Multiple Representations in Physics Education*, Cham, Switzerland: Springer, pp. 183–206.

# PART 2
# IMPLEMENTING THE ART OF TEACHING SCIENCE

# CHAPTER 5
# Contemporary Science Curricula in Australian Schools

Vaille Dawson, The University of Western Australia, and Angela Fitzgerald, University of Southern Queensland

## GOALS

The goals for this chapter are to support you to:

- Understand the importance of school science education in Australia and the role of curriculum
- Understand the purpose of science-curriculum documents and how they can inform practice at a planning level
- Be familiar with the rationale, scope and sequence of the Australian Curriculum in science, including the opportunities in the general capabilities and cross-curriculum priorities

Australian Professional Standards for Teachers—Graduate Level:

- Standard 2: Know the content and how to teach it (Focus areas 2.1, 2.3, 2.5, 2.6)
- Standard 3: Plan for and implement effective teaching and learning (Focus area 3.2)

# INTRODUCTION

A quality education in science is a crucial outcome of schooling. All young people need a deep understanding of how the practice of science enables humans to make sense of the world around them. The knowledge produced by science allows us to solve problems and make informed, evidence-based judgements to improve our lives and those of others. For example, our understanding of science allows us to develop drugs to treat diseases, build telescopes to search the outermost parts of the universe, predict weather patterns and explain why certain chemicals react with each other in predictable ways. Many of the global problems facing humanity (for example, climate change and food, water and energy shortages) require science and technology-based solutions.

There are two key purposes of school science education in Australia. The first is to provide future scientists with a firm grounding in scientific concepts, skills and attitudes so that they have the background to continue with science study beyond the compulsory years of schooling. The second—and arguably the more important purpose—is to develop scientific literacy in all young people. Science teaching should promote the development of scientific literacy and assist students in the process of actively making informed decisions about science-based issues impacting on them at a public level and a personal level (Millar 2006).

If we consider that our young people will need to tackle a range of future issues at local, national and global levels, then it is crucial that the school science curriculum includes the necessary understandings, skills and values and be implemented in an engaging and inclusive way to enable students' development as scientifically aware and literate citizens. This chapter starts by unpacking what curriculum is before examining the science curriculum specifically and how it can be used to inform science learning and teaching practices. The intention of this chapter is to provide you with details and insights into curriculum in general, and the Australian science curriculum in particular, to assist you in being able to navigate these documents effectively. Ultimately, the intention is to support you in the development and implementation of meaningful science-learning experiences for your students.

## WHAT IS CURRICULUM?

The type of learning offered to students is dictated through curriculum documents. Before considering Australian science-curriculum documents, the term, *curriculum*, is defined and explained. A simple definition coined by Decker Walker, Emeritus Professor of Education at Harvard University, is that 'the curriculum refers to the *content* and *purpose* of an educational program together with their *organisation*' (2003, p. 5). The *content* of a curriculum refers to the components or topics. In science, there are typically knowledge and understanding aspects (for example, physics, chemistry, biology, earth science and astronomy concepts), process skills (for example, posing questions, collecting and analysing data and constructing arguments) and affective factors (for example, scepticism and valuing living organisms). The *purpose* of the curriculum refers to the aims or objectives and is usually linked to an overarching goal of preparing the next generation of young people to achieve their full potential, live fulfilling lives and participate fully in society. The *organisation* refers to the structure (for example, simple to complex understandings), scope (breadth of content) and sequence (order and timing of content). The purpose, organisation, and content of the Australian Curriculum in science will be described in detail later in this chapter.

There are different forms of curriculum, depending on the audience (Van Den Akker 1998). For example, and in brief, there is the *ideal* curriculum (underlying philosophy of the curriculum), the *formal* curriculum (mandated curriculum documents or frameworks), the *perceived* curriculum (curriculum as interpreted by teachers), the *enacted* curriculum (the teaching strategies used by teachers in the classroom), the *experiential* curriculum (learning activities experienced by students) and, finally, the *attained* curriculum (the actual learning by the students). Alignment across these various levels of curriculum is not always evident, as the things that students actually learn can be quite different from the ideal curriculum. It is important for teachers to keep this factor in mind, as they are the key people responsible for interpreting and enacting the curriculum in ways that both reflect its intention and make sense for their students.

## USING SCIENCE CURRICULUM DOCUMENTS

When you commence your first job as a beginning teacher, a question uppermost in your mind is likely to be, 'What do I actually teach these students?' You will most likely have a good sense of how to construct a lesson plan or sequence of lessons, but might feel uncertain about what content needs to be explored and where to access this information.

In some schools, especially larger ones, there may be well-documented teaching programs that set out a sequence of learning and teaching activities. Other schools may have little to draw upon. However, it can be difficult to pick up another teacher's program and use it without understanding why particular outcomes, learning activities or assessments are specified. It is a bit like following a knitting pattern without having a picture of the whole garment. Who knows what the final product will look like? You need to be aware of what your students might already know from primary school and what they will need to know by the time you have finished working together. The most important source of information about *what* to teach, and *how* and *why*, will be *formal* curriculum documents.

*Formal* curriculum documents are provided to teachers by government educational jurisdictions to help them to know *what* to teach and *why*. These documents may be supported by a syllabus that prescribes in greater detail *what* is taught and *how*. The curriculum documents help teachers to plan teaching programs and lessons, select curriculum resources, develop learning activities and assess students' learning. Science curriculum documents provide information about the sequence, breadth and depth of science learning at each year level. Typically, scientific concepts are revisited throughout the years of schooling so that students are exposed to similar concepts in increasing complexity as they progress. Although the terminology varies, the content areas of biology, chemistry, physics, and earth and space science, and the process areas of laboratory skills, scientific inquiry, nature of science and the role of science in society, are generally included in formal curriculum documents worldwide.

The *experiential* curriculum (in other words, the learning activities that students participate in) depends not only on the *formal* curriculum but also on a number of other factors, including:

- curriculum-support documents provided by the education sector (e.g. government, Catholic, independent);
- curriculum resources (e.g. laboratory equipment, textbooks, science garden, animals) available at the school;
- ICT resources and support (e.g. laptops, mobile technologies);
- technical support (e.g. laboratory technicians);
- the priority given to science compared with other curriculum areas in your school and state/territory;
- time allocation (e.g. single periods, block time);
- financial budget allocated to science in the school;
- teacher background, experience, expertise and interest;
- teacher beliefs about how science should be taught;
- student factors, such as achievement levels, aspirations, previous science experiences and attitudes to science; and
- community and parental expectations.

To summarise, *curriculum* provides big-picture information about what to teach and why, whereas *syllabus* enables the drilling down to provide greater detail about what to teach and how. Both curriculum and syllabus documents are drawn upon to inform the development of *unit* or *program* outlines, which unpack the content to be taught and provide a learning sequence, and the creation of *lesson plans*, which provide guidance on how content is delivered on a daily basis.

## THE AUSTRALIAN CURRICULUM IN SCIENCE

As of 2019, the Australian Curriculum: Science is fully implemented in government schools in its intended form in five of the eight states and territories—the Australian Capital Territory (ACT), the Northern Territory, Queensland, South Australia and Tasmania. The science-curriculum document is available in both a paper-based and a hyperlinked web-based version. The online version has functionality that allows users to search according to their needs (for example, specifying particular year levels or strands of science).

While all states and territories have endorsed the Australian Curriculum, not all have adopted it in its entirety. The states of New South Wales, Victoria and Western Australia each have their own version of curriculum documents for teachers in their state jurisdictions, guided respectively by:

- the New South Wales Syllabus (https://syllabus.nesa.nsw.edu.au/science/);
- the Victorian Curriculum (http://victoriancurriculum.vcaa.vic.edu.au/science/introduction/rationale-and-aims); and
- the Western Australian Curriculum (https://k10outline.scsa.wa.edu.au/home/teaching/curriculum-browser/science-v8).

These curricula encompass and are largely consistent with the Australian Curriculum, but have been contextualised to suit the setting or draw upon agreed aspects. The Catholic and independent education sectors in all states and territories work in a similar way, by linking to the Australian Curriculum within their own versions in ways that make sense in terms of their ethos, communities and students' needs. It should be acknowledged that education settings drawing on particular philosophical approaches to learning and teaching (for example, Montessori and the International Baccalaureate) use different curriculum guidelines and tend to not make direct links with the Australian Curriculum.

For the purpose of this chapter, and given its pivotal role in curriculum development and implementation regardless of location or jurisdiction, the Australian Curriculum: Science will be the focus for the remainder of this chapter. Drawing on Walker's (2003) definition of curriculum, introduced earlier in this chapter, the purpose, organisation and content of the Australian science curriculum are summarised below.

## Purpose

The Australian science curriculum describes the rationale and aims of school science education from Foundation (the year prior to commencing Year 1) through to Year 12. In the rationale, science is described as a 'dynamic, collaborative and creative human endeavour arising from our desire to make sense of our world through exploring the unknown, investigating universal mysteries, making predictions and solving problems' (ACARA 2018, Rationale). Linking back to the purpose of science education in schools as briefly explored in the introductory section of this chapter, this quote provides insights into the intentions of the science curriculum to support students in becoming scientifically literate. It aims to achieve this through the provision of a strong grounding in the conceptual understandings of science as well as scientific methodologies, and the development of critical and creative thinking skills that build students' capabilities to investigate the world around them.

Arising from these intentions, there are seven aims of the science curriculum across all year levels. They are summarised as:

1. an interest in science;
2. an understanding that science explains the living and non-living world;
3. an understanding of scientific inquiry;
4. an ability to communicate scientifically to a range of audiences;
5. an ability to solve problems and make informed, evidence-based decisions;
6. an understanding of historical and cultural contributions to science; and
7. a knowledge base in biological, chemical, physical and earth and space sciences.

The way the Australian science curriculum is organised, as explored in the next section, helps to explain how these intentions are realised.

## Organisation

The curriculum is organised into three interrelated *strands*: *Science Understanding, Science as a Human Endeavour* and *Science Inquiry Skills*. Together, these strands unpack the understandings, knowledge, and skills that learners need to develop a scientific understanding of their experiences and the world. Individually, each strand has a particular purpose, which will be briefly outlined. *Science Understanding* (SU) focuses on the content required to address the key ideas and skills of science and is situated within appropriate contexts for the learner (for example, year level, needs and settings). *Science as a Human Endeavour* (SHE) supports students in connecting with science as a way of knowing and doing, and highlights the role of decision-making and problem-solving in science, but in ways that take into account ethical and socially responsible practices and implications. *Science Inquiry Skills* (SIS)—see Chapter 8—enables students to develop the thinking and procedural tools needed to move towards deeper, more meaningful conceptual understandings of science, such as questioning, predicting, organising data, making sense of findings and ways of communicating their ideas and understandings.

Each of these strands is further divided into *sub-strands*. SU has four sub-strands, SHE is divided across two areas and SIS has been broken down into five parts. The sub-strands are described in more detail in the content section below, but essentially they build upon each other conceptually and in complexity across the years of schooling. It is intended that the strands are taught in an integrated way.

In addition to the strand and sub-strand structure inherent in the Australian science curriculum, there are six *overarching ideas* that are fundamental to science education. In particular, they highlight the key aspects of a scientific worldview and bridge understanding and knowledge dimensions across the science strands and sub-strands. The overarching ideas, with a brief description of what they cover, are:

1. patterns, order and organisation—recognising patterns in the world, along with ordering and organising science phenomena using meaningful scales of measurement (e.g. states of matter, the seasons, biological classification, sub-atomic particles);

2. form and function—form refers to the characteristics of an object/ organism, whereas function refers to how those characteristics impact on its use (e.g. biological adaptations, atomic structures, energy and matter flow, interaction of forces);
3. stability and change—understanding that some phenomena are stable over time, while others change (e.g. relationships between organisms, chemical reactions, building and erosion of mountains, impact of force);
4. scale and measurement—articulation of time and scale is important in the development of science understanding, as it provides a benchmark for comparisons (e.g. geological time, biodiversity, size of atoms, distances in space, quantum physics);
5. matter and energy—the ability to describe observations of and changes in phenomena using the terminology of matter and energy (e.g. matter recycling and energy flow, energy transfer and transformation, cellular respiration); and
6. systems—making sense of phenomena (including predicting what will happen) by exploring, describing and analysing systems (e.g. organ systems, carbon cycle, opposing forces, chemical reactions).

In examining the organisational aspects of the curriculum in greater detail, across all learning areas of the Australian Curriculum (science included), there are broad skills and behaviours that are considered important for all young people to achieve. These skills and behaviours are referred to as *general capabilities* and are embedded in the content of all curriculum areas. They are intended to provide opportunities to add richness and depth to student learning within the different key learning areas, which in this case is science. The seven general capabilities and examples of how they might be understood in reference to science learning and teaching are:

1. literacy—e.g. interpreting media articles, presenting claims, formulating hypotheses, using technical science vocabulary accurately and using language appropriate for the context and audience;
2. numeracy—e.g. measurement (use of formal units), representing data (tables and graphs), identifying patterns and trends in numerical data and the statistical analysis of data;

3. ICT competence—e.g. accessing information, representing science phenomena and using technology as a digital aid (i.e. creating animations and simulations) and for communicating science understanding;
4. critical and creative thinking—e.g. generating new or novel ideas and solutions, encouraging open-mindedness in making sense of the world and enabling active inquiry (e.g. predicting, speculating);
5. personal and social capability—e.g. taking the initiative, applying scientific knowledge to daily life, displaying curiosity, questioning and making informed decisions about issues that impact their lives;
6. ethical understanding—e.g. forming and making ethical judgements, understanding integrity in science, applying ethical guidelines and using scientific information to inform ethical decision-making processes; and
7. intercultural understanding—e.g. appreciating the contribution of different cultural perspectives to science knowledge, being aware of culturally diverse ways of making sense of the world and demonstrating cultural sensitivity in relation to some areas of debate in science.

Finally, while we are still thinking about curriculum organisation from a bigger-picture perspective, there are three *cross-curriculum priorities* that need to be included in all learning areas, including science. The inclusion of these priorities stems from the *Melbourne Declaration* (Ministerial Council on Education, Employment, Training & Youth Affairs [MCEETYA] 2008), a statement and commitment from all state and territory governments that led to a set of goals to ensure high-quality schooling for all young Australians. This included the development of a curriculum, from which the Australian Curriculum arose, which is relevant, contemporary and engaging for students. From this declaration, three key areas were identified and intended to be interwoven through the curriculum for the benefit of individuals and Australia collectively, as they draw on regional, national and global components to enrich and enliven learning.

The cross-curriculum priorities in brief are:

1. Aboriginal and Torres Strait Islander histories and cultures—provision of opportunities to deepen knowledge and understanding through the elements of identity and living communities by drawing on insights from three key ideas: country/place, people and culture;
2. Asia, and Australia's engagement with Asia—building on and extending regional connectedness by developing an understanding through three key concepts: Asia and its diversity, achievement and contributions of the peoples of Asia and Asia–Australia engagement; and
3. sustainability—with a focus on more sustainable patterns of living, there are three underlying conceptual areas to connect with in terms of how humans interact with each other and their environments: systems, worldviews and futures.

Within each curriculum area, icons are used to indicate opportunities to develop or apply one or more of these cross-curriculum priorities as a way to enhance the learning of a particular topic or content. It is worth noting that not all content descriptors within the Australian science curriculum lend themselves to a connection with a priority area, and that they are only identified when relevant. There are, however, greater opportunities to link with many, if not most, of the general capabilities on a more regular basis.

## Content

### *Foundation to Year 10*

As identified previously in this chapter, the science curriculum from Foundation to Year 10 comprises the three interrelated strands of *Science Understanding, Science as a Human Endeavour* and *Science Inquiry Skills*. Each strand is further divided into sub-strands. For example, in Years 7 to 10, *Science Understanding* is divided into four sub-strands—biological, chemical, earth and space, and physical sciences. Figure 5.1 summarises the strands, sub-strands and key concepts in the Australian science curriculum.

**FIGURE 5.1:** Strands, sub-strands and key concepts of the Australian Curriculum: Science

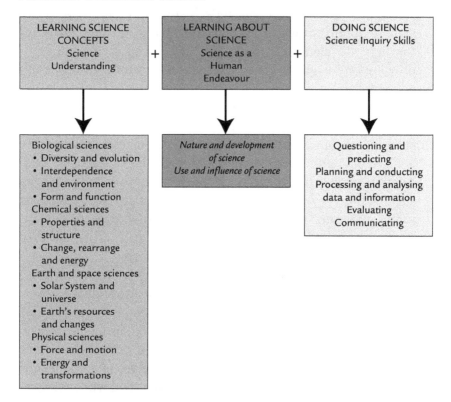

For each year level from Foundation to Year 10, there is a *year level description*, a *year achievement standard* and a number of annotated *work samples*. These work samples provide evidence of student learning in relation to the required achievement standard and illustrate satisfactory, above satisfactory and below satisfactory student achievement. This is intended to assist teachers in making judgements about the quality of their students' achievement. There are also *content descriptions* for each of the sub-strands, which identify key conceptual understandings and knowledge. *Elaborations* associated with each content description provide further insights and examples of the content to be addressed. Although these terms may initially seem confusing, they are used consistently throughout the curriculum documents and will become familiar through regular use.

In developing and implementing quality science-learning opportunities at a secondary level, it is useful to understand the science-education approaches many students would have experienced during their primary schooling. From the outset, it is important to recognise that primary teachers are educated to be generalists rather than (content) specialists, as is the focus in secondary contexts. This means that their initial teacher education has equipped them to teach across all learning areas and develop significant pedagogical expertise. While primary teachers might not feel entirely confident about their level of science knowledge at times, they have an in-depth understanding of how to foster the conditions required to promote quality science-learning practices in their classrooms (Fitzgerald & Smith 2016). These practices include developing a questioning mind and the ability to work collaboratively, gathering evidence through use of the senses, and connecting science with the students' lived experiences. Science learning in primary classrooms is often experienced through the lens of inquiry-based approaches (for example, as used to scaffold the *Primary Connections* (Australian Academy of Science [AAS] 2018) resources) and connected with overarching topics or issues (for example, sustainability, water, diversity). Making links with the community and relevant expertise (for example, parents, scientists, researchers) to enhance what is happening in science lessons is also a common practice adopted by primary teachers (Smith et al. 2018).

### Years 11 and 12

In the Australian Curriculum: Science, there are four science subjects: biology, chemistry, physics and earth and environmental science. The content of each subject aligns closely with the current senior secondary subjects of biology, chemistry and physics as it is offered in all states and territories, and earth and environmental science as offered in Western Australia and New South Wales. Psychology is taught as a science subject in Years 11 and 12 (earlier in some instances) in the Australian Capital Territory, the Northern Territory, South Australia, Tasmania, Victoria, Western Australia and, as of 2019, Queensland. Human biology is taught as an additional science subject in Years 11 and 12 in Western Australia. Each of the subjects is divided into four units (one per semester across the two years of study) and the content is organised under the same three strands as the Foundation to Year 10 science curriculum— *Science Understanding*, *Science as a Human Endeavour* and *Science Inquiry Skills*. At the end of Year 12, students complete an external examination that contributes to an Australian Tertiary Admission Ranking (ATAR) for university admission.

## SUMMARY OF KEY POINTS

This chapter describes the purpose of science education and argues that a quality curriculum is essential to develop the next generation of scientists and to ensure all Australians have a high level of scientific literacy. The purpose, organisation and structure of a curriculum are discussed, and details of the Australian science curriculum, including aspects of the content, are described. Although the Australian Curriculum documents may initially seem daunting, it is important to realise that support is available from state curriculum bodies, education sectors, professional associations and colleagues.

## DISCUSSION QUESTIONS

5.1 Visit the website of the Australian Curriculum (www.australiancurriculum.edu.au). Select a year level, strand, sub-strand and science-content description. Look at the elaborations to assist you to identify three learning activities that you could use in teaching this part of the curriculum.

5.2 Consider a unit of work on human-body systems to be taught in Year 9 science. What opportunities might there be to integrate some of the general capabilities into this learning experience? What connections could be made to one or more of the cross-curriculum priorities?

5.3 Identify a contemporary issue in your community (for example, single-use plastics) and investigate the ways in which it might connect with the strands and sub-strands in the Australian

Curriculum: Science. How might you leverage this real-world problem to create a meaningful science-learning and teaching opportunity?

## REFERENCES

Australian Academy of Science (AAS), 2018, *Primary Connections— Curriculum Resources,* <https://primaryconnections.org.au/curriculum-resources>, accessed 13 January 2019.

Australian Curriculum, Assessment and Reporting Authority (ACARA), 2018, *Australian Curriculum: Science,* <www.australiancurriculum.edu.au/f-10-curriculum/science/>, accessed 13 January 2019.

Fitzgerald, A. & Smith, K., 2016, 'Science that matters: Exploring science learning and teaching in primary schools', *Australian Journal of Teacher Education,* vol. 41, no. 4, pp. 64–78.

Millar, R., 2006, 'Twenty first century science: Insights from the design and implementation of a scientific literacy approach in school science', *International Journal of Science Education,* vol. 28, no. 13, pp. 1499–1521.

Ministerial Council on Education, Employment, Training and Youth Affairs (MCEETYA), 2008, *Melbourne Declaration on Educational Goals for Young Australians,* Carlton: Author.

Smith, K., Fitzgerald, A., Deefholts, S., Jackson, S., Sadler, N., Smith, A. & Lindsay, S., 2018, 'Reinvigorating primary school science through school–community partnerships', in D. Corrigan, C. Buntting, A. Jones & J. Loughran (eds), *Navigating the Changing Landscape of Formal and Informal Science Learning Opportunities,* Cham, Switzerland: Springer, pp. 87–103.

Van Den Akker, J., 1998, 'The science curriculum: Between ideals and outcomes', in B.J. Fraser & K.G. Tobin (eds), *International Handbook of Science Education,* Dordrecht, The Netherlands: Kluwer, pp. 421–47.

Walker, D.F., 2003, *Fundamentals of Curriculum: Passion and Professionalism,* 2nd ed., Mahwah, NJ: Lawrence Erlbaum Associates.

CHAPTER 6

# Planning in Secondary-School Science

Donna King and Reece Mills, Queensland University of Technology

## GOALS

**The goals for this chapter are to support you to:**

- Understand the benefits of planning in secondary-school science
- Design a science-teaching program that uses constructivism as a referent
- Plan and prepare lessons that support a learner-centred approach to teaching and learning science

**Australian Professional Standards for Teachers—Graduate Level:**

- Standard 3: Plan for and implement effective teaching and learning (Focus areas 3.1, 3.2, 3.3, 3.4, 3.5)

## INTRODUCTION

Planning is an important part of learning to be a secondary-science teacher. Effective planning requires teachers to design logical and coherent learning experiences that engage and challenge students.

This chapter outlines methods of planning secondary-science units and lessons based on a constructivist framework. While constructivism comprises a family of theories (see Chapter 3), they all have in common the centrality of the learner's activities in creating meaning. In this chapter, constructivism will be used as a referent (Tobin 2012) for planning teaching sequences that give students opportunities to construct knowledge through individual and group activities. Important steps in the planning process will be highlighted, such as the consideration of students' pre-instructional knowledge, recognition of the variety of teaching and learning strategies available and the inclusion of ongoing assessment.

Planning for teaching science in secondary schools requires three levels of consideration. Firstly, at the macro-level, broader planning occurs at the whole-school level. Secondly, at the meso-level, unit plans are developed for a particular topic and year level. Thirdly, at the micro-level, lesson planning occurs. This chapter discusses these three levels, including examples or snapshots of teachers' planning documents to highlight the differences between the levels.

# WHOLE-SCHOOL PLANNING

The first planning document that science teachers use in their schools is the science curriculum or syllabus, which is the mandatory document devised by a government body associated with the relevant state or territory authority. Nationally, we have the Australian Curriculum, Assessment and Reporting Authority curriculum (ACARA 2018), which is mandated across Australia. A detailed explanation of the Australian Curriculum: Science is presented in Chapter 5.

## Science Curriculum Whole-school Plan

Teachers use the ACARA curriculum document for the first broad, macro-level planning, where core science content applicable to specific student year levels is obtained. Once the curriculum

THE ART OF TEACHING SCIENCE 3RD EDITION

document has been scrutinised, a school science curriculum, or *whole-school plan*, is developed. This document includes content, pedagogy and assessment linked to achievement standards and school policies. In larger secondary schools, it is often the responsibility of the head of science to coordinate the planning of the curriculum with the teachers for each year level.

The whole-school plan ensures all concepts are addressed and directs teachers to the topics and key ideas they will address when planning units of work. Generally, the whole-school plan is developed in specific year levels and incorporates the sequential development of science concepts from each of the various science-knowledge areas (or strands) mandated by the syllabus. Snapshot 6.1 presents a section of a school's science-curriculum plan for Year 8. At a glance, any teacher of Year 8 science in that school can see the topics, strands and content descriptors that they will include in their units of work and lesson plans.

---

**SNAPSHOT 6.1:** A section of a Year 8 whole-school curriculum plan

The table below shows an example of part of a plan over a time period of approximately 4–5 weeks. This is what suits a particular school and is not a definitive plan to be followed. It is an exemplar to show how such planning can be accomplished. In this plan the school has opted to spend more time on chemical sciences than the other substrands of the *Science Understanding* strand. This may not suit all schools.

| Unit Name | Strand | Content Descriptors |
|---|---|---|
| Science is Matter | Chemical sciences | • Properties of the different states of matter can be explained in terms of the motion and arrangement of particles |

| What is a Reaction? | Chemical sciences | • Differences between elements, compounds and mixtures can be described at a particle level<br>• Chemical change involves substances reacting to form new substances |
|---|---|---|
| Cells and Systems | Biological sciences | • Cells are the basic units of living things; they have specialised structures and functions<br>• Multicellular organisms contain systems of organs carrying out specialised functions that enable them to survive and reproduce |
| Energy to Burn | Physical sciences | • Energy appears in different forms, including movement (kinetic energy), heat and potential energy, and energy transformations and transfers cause change within systems |
| How are Rocks Formed? | Earth and space sciences | • Sedimentary, igneous and metamorphic rocks contain minerals and are formed by processes that occur within Earth over a variety of timescales |

There are many aspects of a whole-school curriculum plan not included in Snapshot 6.1 (for example, aims and rationale, specific objectives, school assessment policy and recommendations for catering for diverse learners). The school's context and culture, available resources and needs of the community must be considered when developing a science curriculum (see Chapter 5). Although schools are required to adhere to the prescribed syllabus, they have the freedom to choose their pedagogical approach and underlying theories of teaching and learning. While not every science teacher in the school may choose the same pedagogical approach, recent research in science education supports a learner-centred approach using constructivism as a referent for practice. Most science educators agree that such a referent encourages the 'active participation of students in the construction of knowledge' rather than students reconstructing knowledge provided by the teacher or a textbook (Gil-Pérez et al. 2002, p. 561).

## PLANNING UNITS OF WORK

A unit of work is a series of science lessons that teaches the concepts in a topic outlined in the science curriculum. This is the *middle picture* or meso-level for planning to teach science in secondary classrooms. Prior to planning the unit, the teacher needs to become familiar with the content, decide on the pedagogical approach that will underpin the learning experiences and identify opportunities for gathering information about the students' learning. To help teachers sequence the learning experiences, there are a number of teaching/learning models that can be used in the planning process. These models help teachers structure the lessons into phases and order activities appropriately. Chapter 7 describes Bybee's (2006) 5E model that can be used for planning a sequence of teaching and learning activities. Models vary in the number of steps or phases utilised. Teachers generally choose the model that is most suitable for their approach to teaching and learning.

Another model has three phases: Orientating, Enhancing and Synthesising. This three-phase approach is designed to orientate students to the problem or phenomenon to be explored, enhance students' understanding of the problem or phenomenon through science inquiry, and synthesise their learning through students' demonstration of what they have learned. Some teachers prefer to use only three phases in the planning of interactive science units and lessons. Although these two models (5E and three-phase) have been

PLANNING IN SECONDARY-SCHOOL SCIENCE 89

described as a linear sequence of steps, there may be *toing and froing* between the various steps as teachers and students revisit stages to reinforce students' learning.

Flexibility and creativity can be incorporated in the stages or phases of the unit plan through innovative pedagogical approaches that provide a wide variety of learning experiences for students. Planning the unit gives teachers opportunities to choose innovative approaches to teaching science, such as problem-based learning (a problem to be solved structures the learning) or context-based learning (a real-world context is central to the learning). Each of these approaches is further elaborated below.

## Problem-based Learning Approach

Problem-based learning (PBL) focuses on a problem to be solved using a science-inquiry approach. The problem may be localised to an area surrounding the school (for example, North Queensland and the Great Barrier Reef):

> Scientists are trying to sustain the long-term health and resilience of the Great Barrier Reef. One problem they are addressing is maintaining the water quality for the sustainability of the coral reefs and ecosystems. One of the main water-quality issues is the increasing concentration of sediment, nutrients and contaminants entering coastal waters in run-off from agricultural, industrial and urban land uses. You are hired by the Great Barrier Reef Marine Authority to write a report about the health of the Great Barrier Reef. The report should include an analysis of the water-quality tests conducted during field work on the school tour. A recommendation is to be made about the sustainability of the Great Barrier Reef.

In such a way, the students are required to design an open inquiry (see Chapter 8) that provides sufficient data to answer the problem that is posed. The teacher structures the unit of work around the problem, supporting students with the design of the inquiry, the experimental work and the analysis of data.

## Context-based Learning Approach

A context-based approach is when the *context* or *application of the science to a real-world situation* is central to the teaching of the science. In such a way, the science concepts are taught on a *need-to-know* basis—that is, when the students require the concepts to understand the real-world application further. While a context-based approach contains characteristics that are similar to PBL approaches, it is not identical to them. In context-based chemistry, for example, students may be required to investigate a project such as the water quality of their local creek, or the context may be centralised around a local shipwreck (for example, *Pandora*—the name of a shipwreck off the North Queensland Coast) where gas laws that affect scuba divers and the process of the ship rusting can be explored (King, Bellocchi & Ritchie 2008). Such projects are central to the context-based unit, connect with students' real worlds and may be student-driven to a significant degree.

## An Integrated STEM Curriculum Approach

Recently, there has been a national interest in STEM (science, technology, engineering and mathematics) education. While there are a variety of definitions for this term, one representation defines STEM as a continuum starting with the separate disciplines of science, technology, engineering and mathematics at one end, moving through multidisciplinary (students learn concepts and skills separately in each discipline in reference to a theme), onto interdisciplinary (students learn concepts and skills from two or more disciplines) and finally ending with transdisciplinary, where students undertake real-world problems or projects applying knowledge and skills from two or more disciplines (Vasquez, Sneider & Comer 2013).

One example of an integrated interdisciplinary STEM unit developed by a school in Brisbane was to provide an extension course for high-achieving Year 9 students interested in a career in engineering and/or IT. The unit was designed to address advanced concepts in digital and design technology, with practical application of concepts in mathematics and science through a PBL approach. For example, students designed and developed a number of complex STEM projects, such as programming drones and designing web pages, bridges and a Ferris wheel. Planning creative and innovative STEM units is becoming necessary to afford students the opportunity to develop 21st century skills. This is discussed more fully in Chapter 14.

## The Planning Process

While there are many ways to plan a unit, teachers generally begin with a list of objectives, specific outcomes and/or key concepts obtained from the syllabus document. The documents in various Australian states and territories may use different terms for *outcomes* (for example, standards, frameworks or descriptors). The next step is to decide on a teaching/learning model that will maximise learning and engagement. Snapshot 6.2 provides a sample unit plan for a Year 9 science class.

When planning a unit of work, teachers access a vast range of resources, including curriculum documents and support materials, multimedia resources such as YouTube and the internet, student textbooks, software, television shows, excursion sites, professional science-teacher associations, colleagues' knowledge and previous science programs. With advances in digital media resources, teachers and students can create their own learning resources for use in their classrooms. For example, in research conducted by one of the authors of this chapter, middle-school students used an iPad application to construct a stop-motion animation to explain the scientific processes that occur at tectonic-plate boundaries (Mills 2017). Good unit plans are working documents that evolve and change as teachers meet the emerging needs of their students. Annotations can be recorded on the unit plan throughout the course of the unit to help the teacher reflect and improve the plan for the next time the unit is taught (Preston & Van Roy 2007).

**SNAPSHOT 6.2:** A contextualised approach to the Year 9 Science (ten-week) Environmental Unit Plan: monitoring the health of Spring Creek

This environmental-science unit adopted a context-based approach to teaching science using the 5E model (see Chapter 7) to structure the teaching sequence. The unit required students to complete a guided inquiry (see Chapter 8) that assessed the health of the local creek (Spring Creek). Students conducted water-quality investigations, analysed primary- and secondary-data sources, and wrote a scientific report that could be communicated to the local community via local government authorities. The report included a summary of the data derived from the water tests, an evaluation of the water quality of Spring Creek based on scientific evidence and a summary of environmental issues affecting the water quality. On each visit to the creek, the groups rotated through activities, including an animal-population study, plant study, soil sampling, drawing a site map, water sampling, water testing and pollution study. The table below shows the Unit plan in detail.

| Objectives | Specific Outcomes | Key Concepts |
| --- | --- | --- |
| • Promote greater interest and hence engagement in science via the use of a context-based approach<br>• Provide students with scientific skills, such as investigation skills<br>• Promote ways of thinking that foster improved scientific literacy | Students will:<br>• Understand factors that affect the environment and specific ecosystems<br>• Evaluate and explain the effects of anthropogenic factors on water quality and ecological systems<br>• Analyse and evaluate data to draw conclusions | • Biotic and abiotic factors<br>• Interactions—food webs/food chains (revision)<br>• Roles in webs (e.g. decomposers)<br>• Habitats<br>• Populations and communities<br>• Natural cycles<br>• Human impacts on ecosystems, including historical land use |

- Afford students opportunities to work collaboratively with their teacher to direct their own learning and develop their own course of work

- Explain the relationships between adaptations/variations of organisms within a specific habitat

- Responsible environmental decision-making
- Adaptations
- Changes in ecosystems
- Water quality analysis

## ACARA Curriculum Links

*Science Understanding*

*Biological sciences: Ecosystems consist of communities of interdependent organisms and abiotic components of the environment; matter and energy flow through these systems* (ACSSU176)
*Chemical sciences: Chemical reactions are important in both non-living and living systems and involve energy transfer* (ACSSU179)

*Science Inquiry Skills*

Questioning and predicting: ACSIS164

Planning and conducting: ACSIS165, ACSIS166

Processing and analysing data and information:

ACSIS169, ACSIS170

Evaluating:

ACSIS171, ACSIS172

Communicating:

ACSIS174

*Science as a Human Endeavour*

*People use scientific knowledge to evaluate whether they accept claims, explanations or predictions, and advances in science can affect people's lives, including generating new career opportunities* (ACSHE160)

Assessment: Students write a report to the local council about the health of the creek, including the analysis of data collected at the creek.

## Breakdown of Unit: Key Questions

| Water Quality | Ecology | The Environment |
|---|---|---|
| What is meant by the term *water quality*? | How do you determine if something is living? | What is an environment? |
| How can we determine the quality of water? (i.e. what tests can be done?) | Can the location in which the organism is living have an effect on the organism (and vice versa)? | What are some major types of environments? |
| What factors affect water quality? | Why are animals living in different habitats not the same? | What are natural cycles, and why are natural cycles important? |
| Are all sources of water (e.g. creeks, rivers) the same? | Is the number of organisms living in an area important? | Can the environment as a whole be affected by the organisms (including humans) living within it? |
| Can human activity affect the water quality of a creek? | Are all of the organisms in a habitat in some way linked (or important) to each other? | |

## Assessment (Summative)

Report on the water quality of Spring Creek, including:

- a site map
- a glossary of key terms
- data collection based on weekly creek visits
- a food-web diagram of organisms identified at the creek
- reflective entries; and
- an interpretation of data and summary of water quality.

### Phase 1: Engage

Students are introduced to the context: the students are considered environmental scientists who have been appointed by Spring Creek Senior High School to monitor the health of Spring Creek. They will develop a *road map* (or *mind map*) for the unit that will determine the direction they will follow for the completion of the task. This will be a teacher-facilitated, whole-class discussion with key questions serving as prompts to elicit prior knowledge.

### Phase 2: Explore

Students will make their first visit to the creek, where they will record observations and formulate questions about the environment and the testing site (bridge near scout hall). Students will be afforded opportunities to use the water-quality analysis equipment. Questions generated from this visit will be addressed in the subsequent lesson in class, identifying what students don't know and what they need to know. The road map will be revisited to allow students opportunities to add questions or ideas to further direct the unit.

### Phase 3: Explain

Weekly visits to the creek will continue, during which students collect the data they need to complete the investigation and begin to determine the health of Spring Creek. When the students demonstrate a *need-to-know* situation, the teacher will guide their learning through appropriate student-centred learning activities (e.g. laboratory activities on water-quality testing will help students understand the water-quality parameters used in the determination of the health of Spring Creek). Information through web-based resources will be accessed when appropriate.

## Phase 4: Elaborate

Students apply the knowledge they have gained of the creek system throughout the unit to draw conclusions about the health of Spring Creek and its related ecology. The assessment item (final report) will provide direction for this phase but will not be the major focus. Extension will be made from the work the students have completed on the creek to other creek/river environments, with a focus on the possible impacts of human activities on those systems. An appreciation of human effects on environments may translate to larger-scale (state, national and global) approaches to environmental and resource management, leading to improved scientific literacy.

## Phase 5: Evaluate

Students reflect on their learning, new understandings and the new skills they have developed. Reflective entries in student learning logs are completed. Students are encouraged to reflect on how they can apply their knowledge to other areas of science, the school community, and their daily lives.

## Learning Experiences

- Student-directed learning
- Case study
- Group work
- Whole-class and small-group discussion
- Student research
- Problem solving
- Practical (i.e. hands-on) investigation and experimentation
- Reflective learning

# LESSON PLANNING

Once the unit overview is written, the individual lesson plans can be created. This is an important step for beginning teachers, since it enables the timing, flow and sequence of activities to be planned. Similar to curriculum plans and unit plans, there are many ways of designing a lesson plan. Templates exist for pre-service and beginning teachers that provide a structure for planning. Generally, teachers modify an existing template to suit their individual needs and the requirements of school policy.

The first step in lesson planning is to determine the intended outcome or achievement standard using the unit plan that was written from the current syllabus mandated by ACARA.

The second step is to determine the key scientific concept that will be explored in the lesson. This is generally presented in one or two simple sentences. Two examples are given below:

1. There are three different states of matter (i.e. solid, liquid and gas).
2. Forces are pushes, pulls and twists.

The key scientific concept states simply and clearly the one main scientific idea you intend students to learn from the lesson. Starting with one key concept enables beginning teachers to focus their planning.

The third step requires a plan of the teaching and learning sequence through the design of learner-centred activities. This step allows a timeframe to be allocated to various parts of the lesson, and the planning of necessary resources. The chosen activities for the lesson will provide the basis for the ongoing assessment for your class. Assessment is discussed in detail in Chapter 9. In broad terms, assessment is information about a students' learning. Since assessment, outcomes, key concepts and the teaching-learning activities are all interrelated, planning the lesson involves a constant interplay between all of these aspects.

An example of a lesson plan from a Year 9 environmental-science unit is presented in Snapshot 6.3. This example occurs in the

# THE ART OF TEACHING SCIENCE 3RD EDITION

**SNAPSHOT 6.3:** Year 9 Environmental Science lesson plan on energy flow into and out of an ecosystem via the pathways of food chains and food webs

This continues from the Unit plan exemplar in Snapshot 6.2 to show how this can be translated into a single lesson plan. Again, the table below is an example, and is not intended to be a definitive format. Every school is likely to have their own preferred format, but if not, this can be used as a template to guide your planning.

| Key Learning Area: Science | Lesson Topic: Energy flow into and out of an ecosystem via the pathways of food chains and food webs | Science *Understanding:* In ecosystems, organisms interact with each other and their surroundings | Time: 45 minutes |
|---|---|---|---|
| Year 9 | | | |

### Learning Outcomes Strand: Biological Sciences

By the end of this lesson, it is expected that students will:

- understand how energy flows into and out of an ecosystem via the pathways of food webs, and how it must be replaced to maintain the sustainability of the system; and
- be able to construct food chains, food webs and energy pyramids to show the direction of the flow of energy.

### Prior Knowledge

- Consumers and producers (Year 8)
- Food webs and chains discussed at the creek while observing the interactions in the creek system

# PLANNING IN SECONDARY-SCHOOL SCIENCE

*Key Concept(s):* A food chain shows how each living thing gets its food. Interconnected food chains form a food web. Energy pyramids show the direction of the flow of energy.

| Resources for Students | Resources for Teachers | Safety |
|---|---|---|
| • Journals, laptops | • Video of animals taken at the creek<br>• Activity of food web in envelopes<br>• Cards with animals and plants for energy-pyramid activity | • Laptops used safely—opened on clean desks |

**Introduction** (5 minutes):
- Students brainstorm animals and plants seen at the three previous creek visits.
- Recorded in their journal, and teacher will record these on the computer projected onto the screen.
- Teacher asks students which animals may be eaten by other animals on the board and which animals may eat plants, and links them using inspiration software.

**Body** (35 minutes):

- Teacher asks students to form groups and decide which of the examples on the board are food chains and which are food webs.
- A whole-class discussion, and a class definition of food chains and food webs is recorded on the interactive whiteboard.
- Terms such as first-, second- and third-order consumers are discussed.
- Teacher shows a video recorded at the creek of animals and asks students to predict a food chain for each (e.g. water-glider insect, crow, carp fish, turtle, butterfly).
- Teacher discusses food chains and food webs for a variety of animals and plants that are in the creek system highlighted in the video.
- Students are split into groups and given cards with a variety of plants and animals found in creek systems. They design an energy pyramid for an ecosystem that classifies the animals and plants found in the envelope as first-, second- or third-order consumers.
- Students examine the distribution of biomass in the ecosystem, and pose questions and hypothesise about the possible impacts of changes to the populations.

**Conclusion** (5 minutes):

- Whole-class discussion on the possible food webs that have been created.
- Teacher reiterates the key concepts learned through whole-class questioning, checking for student understanding.
- Teacher asks students to hand in their final energy pyramid for formative assessment.
- Students are reminded to look for evidence of these food chains and food webs and to discuss energy flow at the next creek visit.

**Assessment:** Energy pyramid created by students, students' responses to questions and discussion, students' questions.

**Evaluation:** Did students achieve the intended outcome(s)? What could be improved? How could I plan this better next time?

There are three stages to this lesson: an introduction, a body and a conclusion. In the introduction, students' prior knowledge is obtained. The body of the lesson involves an interactive activity, where students work in groups. Finally, during the conclusion the teacher sums up the intended outcomes of the lesson, formatively assessing students' understanding through questioning. Effective teachers use a variety of teaching strategies in their lessons. At the end of the lesson, the teacher can evaluate or reflect on students' learning by asking: did students achieve the intended outcome(s)? What could be improved? How could I plan this better next time?

*Explain* phase of the 5E model in the unit plan and represents one of the many styles for presenting a lesson plan.

## Health and Safety

Often, science lessons involve work that requires teachers to plan the health and safety aspects of the lesson very carefully. When constructing your lesson plan, always include the health and safety requirements for the lesson, since your students' wellbeing must be your first priority. For example, in the Year 9 environmental-science unit, the creek visits required the teacher to explain carefully the students' expected behaviour at the creek. They recorded the health and safety requirements in their journals prior to the first creek visit.

Health and safety are important considerations for lessons both inside and outside the classroom. Often, science lessons involve laboratory activities that need to be prepared carefully. Think about the basic steps of the activity, and record any potential hazards in the lesson plan. Check with a laboratory technician or an experienced teacher if in doubt about potential hazards. Allocate time for explaining the health and safety requirements to the students prior to the activity. As a beginning teacher, it is important to remember that your students' health and safety is part of your duty of care and legal responsibility.

## SUMMARY OF KEY POINTS

Planning for the teaching of science in secondary schools requires three levels of planning: macro (whole-school planning), meso (unit planning) and micro (lesson planning). Teachers who adopt a learner-centred approach—using constructivism as a referent—plan for eliciting students' pre-instructional knowledge, design interactive activities that challenge and engage students in the learning of key concepts, and conclude with a summary and assessment of what has been learned. Reflecting on whether students achieved the intended outcome(s) is the last stage in effective planning.

## DISCUSSION QUESTIONS

6.1   What are the benefits of planning in secondary science?
6.2   What does it mean to use constructivism as a referent when planning secondary-science lessons?
6.3   How do effective teachers improve their practice in secondary-science classrooms?

## ACKNOWLEDGEMENTS

The environmental-science unit examples came from a project funded by a Queensland University of Technology early-career research grant and conducted with a Year 9 science class and their teacher, Evan Winner. The Year 8 unit examples were summarised from the units of work at Pimlico Senior High School in Queensland. The example STEM unit was designed by a Brisbane teacher, Bradley Nielsen. Thank you to Dr Christine McDonald, who read earlier versions of the original chapter and provided constructive feedback.

## REFERENCES

Australian Curriculum, Assessment and Reporting Authority (ACARA), 2018, *Australian Curriculum: Science,* <www.australiancurriculum.edu.au/f-10-curriculum/science/>, accessed 27 April 2018.

Bybee, R.W., Taylor, J.A., Gardner, A., Van Scatter, P., Carlson Powell, J., Westbrook, A. & Landes, N., (2006), *BSCS 5E Instructional Model: Origins and Effectiveness. A Report Prepared for the Office of Science Education, National Institutes of Health.* Colorado Springs, CO: BSCS.

Gil-Pérez, D., Guisasola, J., Moreno, A., Cachapuz, A., Pessoa De Carvahho, A.M., Martínez Torregrosa, J., Salinas, J., Valdés, P., González, E., Gené Duch, A., Dumas-Carré, A., Tricárico, H. & Gallego, R., 2002, 'Defending constructivism in science education', *Science & Education*, vol. 11, no. 6, pp. 557–71.

King, D., Bellocchi, A. & Ritchie, S., 2008, 'Making connections: Learning and teaching chemistry in context', *Research in Science Education*, vol. 38, no. 3, pp. 365–84.

Mills, R., 2017, 'Representing earth science concepts using slow-mation: Influences of middle school students' conceptual change', unpublished PhD thesis, Queensland University of Technology.

Preston, C. & Van Rooy, W., (2007), 'Planning to teach primary science', in Dawson, V., Venville, G. (ed), *The Art of Teaching Primary Science*, Sydney: Allen & Unwin, pp. 87–107.

Tobin, K., 2012, *The Practice of Constructivism in Science Education*, New York, NY: Routledge.

Vasquez, J., Sneider, C. & Comer, M., 2013, *STEM Lesson Essentials, Grades 3–8: Integrating Science, Technology, Engineering, and Mathematics*, New York, NY: Heinemann.

# CHAPTER 7
# Principles of Effective Science Teaching and Learning

Denis Goodrum, University of Canberra

## GOALS

The goals for this chapter are to support you to:

- Use knowledge of scientific literacy and student-learning theory to understand what makes teaching strategies effective
- Adopt an inquiry-based approach to teaching, including the 5E model
- Organise student teams and develop specific strategies for inquiry-based teaching

Australian Professional Standards for Teachers—Graduate Level:

- Standard 2: Know the content and how to teach it (Focus areas 2.1, 2.2)
- Standard 3: Plan for and implement effective teaching and learning (Focus areas 3.1, 3.2, 3.3, 3.4, 3.5)
- Standard 4: Create and maintain supportive and safe learning environments (Focus areas 4.1, 4.2)
- Standard 6: Engage in professional learning (Focus area 6.2)

## INTRODUCTION

The purpose of this chapter is to provide some simple and practical advice on how to maximise the quality of teaching, which will result in better learning by your students. To understand the evolving development of teaching strategies, it helps to appreciate the influence of two significant forces that have emerged in recent years.

The first issue to consider is why science is taught in our schools. In previous years, the prevailing view was that school science was necessary for the initial preparation of scientists or science-related careers. Notwithstanding the importance of this consideration, today educators generally believe that the purpose of teaching science in our schools is to promote scientific literacy. In simple terms, scientific literacy refers to the extent to which people are able to use science in their daily lives. This shift in focus has had a profound impact on what we teach and how we teach.

The second major influence on teaching approaches revolves around the developing understanding of how people learn science. Chapters 3 and 4 explain in detail the current ideas on learning and the factors that affect learning. While there is much unknown about learning, the research of the past 50 years has shown the limitations of previous teaching practices. Present views on learning provide some valuable insights into the types of teaching strategies educators need to employ to provide opportunities that will result in more meaningful learning by students.

## WHAT IS SCIENTIFIC LITERACY?

There is widespread agreement within the education and broader community that the purpose of science education is to develop scientific literacy. According to the authors of the national review of Australian science teaching and learning (Goodrum, Hackling, & Rennie 2001), scientifically literate people:

- are interested in and understand the world around them;
- engage in discussions of science matters;

- are sceptical and questioning of claims made by others about science matters;
- can identify questions, investigate, and use evidence to conclude; and
- make informed decisions about the environment and themselves.

These attributes inform the type of learning expected from the compulsory years of schooling. For this learning, it is important for a teacher to be able to relate learning to a real-world context that is meaningful for the student. Obviously, students who seek occupations in science-related fields would pursue their interest in post-compulsory studies. All students, however, have the right to a science education that enables them to feel confident and able to deal with the scientific issues that impact on their lives.

If you believe in a science education that promotes the development of scientific literacy, then there are some expectations about the way the science is taught. Many of these expectations are embedded in what is called in this chapter an *inquiry-based approach*. Table 7.1 outlines some of the changes required to teaching when there is a commitment to inquiry-based teaching. If you are committed to inquiry-based teaching, there should be less emphasis on memorising the names of scientific terms and more emphasis on learning broad concepts that can be applied to new situations. But there will still be some scientific terms that are useful for a student to know and apply. Chapter 8 provides an outline of different types of science inquiry. In this chapter, however, I generally refer to a guided inquiry-based approach.

## SUPPORTING STUDENT LEARNING

A teacher's understanding of how students learn affects the way in which they teach. In previous years, the transmission model of learning influenced teaching. In this model, it was believed that the mind of a student was empty and the role of the teacher was to fill it with scientific facts and principles. Teaching was equated with telling. This teacher-telling or didactic approach became entrenched

# THE ART OF TEACHING SCIENCE 3RD EDITION

**TABLE 7.1:** An outline of inquiry-based teaching

| Inquiry-based teaching requires more emphasis on: | Inquiry-based teaching requires less emphasis on: |
| --- | --- |
| • science being interesting for all students | • science being interesting for some students |
| • studying a few fundamental concepts | • covering many science topics |
| • content that is meaningful to the student's experience and interest | • theoretical, abstract topics |
| • guiding students in active, extended student activity | • presenting science by talk, text and demonstration |
| • providing opportunities for discussion among students | • asking for recitation of knowledge |
| • groups working cooperatively to investigate problems or issues | • individuals completing routine assignments |
| • some open-ended activities that investigate relevant science questions | • activities that demonstrate and verify science content |
| • learning broader concepts that can be applied in new situations | • memorising the name and definitions of scientific terms and facts |
| • learning science actively by seeking understanding from multiple sources of information, including books, internet, media reports, discussion and hands-on investigations | • learning science mainly from textbooks provided to students |
| • assessing learning outcomes that are most valued | • assessing what is easily measured |
| • assessing understanding and its application to new situations, and skills of investigation, data analysis and communication | • assessing recall of scientific terms and facts |
| • ongoing assessment of work and the provision of feedback that assists learning | • end-of-topic multiple-choice tests for grading and reporting |

in our school system, along with a related content-based testing regime. Even today, some secondary-school teachers are influenced by the simplicity of this approach, despite all that is known about how students learn.

The prevailing view of learning, explained in previous chapters, is that people construct meaning using their prior knowledge and any new information they encounter. Learning is an active process. Learners make sense of their world by developing meaningful constructions between what they know and the new experiences that change what they know. Learning is therefore a continual incremental process of comparing, testing and adapting. To learn new ideas and skills takes time, which varies with individuals. The inquiry-based approach reflects the current understanding of how students learn and outlines some important teaching principles that have a profound impact on the way teaching occurs.

## Explore Before Explain

Unfortunately, some teachers explain scientific ideas to students with no context or experiential base for the students. The impact of such explanations is minimal. For a scientific explanation to be effective, a teacher must first create or tap into experiences upon which the explanation is based. Such an approach has a stronger chance of providing meaning to the student.

There are many ways teachers can provide experiences or help students relate to previous experiences. The most common approach is to provide hands-on activities that allow students the opportunity to inquire and investigate. For example, if a person is to develop an understanding of floating as a concept, they need to have experience with objects that float and objects that sink, or with sinking objects that could be made to float. Through questioning, discussion and explanation, the ideas associated with floating can be developed from the direct hands-on experiences of the student.

# THE ART OF TEACHING SCIENCE 3RD EDITION

## Recognising Pre-instructional Knowledge and Experience

Research shows that all students come to any learning situation with some preconceived ideas. These ideas and experiences have an impact on how and what students learn. A teacher needs to not only discover the pre-instructional ideas held by students but also know how to build on this understanding.

There are a number of simple strategies a teacher can use to identify the ideas or experiences students have. One approach, at the beginning of a new topic, is to ask students to write a sentence or two (or draw a picture) to describe their initial understanding of the new concept. For example, in introducing a unit on energy, students could be asked to write a simple sentence containing the word energy and then answer the question, *What is energy?* Another approach is to pose a problem, perhaps using a picture as a stimulus. Students could, as a class or in small groups, discuss possible solutions. For example, Allan said he got his energy from sleeping, but John said he got his energy from food. Who is right?

As a general principle, a teacher should always allow time to revise the previous lesson before starting a new lesson. This could be as simple as a quick three-question quiz at the beginning of the lesson. Not only will this settle the class and prepare them for work, but the students' responses will also give insights into what they remember and understand from the previous lesson.

## Ensuring Student Involvement

Students need to be interested and engaged if they are to learn. Good teachers continually attempt to spark curiosity by relating learning to current events or personal experiences. The experiences and events provide context and serve as *hooks* on which students can hang new learning and ideas. For example, a recent television show might provide the basis for raising an issue related to the given topic. Creative teachers are effective in using popular activities and events to illustrate teaching ideas.

Hands-on activities enhance student understanding. For example, to understand the idea of electrical current or voltage, teachers need to provide opportunities for students to play with batteries (dry cells) and light globes. The more personal the concrete involvement, the greater the potential for learning.

## Encouraging Student Discussion

In previous years, it was believed by some that the quietness of a teacher's class was a measure of teaching quality. Today, educators realise that quietness is not necessarily correlated with learning. This does not diminish the importance of classroom-management skills, but the significance of student discussion in facilitating learning is much more appreciated.

As students attempt to construct meaning and understanding, they need to test and verify their thoughts by discussing them with their peers and their teacher. By chatting about their ideas in small groups or as a class, students can refine and adjust the conceptual pictures they create in their minds. Ideas need to be related to evidence, and views need to be justified. This does not mean that teacher explanation is not important. It is, but it needs to be used judiciously for maximum impact. In an effective classroom, there is a balance between teacher explanation and student discussion.

The other important skill a teacher needs to develop is the skill of summarising the ideas generated from student discussion in a coherent manner. A whiteboard summary of these ideas is a good way to provide worthwhile notes for students. In developing this summary, a teacher can challenge and refine possible alternative conceptions or inaccurate information.

## Developing Conceptual Understanding

Intellectual rigour is an important issue in learning. Many science educators believe that rigour is measured not by the amount of scientific facts that are memorised but by the depth of conceptual understanding. There is a difference between learning for memorisation and learning for understanding. If you understand a concept, you can apply this understanding to a new situation. Many present-day curriculum documents outline learning outcomes in terms of developing levels of conceptual understanding rather than lists of science content to be covered.

## The Role of Questions and Questioning

In traditional lessons, the driving force of teaching is teacher explanation. In inquiry-based teaching, the main engine for facilitating learning is the use of questions and discussion. Teachers need to develop an effective questioning technique to be successful.

To improve your questioning technique, use the following simple but powerful skills.

- *Ask a balance of broad and narrow questions.* Broad questions such as 'What do you observe about this flower?' and 'Why are the parts of a flower arranged as they are?' stimulate thinking among students. In traditional classes, narrow or closed questions usually dominate, and these are mainly used to challenge students to recall information. In a discussion, there are occasions when there is value in the teacher focusing a student's thinking with a narrow question. Unfortunately, many teachers only ask narrow questions. In inquiry-based lessons, it is better to have a balance of questions that range between broad and narrow.
- *Allow for sufficient wait time.* Wait time is the time that you, as a teacher, are willing to wait for students to answer a question. Research strongly indicates that if you allow three seconds or so, students will learn better. This time provides the opportunity for student reflection and comparison. If a student answers quickly, you should allow another three seconds. Hence, students will be able to think further about the question. Remember that you, as the teacher, control the wait time, not the students.
- *Use evaluation-free responses.* To develop a better inquiry atmosphere in a class, it has been suggested that it is better to avoid comments such as 'Good boy', 'Great answer' and 'Well done'. Rather, responses are accepted or rejected on available evidence. By using an *evaluation-free* style of responding to students, a more normal discussion results. For example, 'That's interesting. I can see how it connects to what we were talking

about' or 'Tell me why do you think that? I haven't thought of that before. Did anyone else think the same or different?' This approach encourages independent thought and inhibits the common classroom game called *guessing what the teacher thinks*. In this game, praise is bestowed on students who are successful in reading the teacher's mind rather than thinking for themselves.

- *Listen*. A good teacher is a good listener. By listening to a student's response, you attempt to understand the thinking behind the answer and, as a result, can ask more thoughtful and effective follow-up questions.

A useful resource for learning more about questioning and opportunities for practice is *Effective Questioning: A Stimulus for Professional Discussion* (Druhan & Goodrum 2011). This resource is found on the Science by Doing website at www.sciencebydoing.edu.au.

# WHAT IS A USEFUL TEACHING MODEL?

To help translate ideas about learning into classroom action, various authors have devised teaching/learning models that suggest how teachers can effectively organise their science lessons. These models tend to emphasise aspects of the previously described principles. While there is a similarity about the models, the differences reflect the varying degrees of emphasis on the principles. To illustrate, the 5E model is described here.

## The 5E Model

The 5E model (Bybee 1997) is a simple model that is commonly used in Australia. It consists of five distinct but interconnected phases.

1. Engage    The interest of students is captured through a stimulating activity or question. Students have the opportunity to express what they know about the

|  | unit topic or concept so that they can make connections between what they know and the new ideas being introduced. |
|---|---|
| 2. Explore | Students explore problems or phenomena through hands-on activities, using their own language to discuss ideas. This exploration provides a common set of experiences that allow the new ideas to make sense. |
| 3. Explain | After they engage with and explore experiences, both explanations and scientific terms are provided to students to help them develop their ideas. |
| 4. Elaborate | Students apply what they have learned to new situations. They have discussions using the newly acquired language to clarify their understanding. |
| 5. Evaluate | Students evaluate what they have learned and learning is assessed. |

While this simple model works effectively in the primary-school setting, the case is different for secondary-school science. In secondary science, learning activities are often better arranged in a more cyclical way rather than the linear progression indicated here. For example, students may go through several cycles of Explore, Explain and Elaborate before moving on to Evaluate. This is due to the increased complexity of scientific concepts covered in the secondary years. Individual activities within a unit do not need to follow the whole 5E sequence. Sometimes an activity focuses on one phase, although commonly more will be involved.

## Curriculum Resources

Some curriculum resources have an embedded teaching model. The Australian Academy of Science has developed two programs—Science by Doing and Primary Connections—that use the 5E model to structure learning activities. Science by Doing is a comprehensive online program for Years 7 to 10 that is available free to all Australian teachers and students, and is supported by professional-learning digital modules. These resources can be found at www.sciencebydoing.edu.au, while resources for Primary Connections can be found at www.primaryconnections.org.au.

# HOW MIGHT I BRING THESE IDEAS TO LIFE IN A CLASSROOM?

## Structuring an Inquiry-based Lesson

One of the major ideas intrinsic to this chapter is that students learn more effectively from activity and experience than from listening to teacher explanation. These activities may involve hands-on science inquiry (see Chapter 8), discussions and information research. Some teachers believe that in moving from teacher-centred to student-centred learning, the teacher has less of a role to play in the student activity. However, the opposite is true. The teacher in student-centred or inquiry-based learning needs to structure situations in which students can learn more effectively through questions and relevant comments.

All activities in an inquiry-based lesson proceed through three simple phases:

1. Introduction
2. Activity
3. Conclusion.

Within any lesson, this sequence may be repeated more than once.

1. Introduce the activity or investigation (brief).
   - Capture the interest of students by
     - relating to personal experiences;
     - asking provocative questions;
     - relating to the previous lesson;
     - using an engaging demonstration;
     - relating to television, film or a recent event.
   - Outline the activity, explaining any necessary advanced organisation.

- Explain the equipment arrangements.
- Outline time and outcome expectations.
2. Student activity (main time allocation).
   - Assist groups or individuals with materials and the activity.
   - Discuss ideas with groups and individuals, challenging them to think more deeply about what they are doing.
3. Conclude activity with discussion (adequate time needs to be allowed).
   - Students share the results of their activity.
   - Use questioning to help students summarise the main ideas.

It should be noted that the last phase is by far the most difficult, even for experienced teachers. Commonly, not enough time is allocated to this phase. Practice and planning are the key to honing one's skills in concluding lessons effectively. Examples of activity lessons structured in this manner are provided in the Science by Doing resource titled *Inquiry-based Teaching: A Stimulus for Professional Discussion* (Goodrum & Druhan 2011a).

## Cooperative Learning and Group Work

Working in a group or team enables students to share their experiences and to consider different points of view and solutions to a problem. Cooperative learning is an approach that encourages students to work together to help them learn better. Teams develop the social skills of sharing leadership, communicating, building trust and managing conflict. These skills take time to develop, but the longer-term benefits are worth the effort.

The benefits of cooperative learning include:

- More effective learning—students learn more effectively when they work cooperatively rather than when they work individually or competitively. They have a better attitude towards their schoolwork.
- Improved self-confidence—all students tend to be more successful when working in groups, and this builds their self-confidence.
- Better class management—when students work in cooperative

PRINCIPLES OF EFFECTIVE SCIENCE TEACHING AND LEARNING 117

groups, they take more responsibility for managing the equipment and their behaviour.

- Teaching students how to work cooperatively—even though in most classes there is a balance between individual, team and class activity, students still need to work together regularly to develop effective team-learning skills.

Use the following ideas in planning cooperative learning with your class.

- Assign students to teams rather than allowing them to choose partners.
- Vary the composition of each team. Give students opportunities to work with others who might be of different ability level, gender or cultural background.
- Allow sufficient time for each team to learn to work together successfully.
- If the number of students in your class cannot be divided into teams of equal numbers, form groups of smaller rather than larger sizes. It is more difficult for students to work together effectively in larger groups.
- Some research suggests that for lower secondary students a group size of four with a gender balance provides a better basis for cooperative learning.
- Consider the use of specific team jobs to help students work together in a team.

### Team jobs

For classes—even lower secondary classes—that have limited experience in working in groups, there is value in considering the use of specific team jobs. While each team member has a specific job, they are accountable for the performance of the team and should be able to explain the team results and how they were obtained. It is important to rotate team jobs each time a team works together to give all students an opportunity to perform different roles. It has been suggested that colour coding could be used to distinguish team jobs (for example, coloured wool bracelets). Possible team jobs depend

THE ART OF TEACHING SCIENCE 3RD EDITION

on the task but could include manager, speaker, equipment manager and report coordinator. Groups can be encouraged to define the role for each team job.

### Team skills

In addition to team roles that help teachers manage the work of small groups, it is important to help students develop skills that make teams more cohesive and improve the learning. Teachers need to assess their students' team skills and focus on each skill that would enhance their work. The choice of skills will depend on the skill level of the particular class. Teachers need to name the skill they wish to develop and then explain to the class what is expected and how the skill will enhance students' group work and learning. In addition to this, teachers need to give regular feedback on students' use of the selected skills. It is better to focus on one skill at a time. Support for embedding cooperative learning into your classroom practice can be found in the Science by Doing resource titled *Student Learning: A Stimulus for Professional Discussion* (Goodrum & Druhan 2011b).

## Specific Teaching Strategies

There is a range of different teaching strategies that support inquiry-based approaches and include collaborative and cooperative learning opportunities. Animated versions of these strategies can be found in the Science by Doing resource titled *Inquiry-based Teaching: A Stimulus for Professional Discussion* (Goodrum & Druhan 2011a).

### Concept maps

Concept maps allow students to represent diagrammatically what they know about the links and relationships between concepts. They allow students to access prior knowledge and provide teachers with feedback on what is known or unknown and/or what is misunderstood, either at a single point or over time. Concept maps are designed to increase the student's ability to organise and represent thoughts and to help with reading comprehension. They have a central concept, such as *energy*, around which related concepts are

PRINCIPLES OF EFFECTIVE SCIENCE TEACHING AND LEARNING 119

drawn. The related concepts are linked to the central concept and to each other with lines that are labelled with an explanation of the relationship between the concepts. Concept maps can be generated by the whole class or by individual students. They are discussed further in Chapter 9, and an example is provided in Figure 9.2.

### Envoy

This strategy encourages students to learn from each other and take responsibility for learning. It helps students to develop listening and oral skills and promotes skills in synthesising and summarising. Students are placed into groups and given a topic to discuss. One student from each group is selected to be the *envoy*. When the group has completed its discussion of the topic, the envoy reports to another group and outlines what was discussed. The envoy also listens to a report from the group they are visiting. The envoy then returns to their original group, which has also received a report from another group's envoy, and the group members exchange new ideas. Each group should now have input from two other groups.

### Gallery walk

Student or group work is placed around the room, and students are given the opportunity to view other students' work and to display their own. Students can use the opportunity to read information prepared by others or consider the way the information is presented. They can collect information from the work of others or peer-assess using a prepared set of guidelines.

### Jigsaw

This strategy provides a structure for group work and also allows students to cover a broad amount of information in a shorter period of time. Students are formed into *home* groups of about five or six. The topic (for example, types of energy) is divided into sections (for example, solar energy and chemical energy), and each student in the home group is given a different aspect of the topic to research. The home groups split up, and the students form into *expert* groups such that all members in one group are researching the same aspect of the topic. Students research their aspect of the topic in the expert groups and prepare to report to their home group. Students return to their home group and take turns to report as the expert on their aspect of the topic.

## SUMMARY OF KEY POINTS

This chapter began with two questions that have a profound impact on teaching. Why do we teach science? How do we learn science effectively? These questions led to the ideas of scientific literacy and inquiry-based learning. From these ideas, a series of teaching principles were inferred and described. These principles were embedded in a teaching model known as the 5E model. Using the principles, a suggested approach to planning lessons was outlined. Advice was provided on how to develop cooperative learning using a team approach and concluded with a variety of specific strategies with relevant examples.

## DISCUSSION QUESTIONS

7.1   What is scientific literacy, and how does it influence science teaching?

7.2   How does an inquiry-based approach differ from the way you were taught science in school?

7.3   How might you use the 5E teaching model when planning a unit of work?

7.4   Describe three different lessons that utilise some of the inquiry-based strategies described in this chapter.

## REFERENCES

Bybee, R.W., 1997, *Achieving Scientific Literacy: From Purposes to Practices*, Portsmouth, NH: Heinemann.

Druhan, A. & Goodrum, D., 2011, *Effective Questioning: A Stimulus for Professional Discussion*, <www.sciencebydoing.edu.au/

professional-learning/effective-questioning>, accessed 20 June 2018.

Goodrum, D., Hackling, M. & Rennie, L., 2001, *The Status and Quality of Teaching and Learning of Science in Australian Schools: A Research Report*, Canberra: Department of Education, Training and Youth Affairs.

Goodrum, D. & Druhan, A., 2011a, *Inquiry-based Teaching: A Stimulus for Professional Discussion*, <www.sciencebydoing. edu.au/professional-learning/inquiry-based-teaching>, accessed 20 June 2018.

Goodrum, D. & Druhan, A., 2011b, *Student Learning: A Stimulus for Professional Discussion*, <www.sciencebydoing.edu.au/professional-learning/student-learning>, accessed 20 June 2018.

# CHAPTER 8
# Science Inquiry: Thinking and Working Like a Scientist

Grady Venville, Australian National University

## GOALS

**The goals for this chapter are to support you to:**

- Justify using a science inquiry approach to science teaching
- Describe different types of science inquiry
- Plan science inquiry activities of different levels of openness to support student learning

**Australian Professional Standards for Teachers—Graduate Level:**

- Standard 2: Know the content and how to teach it (Focus areas 2.1, 2.2)
- Standard 3: Plan for and implement effective teaching and learning (Focus areas 3.2, 3.3)

## INTRODUCTION

You may recall anticipation and excitement when you were in high school and your science teacher said that the class would be 'doing an experiment' or 'doing a practical activity'. School science practical work can be used to help students achieve a number of learning outcomes, including getting a feel for natural phenomena; developing conceptual understanding and skills; and giving students a sense of the nature of science, and the excitement of inquiry and discovery. There are strong arguments from research that to maintain students' interest in the study of science, to enhance their learning and to ensure they become scientifically literate citizens, the curriculum needs to be more inquiry-orientated (Furtak, Seidel, Iverson & Briggs 2012; Tytler, Osborne, Williams, Tytler & Cripps Clarke 2008).

The Australian Curriculum: Science is structured around three strands: *Science Understanding, Science as a Human Endeavour* and *Science Inquiry Skills*. These are interrelated, because the intention is that students will develop an understanding of science concepts and the nature of science through science inquiry processes (ACARA 2018; see also Chapter 7). The centrality of inquiry is highlighted in the curriculum, which includes developing an understanding of scientific inquiry methods such as questioning and predicting, planning and conducting, processing and analysing data and information, evaluating investigations, and communicating ideas, findings and evidence-based solutions (ACARA 2018).

This purpose of this chapter is to present an argument that science inquiry is beneficial for students. The chapter also provides practical ideas about science inquiry to help you plan to teach in this way and scaffold your students' learning.

## INQUIRY: WORKING AND THINKING LIKE A SCIENTIST

There are many different forms of practical work that can enhance student engagement in science lessons, including demonstrations, explorations, observations, experiments, investigations and projects. In this chapter, I focus on a *science inquiry* approach to the practical side of science teaching, because I am convinced by research that this approach supports student learning and engagement with science (Furtak et al. 2012).

## What is Scientific Inquiry?

'Scientific inquiry, in short, refers to the systematic approaches used by scientists in an effort to answer their questions' (Lederman 2018, p. 2). Scientific inquiry encompasses all of the complex processes that scientists undertake as part of their work, including the ways they think and the ways they work.

In practice, scientists use a wide range of types of scientific inquiry to answer their questions. As a teacher, it is important that you help your students understand that scientists' questions guide the particular methodological approach taken to their inquiry. For example, a medical scientist may use a carefully designed experiment with controlled variables to determine the effect of a new drug on blood pressure. An astronomer may use descriptive methods to document their observations and measurements of exoplanets. A population-health scientist may use predictive health modelling to determine the expected prevalence of childhood obesity in Australia in the future. An environmental scientist may use a correlation method to determine a relationship between ocean temperature and the average number of eggs in females of a species of crustacean.

Scientific inquiry is about how scientists think and work, but you may well be wondering, 'What has that got to do with how to teach science in schools?' The next section provides some answers to this question.

## Why Science Inquiry in Schools?

The basic principle of a science inquiry approach is that it enables students to learn science through essentially copying what scientists do—they learn science by thinking and working just like scientists! In the next few sections, I elaborate on this idea and provide you with some arguments about how a science inquiry approach to practical work is beneficial. To illustrate my arguments, see Snapshot 8.1 about an inquiry astronomy program provided to interested secondary-school students in an after-school club. I argue that a science inquiry approach enhances the authenticity of scientific conceptual learning, motivation and engagement, scientific literacy and the nature of science.

## SNAPSHOT 8.1: An inquiry astronomy program

Ms Henson started a science inquiry-based after-school program on astronomy at Barton High School because she wanted to improve students' understanding of and attitude towards science. The formal part of the program was a weekly one-hour session presented as an after-school activity for students from Years 8 to 11 who were interested. The astronomy program involved students learning how to locate, image and analyse asteroids, and designing and enacting their own asteroid project, as if they were scientists. The scientific question was: 'Where are previously undiscovered asteroids located?' To answer the question, the students remotely used a 1-metre telescope that was physically located in a purpose-built observatory about 50 kilometres from the students' school. Ms Henson and the students kept journals during the program, and the following account is based on the information recorded in their journals, in the students' work and in the computer software used by the students.

The students worked in groups and used three main computer programs when working to achieve their goals. They gathered their ephemerides from the Minor Planet Centre, used Stellarium to place their object in the night sky and utilised the Zadko Robotic Telescope site to request and view an image. Having access to the Zadko Robotic Telescope was one of the highlights of the astronomy program. This telescope is one of five fully robotic observatories linked to a central observatories coordinator, CADOR, based in France.

The students had to master all of the required skills during the program, and they tended to move freely between computer screens, manipulating the computer programs as required. The students applied new knowledge and skills when completing activities. For example, to view the asteroid's position in the night sky in real time using the Stellarium software, the students first set the date and time and then entered the right ascension and declination. To request an observation, the students were required to follow several complicated steps.

Student collaboration was fundamental to their success. They worked in teams of about three, and the approach used by each group evolved to meet their common goal and changed according to needs. For example, one group of students—Mary, Sydney and Peta (pseudonyms)—discussed the astronomical data they needed to send a request to the Zadko Robotic Telescope so they could search for asteroids. Mary entered the URL for the Minor Planet Centre and began the search for a suitable asteroid to image. As soon as she found an appropriate asteroid, she gave its minor planet designation to Sydney and then continued to look for more viable targets. Finding the asteroid's position in the sky was the next step and was completed by Sydney. She entered the ephemerides obtained from Mary to do a position search using the planetarium software, Stellarium. Robotic telescope access was the most complicated step and, in this example, was carried out by Peta. She logged into the CADOR site and worked through the procedure for requesting an image. The students communicated with each other throughout the process. They checked their work, revised the data, discussed the observation requests and supported each other. Their group work proved to be so efficient that they were able to make several observation requests during each session.

The students developed mind maps during the program. Peta's first two mind maps showed the rapid development of her knowledge and her connections between concepts.

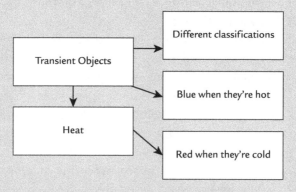

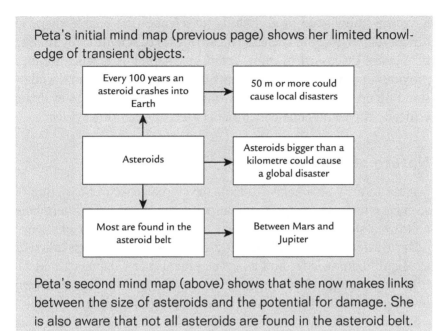

Peta's initial mind map (previous page) shows her limited knowledge of transient objects.

Peta's second mind map (above) shows that she now makes links between the size of asteroids and the potential for damage. She is also aware that not all asteroids are found in the asteroid belt.

## Authenticity

One of the arguments to support a science inquiry approach to science education is that it is *authentic*. The reason I want school students to have an authentic experience of science is twofold: first, it brings about authentic learning; second, it brings about authentic motivation and engagement in science, as demonstrated in Snapshot 8.1. Involving school students in science inquiry gives them the experience of thinking and working like a scientist, which they don't get if they only participate in recipe-style practical activities.

## Scientific Literacy

There is an international consensus that the purpose of teaching and learning science in the compulsory years of schooling is the development of scientifically literate citizens. The importance of scientific literacy is another argument that supports the use of a science inquiry approach in schools. Scientifically literate citizens have the knowledge of and skills in science that enable them to function effectively in society. The attributes of scientifically literate people are discussed in more detail in Chapter 7. Science inquiry provides opportunities for students to develop the skills and understanding needed to conduct scientific investigations and to evaluate critically the claims made by others based on scientific evidence.

## Nature of Science

Science inquiry also helps students develop a sense of the nature of science, which is an important component of the *Science as a Human Endeavour* strand of the Australian Curriculum. The nature of science refers to science as a way of knowing, or the values and beliefs inherent to scientific knowledge and its development (see Chapters 1 and 2). It is only when students practise as scientists conducting their own investigations that the nature of science becomes evident to them.

An important characteristic of scientific knowledge is that it is evidence-based. To be scientifically literate, students need an understanding of the nature of scientific evidence (for example, accuracy, uncertainty). Students need opportunities to develop the understanding and skills associated with the collection, validation, representation and interpretation of evidence. Students who understand the nature of scientific evidence should be able to detect when poor experimental design, inadequate control of variables or inappropriate sampling reduces the reliability of data and when conclusions are not consistent with the data. Evidence-based drawing of conclusions is central to making credible knowledge claims in science. Practising science inquiry, therefore, helps students to understand the difference between science and other ways that humans make sense of their world, such as through social and cultural customs, folklore and religion.

## LEVELS OF SCIENCE INQUIRY

Students need to build a foundation of skills, understanding and confidence before attempting more complex investigations and projects. Table 8.1 illustrates a sequence of levels of science inquiry that may

**TABLE 8.1:** A learning sequence that prepares students for more complex forms of practical work in science, based on Lederman (2018)

| Exploration | Direct science inquiry | Guided science inquiry | Open-ended science inquiry |
|---|---|---|---|
| Students get a feel for the phenomenon. Often causes students to become more curious and ask questions. | The problem and procedure are provided by the teacher. Students can make predictions but analyse the data and come up with their own evidence-based conclusion. Students learn techniques and processes. | The problem or question is provided, but students devise their own methods and solutions. They will also need to devise approaches to data analysis and presentation. Students learn how to plan and conduct a systematic inquiry. | The problem, methods and solution are open for the students to determine. The students take all responsibility for the inquiry. An extended inquiry may involve a review of existing knowledge, investigation of several variables and reporting of findings to stakeholders. |

be used by teachers to scaffold and prepare students for the more demanding tasks.

## Exploration

Exploration (see Table 8.1) is an unstructured mini-investigation where students have the opportunity to *play* with materials and have concrete experiences. Explorations are used to allow students to directly observe and get a feel for phenomena such as magnetic attraction, heat transfer or states of matter. Exploration-type activities might include dissection of a sheep's heart, observation of the phases of the moon through a telescope or comparing the viscosity of different liquids.

# THE ART OF TEACHING SCIENCE 3RD EDITION

In all of these activities, the practical nature of the work can be used as an advance organiser to increase students' curiosity, to get them to ask questions or to reinforce scientific knowledge and concepts they have already learned in a theoretical way. Students can also learn inquiry skills such as observation and measurement, and how to use scientific equipment such as microscopes, thermometers and Bunsen burners. While explorations allow all of these types of learning, they don't enable students to ask their own inquiry questions or design their own scientific method to answer their questions. To be able to learn how to do these things, students need to be included in higher levels of inquiry.

## Direct Science Inquiry

Most practical work conducted in secondary-school science takes the form of routine laboratory exercises, or direct science inquiry (see Table 8.1), in which students follow a procedure prescribed by the teacher to investigate a question set by the teacher (Hackling, Goodrum & Rennie 2001). Students follow the teacher's instructions to set up the prescribed equipment and make measurements and observations, sometimes called a *recipe-style* laboratory activity, and data interpretation is often structured by questions set by the teacher. For example, secondary-school students often conduct a laboratory exercise on the electrical conductivity of different materials. Upper secondary-school biology students conduct laboratory exercises on enzyme action, and chemistry students conduct titration exercises. These exercises provide opportunities for students to practise experimental techniques associated with data collection and gain skills associated with data analysis and interpretation. There is, however, no opportunity for students to develop skills associated with formulating a research question, identifying and manipulating variables or planning how to control variables.

## Guided Science Inquiry

An alternative approach to recipe-style laboratory exercises is to enable the students to participate in guided science inquiry (see

Table 8.1). Guided science inquiry allows students to plan and conduct their own experiments within a context and boundaries set by the teacher. Guided science inquiry provides a more authentic experience of the nature of science and requires students to both think and work like a scientist. Guided science inquiry practical work has been shown to produce higher-order learning outcomes than traditional closed recipe-style laboratory exercises (Furtak et al. 2012; Minner, Levy & Century 2010).

Guided science inquiry involves unstructured problem-solving tasks that require students to take the initiative to devise an appropriate approach to the problem, experimental design and techniques. Many students need considerable support if they are to engage successfully in these tasks. Support can be provided by breaking the task into a series of steps and by modelling some of the more difficult inquiry skills.

## Open-ended Science Inquiry

Open-ended science inquiry (see Table 8.1) is a more extended form of science inquiry often involving a review of existing knowledge, investigation of several independent variables and reporting of findings to stakeholders. Projects often extend over several weeks, as they involve extensive field work, observations or several experiments. For example, Year 9 students might conduct an extended project on wind turbines where they do background research about the efficiency and effectiveness of the power generation, survey local residents about health fears with regard to the turbines and conduct experiments to determine the noise levels produced by the turbines in comparison with other noise in the environment, such as highways. Snapshot 8.1 is an example of an open-ended inquiry activity where the students participated in searching for asteroids.

# IMPLEMENTING SCIENCE INQUIRY IN YOUR CLASSROOM

Your own memory of science in school may not be consistent with an inquiry approach to science education. Moreover, many textbooks,

THE ART OF TEACHING SCIENCE 3RD EDITION

laboratory manuals and digital curriculum materials may also not be inquiry-based. It is challenging in some contexts, therefore, to adopt a science inquiry approach. The following sections will support you in your endeavours.

## Transitioning to Science Inquiry

To improve the curriculum in secondary science, many of the traditional laboratory exercises should be replaced with guided inquiry so that students can learn how to plan their own experiments and investigations. The easiest way to do this is to simply remove the detailed procedural instructions from some of the exercises to open them up and turn them into guided inquiry investigations. For example, lower-secondary students could be required to plan their own investigation on the electrical conductivity of different materials rather than being given a *recipe* about how to do this.

## Science Inquiry Planning and Report Sheets

Planning and report sheets guide students through a sequence of steps, providing structure and scaffolding while giving them the responsibility for the decision-making. These scaffolds are structured by a sequence of questions and prompts. One scaffold, suitable for students in Years 7 to 10, is illustrated in Table 8.2.

Scaffolds such as the one illustrated in Table 8.2 lead students through the science inquiry process and elicit from them information about their thinking and what they are doing at each stage. Scaffolds therefore provide support to students, and the written record of the investigation provides information needed by teachers to assess students against the outcomes of the inquiry strand of the Australian Curriculum. A number of planning and report sheets suitable for scaffolding primary, lower-secondary and upper-secondary students' inquiry can be downloaded in electronic form from Hackling (2005).

## TABLE 8.2: Questions used to scaffold science inquiry for secondary-school science students

| Question or prompt | Instructional purpose of the question or prompt |
| --- | --- |
| What question or hypothesis are you going to investigate? | Students focus on the problem and formulate a question or hypothesis for investigation. |
| What do you think will happen? Explain why. | Students make a prediction and justify their prediction— this activates pre-instructional knowledge for the investigation. |
| Which variables are you going to:<br>• change?<br>• measure?<br>• keep the same? | Students identify and operationalise the key variables. |
| How will you make it a fair test? | Students reflect on their plan and ensure that variables are controlled. |
| What equipment will you need? | Students think about the apparatus they will require to conduct the investigation. |
| Describe your experimental set-up using a labelled diagram, and explain how you will collect your data. | The plan is set out in detail using a diagram and steps for their procedure. |
| Did you carry out any preliminary trials of your procedure to see if your planned method of data collection would work?<br><br>Were there any problems?<br><br>What changes did you make to fix the problems? | These questions provide an opportunity for students to demonstrate that they conducted preliminary trials and have refined their procedure based on what they learned from the trials. |
| What happened? Describe your observations, and record your results. | This prompts students to record their measurements and/or observations. |

## THE ART OF TEACHING SCIENCE 3RD EDITION

| Question or prompt | Instructional purpose of the question or prompt |
|---|---|
| Can your results be presented as a graph? | This prompts students to decide whether it would be worth graphing their data. |
| What do your results tell you? Are there any relationships, patterns or trends in your results? | These questions prompt students to search for patterns in the data. |
| Can you explain the relationships, patterns or trends in your results? Use some science ideas to help explain what happened. | These questions prompt students to explain the patterns in their data using science concepts. |
| What did you find out about the question you investigated? Write your conclusion. Was the outcome different from your prediction? Explain. | These questions prompt students to summarise their findings as a conclusion and to compare their findings with their prediction. Discrepancies often occur between predictions and findings due to students' pre-instructional knowledge. Such discrepancies may cause students to reflect on their beliefs. |
| What difficulties did you experience in doing this investigation? | This question prompts students to reflect on the processes used in the investigation and to identify any difficulties that were experienced. |
| How could you improve this investigation (e.g. fairness, accuracy)? | This question helps students focus on what they have learned about improving their investigation processes. |

## Operationalising Variables

To understand the design of controlled experiments as one of the forms of scientific inquiry, students need to be able to work with the three types of variables—the *dependent variable* (DV), the *independent variable* (IV) and *controlled variables* (CV)—and the relationships between them. One way of helping students understand the relationships between variables in a controlled experiment is to use a variables table. An example of a variables table is illustrated in Figure 8.1.

**FIGURE 8.1:** An example of a variables table

| Research question: How does the amount of light affect the growth of seedlings? | | |
| --- | --- | --- |
| What I will keep the same? | What I will change? | What I will measure? |
| • type of seeds<br>• type of soil<br>• amount of water<br>• amount of fertiliser<br>• size of container<br>• planting depth of seeds | the amount of light (i.e. dark, partial shade, full sun) | the height of the seedlings |
| Controlled variables | Independent variable | Dependent variable |

Variables tables can be completed on a whiteboard using questioning to elicit the variables from students. In this way, the process of designing a controlled experiment can be modelled for students. In summary, in a controlled experiment, the independent variable is changed to see what effect it has on the dependent variable, while all other variables that could potentially affect the dependent variable are kept the same.

## Writing Research Questions and Hypotheses

Many students experience difficulty in writing testable research questions and hypotheses. Students need plenty of experience working with research questions before they are introduced to hypotheses. Research questions focus on the possible relationship between an independent variable and a dependent variable. They can be written in a standard form that can be structured using the following algorithm:

What happens to _____ (DV) when we change _____ (IV)?

For example:
What happens to *the growth of wheat seedlings* when we change *the saltiness of the water*?

OR
What effect does _____ (IV) have on _____ (DV)?

For example:
What effect does *the saltiness of water* have on *the growth of wheat seedlings*?

Hypotheses are tentative declarative statements, based on observations, which can be supported or refuted by experiment. Hypotheses can be written in the following form:

This change to the independent variable
  + will cause this to happen to
    + the dependent variable.

For example:
Increasing the salinity of water (IV) will reduce (relationship) the growth of wheat seedlings (DV).

As many secondary-science students are focused on *getting the right answer* in their practical work, because of their extensive experience of closed laboratory exercises, hypotheses can cause problems for the students when their data do not support their hypothesis. Students might be tempted to *fudge* or make up their data to match the hypothesis in order to give the appearance of getting the right answer. To write a hypothesis assumes that students have some knowledge about the phenomenon and the relationships between the associated variables.

### Types of Data and Ways of Representing Data

It is important to include a range of science inquiry types so that students are exposed to repeat trials, replication, discrete and continuous variables, and bar and line graphing.

Investigations common in primary-school science tend to use discrete independent variables (in categories such as colour, month or species of animal), and data are presented using bar graphs. In secondary school, it is important to use continuous independent variables (in other words, data are continuous on a measurement scale, such as length or mass), where the data are represented on line graphs. Students should also be taught how to use graphing software programs and other data-representation tools in ways that are appropriate to the types of data being represented.

## SUMMARY OF KEY POINTS

Practical work is an essential component of science programs for school students. It is through science inquiry that scientists test ideas and generate new knowledge. By conducting science inquiry, and working and thinking like scientists, students can get a sense of the nature of science and learn the skills and understandings that are at the heart of scientific literacy. Inquiry-orientated and investigative science programs actively engage students in learning, increasing their interest in science and developing those inquiry skills linked to reasoning with scientific processes, ideas and evidence.

## DISCUSSION QUESTIONS

8.1  How would you justify to a colleague your decision to include in your teaching program more science inquiry activities at the expense of covering content?

8.2  Design a science inquiry task that will engage students in authentic science in a real-world context. Your science inquiry task should develop important inquiry skills and provide a platform of experience on which one of the fundamental concepts of science can be developed.

8.3 What strategies could you use to help students understand and remember the difference between independent, dependent and controlled variables?

8.4 What would you say to a student who you discovered had changed the data from her investigation so that her hypothesis was supported rather than refuted? Can you give examples of scientists whose hypotheses were not supported by evidence but who went on to make great discoveries or contribute to science in profound ways?

## REFERENCES

Australian Curriculum, Assessment and Reporting Authority (ACARA), 2018, *Australian Curriculum: Science*, <www.australiancurriculum.edu.au/f-10-curriculum/science/>, accessed 29 June 2018.

Furtak, E.M., Seidel, T., Iverson, H. & Briggs, D.C., 2012, 'Experimental and quasi-experimental studies of inquiry-based science teaching: A meta-analysis', *Review of Educational Research*, vol. 82, no. 3, pp. 300–29.

Hackling, M.W., 2005, *Working Scientifically: Implementing and Assessing Open Investigation Work in Science* (Rev. ed.), <www.watersciencelab.com.au/assets/working-scientifically_by-mark-hackling-2005.pdf> accessed 16 January 2019.

Hackling, M.W., Goodrum, D. & Rennie, L., 2001, 'The state of science in Australian secondary schools', *Australian Science Teachers' Journal*, vol. 47, no. 4, pp. 6–17.

Lederman, J.S., 2018, *Teaching Scientific Inquiry: Exploration, Directed, Guided, and Open-ended Levels*, <https://NGL.Cengage.com/Schools>, accessed 29 June 2018.

Minner, D.D., Levy, A.J. & Century, J., 2010, 'Inquiry-based science instruction—what is it and does it matter? Results from a research synthesis years 1984 to 2002', *Journal of Research in Science Teaching*, vol. 47, no. 4, pp. 474–96.

Tytler, R., Osborne, J., Williams, G., Tytler, K. & Cripps Clark, J., 2008, *Opening Up Pathways: Engagement in STEM Across the Primary–Secondary School Transition*, <https://docs.education.gov.au/system/files/doc/other/openpathinscitechmathenginprimsecschtrans.pdf>, accessed 16 January 2019.

# CHAPTER 9
# Assessment, Learning and Teaching: A Symbiotic Relationship

Debra Panizzon, Monash University

## GOALS

The goals for this chapter are to support you to:

- Explain the central role of assessment to learning and teaching
- Distinguish between different types and purposes of assessment
- Recognise how assessment can be used to monitor students' progress
- Describe the key components of quality assessment processes
- Recognise how increasing accountability can influence teacher assessment practices

Australian Professional Standards for Teachers—Graduate Level:

- Standard 1: Know students and how they learn (Focus areas 1.3, 1.5)
- Standard 2: Know the content and how to teach it (Focus area 2.3)
- Standard 5: Assess, provide feedback and report on student learning (Focus areas 5.1, 5.2, 5.3)

# INTRODUCTION

Assessment generally refers to the gathering and interpreting of information about students' learning (Resnick & Schantz 2017). In science, *student learning* includes scientific understandings, processes, skills, attitudes and values—much more than measuring the content that students acquire. Unfortunately, though, knowledge acquisition often remains a focus in secondary science, which limits the types of tasks used by teachers to assess their students (for example, tests and scientific reports). Ultimately, this can lead to skewed perspectives about what students know, understand and can actually do in science (Panizzon & Pegg 2008).

The link between student learning and assessment is fairly straightforward, but less so is the critical role of assessment in guiding teacher practice. As explained by Cross (1998, p. 6):

> Classroom assessment informs teachers how effectively they are teaching and students how effectively they are learning. Through classroom assessment, teachers get continual feedback on whether and how well students are learning what teachers hope they are teaching. And students are required, through a variety of classroom assessment exercises, to monitor their learning, to reflect on it, and to take corrective action while there is still time left.

In order to put the spotlight on this complex interplay between assessment, learning and teaching, the metaphor of a *symbiotic relationship* is used in the title of this chapter. Symbiosis is a biological term that refers to a mutually beneficial relationship between different organisms, people or groups living in close proximity. Thinking of assessment in this manner moves it from being viewed as a task that occurs at the end of some kind of teaching sequence to an ongoing process that enables teachers to monitor student learning and progress. The pivotal role of assessment to teaching and learning is visualised in Figure 9.1. As demonstrated here, assessment provides important feedback to the teacher in an ongoing manner to inform future learning opportunities for students (1).

**FIGURE 9.1:** Symbiotic relationship between assessment, learning and teaching

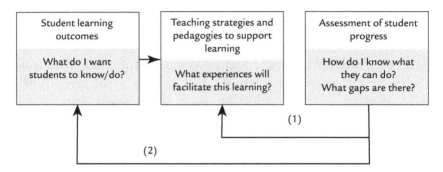

It also enables monitoring of student progress against the intended learning outcomes, which is beneficial for both students and teachers (2).

What this relationship looks like and how it might be achieved in the science classroom to ensure equity for students are the foci of this chapter. Initially, the various types of assessment and their purposes in education are described. Following this, possible tasks and activities for assessing students' learning in science are presented. Ways of ensuring quality and equitable practices are then discussed in the context of building teacher professional judgement. Finally, some of the pressures impacting teachers as they juggle classroom assessment practices with the increasing demands exerted by high-stakes testing are also explored. This chapter deliberately sets out to inform and, importantly, to challenge your current views of assessment and its role in learning and teaching.

## DIFFERENT TYPES OF ASSESSMENT: FIT FOR PURPOSE

Traditionally, assessment has been categorised as diagnostic, formative, summative or evaluative, depending on its intended purpose. In the late 1990s, different categories emerged from the work of Black and Wiliam (1998), who preferred *assessment for learning*, *assessment of learning* and *assessment as learning*. The alignment between these categories and their purposes is summarised in Table 9.1.

**TABLE 9.1:** Assessment types and purposes

| Types | | Purpose |
|---|---|---|
| Black & Wiliam (1998) | Traditional | |
| Assessment for learning | Diagnostic | Identify the preconceptions held by students at the beginning of a teaching sequence so that activities and opportunities can be planned to build on the current conceptions of students. Activities that explore the alternative conceptions of students, such as concept cartoons and two-tier multiple-choice items, are widely available. |
| Assessment for learning | Formative | Provide informal and ongoing feedback to students about their learning progress in science. A critical component of this is to provide positive encouragement but also guidance as to how students might improve their work. The other focus of Black and Wiliam is the way that teachers use the insights gained from assessment to guide their own practice to support and encourage student learning. |
| Assessment of learning | Summative | Collection of evidence using different tasks to assess students formally against outcomes/achievement standards. Marks are allocated and recorded to determine grades that are reported to the student and parents/guardians. This is the most common type of assessment. |

# THE ART OF TEACHING SCIENCE 3RD EDITION

| Types | | Purpose |
| --- | --- | --- |
| Black & Wiliam (1998) | Traditional | |
| Assessment as learning | | Encourage students to reflect and/ or evaluate their own learning. What are their strengths and weaknesses? This is extremely powerful, because it helps students become metacognitive and knowledgeable about how they learn. |
| | Evaluative | Not of direct relevance to the classroom teacher of science but about the measurement and assessment of student learning generally. It involves tracking and monitoring cohorts of students over time and analysing changes in the patterns or trends in the data. This type of assessment is solely for accountability measures so that systems and schools can be measured against specified standards. |

While there is clearly an overlap between the more traditional terms used for assessment and those that emerged from the work of Black and Wiliam (1998), there are three critical points of difference:

1. An emphasis on assessment as being integrated with not only student learning but also with the actual process of teaching. For Black and Wiliam, assessment informs teachers about what students can do but also highlights gaps in learning, which then provides advice about where to target subsequent teaching.
2. Recognition that assessment for learning is pivotal in supporting student learning, because ongoing feedback provides valuable advice that helps students know where to focus attention to enhance their own learning.
3. The emergence of assessment as learning acknowledges that students, too, have responsibility for their learning. Once they

are introduced to strategies that encourage thinking about how they learn, students become metacognitive and self-regulated in their own learning, which is extremely powerful.

## DIVERSITY OF ASSESSMENT TASKS AND STRATEGIES

Many teaching strategies are also effective ways of assessing the progress of our students. Critically, the types of activities, tasks or strategies selected should depend on the purpose of assessment, the year level of your students and the intended learning outcomes. For example, student presentations to the class could be used as *assessment for learning,* with teachers and other students providing constructive feedback resulting in further development of the work. Alternatively, this same task could be used as *assessment of learning,* with marks allocated by the teacher and recorded for reporting purposes. This is an important point to grasp, because in schools there are often prevailing cultures about the types of tasks used for assessment. In the case of secondary science, teachers often revert to tests, examinations and scientific reports for *assessment of learning,* even though this does not have to be the case. It is known from research that student presentations, digital products (for example, videos) and portfolios are extremely useful in providing evidence about what secondary students know and can do in science (Fensham & Rennie 2013). Ultimately, it is the classroom teacher who makes these types of professional decisions regarding the most appropriate tasks for assessing their students as part of their professional judgement.

In acknowledging teacher judgement, little attempt is made in this section to specifically align assessment tasks to a particular type of assessment. This is because there are no rules or specifications about what tasks teachers should use when *assessing of* or *for learning.* The only exception to this is with senior secondary-science students, where curricula might direct teachers to use particular types of assessment, such as scientific reports or examinations.

## Assessing Students' Initial Ideas: Concept Maps

The purpose of assessment activities used at the beginning of a teaching sequence is to ascertain students' existing understandings. This diagnostic purpose enables the teacher to design activities to stimulate students to continue building and restructuring their existing scientific understanding or to remediate alternative conceptions (in other words, teaching based on the theory of constructivism—see Chapter 3). For example, visual displays, such as concept maps, encourage students to demonstrate links and connections between different concepts (see Figure 9.2). By developing maps at the beginning of a teaching sequence in one colour and then reviewing these at the end using another colour, students can compare and contrast the maps, identifying additions, changes and improved depth in their own understanding. For example, the concept map in Figure 9.2 might be expected initially but should become more complex as students learn about energy transformations. It encourages them to reflect on their own learning.

**FIGURE 9.2:** An example of a concept map on the concept of *ecosystem*

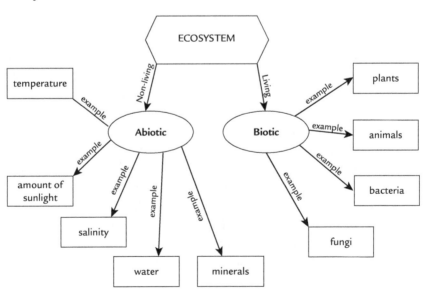

## Observations and Conversations with Students

Teachers make observations of what is happening in their class-rooms all the time. However, by focusing on individual students, it is possible to gain a sense of progress through their engagement with written tasks, in their development of scientific skills (such as measuring, collecting data) or with their scientific communication. Time spent asking students questions and carefully listening to their answers immediately highlights areas of difficulty; this is an opportunity for the teacher to provide constructive feedback to enhance learning.

## Student Voice: Oral or Written

Oral and written assessment tasks require students to internalise what is being asked and produce a considered response. This work should be less about regurgitation of facts or information and more about students demonstrating their ability to apply, critique, synthesise and challenge the topic being explored as part of their assessment. While usually termed *assignments*, oral and written tasks can be quite diverse in nature.

- *Research a topic*: Teachers identify a particular area for exploration. In junior secondary science, it could be about famous scientific discoveries and their impact on humanity. In preparing to assess students, the teacher must think carefully about the learning outcomes targeted so that appropriate points to be addressed or questions to be answered are posed for students. Without this type of direction or scaffolding, many students are left to their own devices with little idea about what is actually required.
- *Reflective journals*: Encourage students to move beyond a diary entry of what is completed during a lesson and towards thinking back over what they have actually learned, noticing how their understandings have changed and evolved. This type of task encourages students to become metacognitive and aware of how they learn in science. With students who are less experienced with reflective journals, it is useful to stimulate their thinking by

using questions that build the skills necessary for reflection on their work.

- *Portfolio*: This represents a selection of student work completed over a period of time, which is used to demonstrate the growth and development of students' scientific understandings and skills. There is a degree of ownership for the student, who chooses the work that best illustrates their achievement. For secondary students a reflective journal might also be undertaken, with the student reflecting on their own progress as represented by the work they have included in the portfolio. Collectively, these become very powerful metacognitive tools for the student while allowing the teacher to assess one or both.

## Investigative Activities

Investigative activities enhance scientific skills and processes while reinforcing students' understandings of scientific concepts. Importantly, they do not have to be based on the collection of firsthand data, with analysis of secondary data also appropriate.

- *Investigations and/or controlled experiments (i.e. fair testing)*: Practical work can involve students completing a specified protocol (i.e. controlled experiment) through to more open-ended investigations where students develop an inquiry question to explore (see Chapter 8). In terms of assessment, there are two aspects to consider: (1) assessing the actual scientific skills of observing, measuring and recording data; and (2) assessing the analysis, synthesis and interpretations of these data. Teachers need to think carefully about how to assess each so that it is appropriate. For example, assessing the preparation of a wet mount for a microscope must be done by observing individual students. Alternatively, laboratory reports demonstrate the extent to which students can communicate the results and draw conclusions about the findings in relation to the aim, hypothesis or question being investigated.
- *Investigative activity*: Instead of a formal practical activity, it might be useful to focus on particular scientific inquiry skills. Predict–Observe–Explain (POE) tasks (see Chapter 4) can be

conducted either as a whole class or in small groups. Responses might be shared to stimulate discussion within the class about the scientific concept being explored (i.e. *assessment for learning*) or written up and submitted as *assessment of learning*.

- *Online interactive simulations*: Access to digital scenarios and tools allows students to manipulate, isolate and alter individual variables so they can explore and better understand their impact on the concept or system being studied. Students can repeat the process a number of times, generating more complex data sets for analysis. These types of tools are equally appropriate to use as *assessment for learning* or *assessment of learning*, depending on the purpose of the work.

## Student Productions

There are a number of different types of student productions that can be used for assessment.

- *Presentations*: Posters, PowerPoints, Prezis and iMovies are relevant ways to assess students. By setting parameters, such as specifying the time allowed or number of slides to be used, this ensures that students are not only synthesising knowledge but also extracting the key points to address the question or topic.
- *Building models/dioramas*: Construction of three-dimensional (3D) models encourages students to demonstrate their scientific understandings through physical representations (e.g. a model of a cell, with students justifying the use of objects to represent organelles).
- *Slowmation*: Derived from 'slow animation', this involves students taking digital still photos and combining them to produce an animation around a particular scientific concept or theme. Snapshot 9.1 explores slowmations as assessment tasks.

## Quizzes, Tests and Examinations

Quizzes, tests and examinations are commonly used with secondary-science students for *assessment of learning*, but they should be used

> **SNAPSHOT 9.1:** An example of using slowmation for assessment
>
> Access the slowmation gallery at https://slowmation.uow.edu.au/gallery/. View the photosynthesis animation. The value of creating animations like this is that students have to:
>
>
>
> - unpack their own understanding of the scientific concept/process and how best to represent it;
> - deconstruct the concept/process into separate components, checking their own understanding; and
> - reconstruct the components of the concept into a sequence that can be understood by others.
>
> The design and development of well-constructed slowmations takes considerable time. As such, they should be used for *assessment of learning*, with marks allocated for the planning and preparation of the animation.

more often as diagnostic assessment or as *assessment for learning*. They usually comprise a set of multiple-choice and extended-response questions. A quiz (a very short test) could be used at the beginning of a topic to identify students' prior learning or at the beginning of a lesson to gauge how much students understand from the previous lesson. Tests and examinations, on the other hand, tend to assess a sequence of work covering an extended period of time.

Tests and examinations can be effective and highly appropriate mechanisms for assessing what students know, understand and can do in particular areas of science *if* used appropriately (Darling-Hammond & Rustique-Forrester 2005). What is pivotal when tests are used as *assessment of learning* is the *quality of the items* and the way in which marks are allocated. For example, items that gauge the ability of students to memorise and regurgitate facts simply reinforce the notion that science is about learning *stuff*. The items used should explore the ability of students to explain and apply their conceptual understandings of science, and allow students to demonstrate their scientific skills, their knowledge of the processes of science, and the ways in which science helps them to interpret their world. An example of how to achieve this is provided in Snapshot 9.2.

---

**SNAPSHOT 9.2:** Quality test items

Multiple-choice items are used in tests and examinations. However, many students are able to recognise words in the items and match them to work covered in class, so they are able to select the correct answer. Consider the following item used by the American Association for the Advancement of Science (2007, p. 5) in a study with high-school students.

Which of the following is an example of a chemical reaction?

A. A piece of metal hammered into a tree
B. A pot of water being heated and the water evaporation rates
C. A spoonful of salt dissolving in a glass of water
D. An iron railing developing an orange, powdery surface after standing in air

Approximately 18 per cent of students selected B, 24 per cent chose C, while 57 per cent opted for D. When the students who selected D were interviewed, only five could explain that a new substance had been formed. Most students admitted to selecting D because they recognised the example of rusting, which was used in class. To overcome this issue, a further question might be added: *Explain why you selected this answer.* Students with limited scientific understanding will not be able to answer this part of the question. By allocating one mark for D but two marks for the explanation, students who understand the chemical process will be rewarded appropriately.

---

## Teacher Questioning

Questioning, whether closed or open, is one of the most powerful strategies for assessing the progress of students on a daily basis. In a nutshell, questions should elicit 'evidence of understanding' in relation to student learning in science (Millar 2013, p. 58). While teaching, the type of responses provided by students along with the number of students prepared to respond gives the teacher immediate feedback about which students are struggling with particular aspects of the lesson (in other words, *assessment for learning*). But equally important is that questioning underpins most of the assessment tasks discussed in this section, because without carefully constructed questions targeting particular learning outcomes, teachers can severely limit and hinder students from demonstrating their actual level of achievement in science (Panizzon & Pegg 2008). The art of constructing and posing questions is addressed in Chapter 7.

## USING PROFESSIONAL JUDGEMENT TO ENSURE QUALITY, EQUITABLE ASSESSMENT PRACTICES

Regardless of which of the above tasks are used for assessment, they must be fair and equitable for all students. Items should provide opportunities for students to explain, demonstrate and communicate their learning in science—*not what they do not know*. Key to this is making certain that students are clear about the expectations and the learning outcomes being targeted, especially with *assessment of learning*. For example, distributing the criteria to be used to assess work from the outset of a teaching sequence provides direction to students about where to focus their learning and reduces anxiety. Some teachers have difficulty with the idea of distributing assessment criteria early in a teaching sequence, because they feel that if students know the criteria they will all achieve highly. Actually, this is not the case, because students respond using their constructed knowledge, which cannot be prompted by knowing the assessment criteria unless the item is merely gauging the student's ability to memorise facts and figures.

## Rubrics

An excellent way to communicate assessment expectations to students is to develop and share *rubrics*. In brief, rubrics help make explicit the outcomes to be achieved along with the steps involved in the learning. A rubric is designed for a specific assessment task and helps to align the assessment criteria to the learning outcomes and the curriculum achievement standards. Each criterion is broken down to identify how marks will be allocated to responses that show different levels of achievement (see Snapshot 9.3).

It is the allocation of marks to a criterion that sends the clearest message to students about what is actually valued by their teacher. For example, if more marks are allocated to the type of output used by the student (such as an iMovie) rather than to the degree to which students can articulate their scientific understandings, students learn quickly that presentation matters most. This is clearly not ideal and will focus students on superficial approaches to their classwork.

## Feedback

With student work assessed, there is still one more crucial step. Much research indicates that a key factor in raising student achievement, regardless of their age, is teacher feedback (Hattie & Timperley 2007). Snapshot 9.4 discusses levels of teacher feedback.

**SNAPSHOT 9.3:** Assessment rubric for data-handling skills

The table below is an example of a rubric and is not intended to be definitive. Some educators prefer this order of grades from lower level (C) to higher level (A) going from left to right; others prefer the opposite order from A to C going from left to right. There are reasons to support either choice, it is a matter of preference.

| Data-handling skills | Grade | | |
|---|---|---|---|
| | C | B | A |
| Measurement | • Measures when required and uses standard units of measure (e.g. cm, kg). | • C-level skill<br>+<br>• Repeats measurements or uses replicates. | • B-level skill<br>+<br>• Reassesses the measuring procedure to enhance accuracy, including selection of most appropriate apparatus (e.g. uses appropriate size of measuring cylinder). |
| Recording | • Data are recorded in a suitable format (e.g. table, drawing, list). | • C-level skill<br>+<br>• Each data trial is recorded separately. | • B-level skill<br>+<br>• Recording of data is done using appropriate conventions (e.g. tables have titles, columns and headings). |
| Graphing | • Constructs bar graphs. | • C-level skill<br>+<br>• Graphs selected depending on the type of data (e.g. line graphs for continuous variables). | • B-level skill<br>+<br>• Graphs plotted using the convention of the dependent variable on the vertical axis and the independent variable on the horizontal axis; appropriate scale is used to reduce vertical exaggeration. |

## SNAPSHOT 9.4: Quality feedback

Hattie and Timperley (2007) identified four non-hierarchical levels of teacher feedback.

Level 1: A focus on how well *the task* is completed (e.g. correct or incorrect), with the teacher providing directions about acquiring more, different or correct information (e.g. 'You need to include more in your description about the importance of plants.').

Level 2: A focus on *the process* required to finish a task or create a product (i.e. model). Feedback targets the processing of information or learning processes required to complete the work (e.g. 'This model will make more sense if you discuss the structures explored during the last practical.').

Level 3: A focus on developing *self-regulation* to enhance confidence and the ability of the student to self-assess (e.g. 'You already know the structure of an atom. Check to see how you have incorporated this idea into your discussion of results.'). This feedback builds student self-efficacy, because it provides clarity and guidance about how students can improve their own learning.

Level 4: A focus on the *personal* or *self*, which is frequently unrelated to the performance on a given task (e.g. 'That's a great response, well done!').

Reflecting on these levels, which do you think are most frequently used by teachers? You probably guessed correctly: Levels 1 and 4. However, it is Levels 2 and 3 that maximise student achievement, because they *empower students to become more effective learners*.

# EXTERNAL ACCOUNTABILITY

In the current educational environment, assessment is often used for different purposes by governments and other stakeholders who have competing agendas. This has resulted in increasing educational and

THE ART OF TEACHING SCIENCE 3RD EDITION

political accountability over the last two decades and is a complex and controversial issue (Klenowski & Wyatt-Smith 2012). An obvious example of this is with Year 12 students and their Australian Tertiary Admission Rank (ATAR), which is partially determined using an externally set and marked examination in all states and territories of Australia. The increasing accountability around the ATAR puts teachers under pressure to prepare their students in ways that will maximise their scores. As a result, many teachers resort to direct instruction and assessments that help students to practise for the exam (for example, use of frequent tests for class assessment).

Other examples include the National Assessment Program— Literacy and Numeracy (NAPLAN) test, with the data often used by the media and government authorities to undermine the community perception of the quality of jurisdictions, schools and individual teachers. The same occurs with international tests, such as Programme for International Student Assessment (PISA) and Trends in International Mathematics and Science Study (TIMSS). These high-stakes tests are implemented for evaluative purposes (see Table 9.1), yet the results are sometimes used to make assumptions about the overall achievement of students in specific classrooms across Australia. These accountability pressures impact teachers in their classroom practices. One of the most immediate outcomes has been a *teaching-to-the-test* mentality (Klenowski & Wyatt-Smith 2012), when teachers' foci should be on the day-to-day progress of their students.

## SUMMARY OF KEY POINTS

Assessment is intrinsically linked to learning and teaching—it is not something that happens at the end of a teaching sequence. Assessment is important not only because it informs students about what they know and can do in science, but also because it helps teachers to plan future lessons. Understanding the different types of assessment and their purposes is pivotal for teachers, who must use their professional judgement to select the most appropriate ways of assessing their students in relation to the targeted learning outcomes. Collecting evidence around student achievement in science requires quality items that are fair and equitable and give all students the chance to achieve in science.

## DISCUSSION QUESTIONS

9.1    Why is it important to use a range of different tasks when assessing students in science?
9.2    How does assessment impact teaching? Refer to your own teaching experiences in discussing this question.
9.3    Fair and equitable assessment is critical. Explain what this statement means in relation to classroom teaching.

## REFERENCES

American Association for the Advancement of Science (AAAS), 2007, 'Science literacy for a changing future', *2061 Today*, vol. 17, no. 1, pp. 1–8, <www.project2061.org/publications/newsletters/2061Today/pdfs/v17n1.pdf>, accessed 26 April 2018.

Black, P. & Wiliam, D., 1998, 'Assessment and classroom learning', *Assessment in Education: Principles, Policy & Practice*, vol. 5, no. 1, pp. 7–74.

Cross, K.P., 1998, 'Classroom research: Implementing the scholarship of teaching', *New Directions for Teaching & Learning*, vol. 75, pp. 5–12.

Darling-Hammond, L. & Rustique-Forrester, E., 2005, 'The consequences of student testing for teaching and teacher quality', *Yearbook of the National Society for the Study of Education*, vol. 104, no. 2, pp. 289–319.

Fensham, P.J. & Rennie, L.J., 2013, 'Towards an authentically assessed science curriculum', in D. Corrigan, R. Gunstone & A. Jones (eds), *Valuing Assessment in Science Education: Pedagogy, Curriculum, Policy*, Dordrecht: Springer, pp. 69–100.

Hattie, J. & Timperley, H., 2007, 'The power of feedback', *Review of Educational Research*, vol. 77, no. 1., pp. 81–112.

Klenowski, V. & Wyatt-Smith, C., 2012, 'The impact of high stakes testing: The Australian story', *Assessment in Education: Principles, Policy & Practice*, vol. 19, no. 1, pp. 65–79.

Millar, R., 2013, 'Improving science education: Why assessment matters', in D. Corrigan, R. Gunstone & A. Jones (eds), *Valuing Assessment in Science Education: Pedagogy, Curriculum, Policy*, Dordrecht: Springer, pp. 55–68.

Panizzon, D. & Pegg, J., 2008, 'Assessment practices: Empowering mathematics and science teachers in rural secondary schools to enhance student learning', *International Journal of Science and Mathematics Education*, vol. 6, no. 2, pp. 417–36.

Resnick, L.B. & Schantz, F., 2017, 'Testing, teaching, learning: Who is in charge?', *Assessment in Education: Principles, Policy & Practice*, vol. 24, no. 3, pp. 424–32.

# CHAPTER 10
# Diversity and Differentiation in Science

Gemma Scarparolo, The University of Western Australia

## GOALS

**The goals for this chapter are to support you to:**

- Explain the Australian Disability Standards for Education legislation and its relevance for education providers
- Describe differentiation and some of the ways that teachers can differentiate
- Explain three instructional strategies for effective differentiation

**Australian Professional Standards for Teachers—Graduate Level:**

- Standard 1: Know students and how they learn (Focus areas 1.1, 1.5)
- Standard 3: Plan for and implement effective teaching and learning (Focus area 3.3)
- Standard 5: Assess, provide feedback and report on student learning (Focus areas 5.1, 5.2)

## INTRODUCTION

The purpose of this chapter is to provide some background knowledge and practical suggestions for how to accommodate diversity within the science classroom through differentiation.

> The students were really nice, but it was difficult because in one class I had three students that were capable of working about two years above, and two students that were working at least a year below. One of these students had very poor literacy skills, and the other student was learning English. Then there was another student who had dyslexia, and there were two students who had ADHD. I tried my best to teach the curriculum and control the class, but I did find it difficult. (Pre-service high-school teacher)

The sentiments expressed by this pre-service teacher are common and reflect the feelings of many pre-service teachers after they have completed a professional practice experience. Generally, pre-service teachers don't anticipate facing such diversity within the one classroom; however, they should expect to see this diversity in every class that they teach. The reality is that regardless of a school's geographical location (rural, remote or suburban) or socio-economic status, the subject or the age of the students, each class will comprise students with various cultural, linguistic, religious and socio-economic backgrounds as well as gifted students and those with specific learning, physical, neurological or developmental disabilities.

Despite the diversity in every classroom, it is common for teachers, especially beginning teachers, to *teach to the middle*. This is a term used when teachers teach the content at the level of the average-ability student in the class, with little to no variation in how the content is presented in terms of the challenge, pace or how the students show what they know and understand. In Australia, teachers are required to cater for diversity as reflected in the Australian Professional Standards for Teachers. Standard 1.5 states that teachers need to provide evidence that they are able to differentiate 'teaching to meet the specific learning needs of students across the full range of abilities' (AITSL 2011, p. 9). While this standard states that differentiation is the way that teachers can cater for diversity within the classroom, Standard 1.3 is also relevant as this standard states that teachers need to demonstrate that they are able to implement teaching strategies that are 'responsive to the learning strengths and needs of students from diverse linguistic, cultural, religious and socio-economic backgrounds' (AITSL 2011, p. 8). Teachers must also be knowledgeable about the cultural and linguistic diversity of Aboriginal and Torres Strait Islander students, and this is reflected both in Standard 1.4 and in the cross-curriculum priority in the Australian Curriculum.

## EQUITY AND DIVERSITY

Globally, there has been a move towards education providers being more inclusive of students with disabilities. Australia has signed two international treaties that relate to the protection and rights of people with disabilities: the *United Nations Convention on the Rights of the Child* (Commonwealth of Australia 1986) and the *Convention on the Rights of Persons with Disabilities Declaration* (Commonwealth of Australia 2009).

While Australia signed both of these international treaties, specific legislation was introduced in Australia in 1992 called the *Disability Discrimination Act* (DDA) to protect people with disabilities in all areas of life (Commonwealth of Australia 1992). Many definitions of disability are provided in Section 4 of the DDA to include people with intellectual, physical, neurological, psychiatric and learning disabilities (Commonwealth of Australia 1992). The definitions of disability provided in the legislation include students with specific learning disabilities (such as dyslexia and dysgraphia), Attention Deficit Hyperactivity Disorder (ADHD), Autism Spectrum Disorder (ASD) and physical disabilities such as cerebral palsy.

In 2005, a sub-legislation of the DDA was introduced in Australia called the *Disability Standards for Education* (DSE) (Commonwealth of Australia 2005). *The Standards,* as they are commonly called, 'provide a framework to ensure that students with disability are able to access and participate in education on the same basis as other students. The Education Standards do this by providing clarity and specificity for education and training providers and for students with disability' (Commonwealth of Australia 2005, p. iii). It is important that education providers, teachers and parents are aware of both the DDA and the DSE legislation to ensure that the rights of students with disability are upheld and that these students have access to enrolment, curriculum delivery, facilities and programs in ways that are accessible and promote participation and achievement.

As part of the Australian Professional Standards for Teachers mentioned previously, teachers are also required to demonstrate evidence of how they accommodate students with disabilities in their teaching. This is reflected in Standard 1.6: Strategies to support full participation of students with disability (AITSL 2011).

## DIFFERENTIATION

The practice of differentiation is not new; catering for students' diversity within the classroom has always been at the core of effective teaching practice. With increasing diversity in classrooms, it is becoming important to formalise this practice and proactively and purposefully plan for diversity through differentiation. Carol Ann Tomlinson (2017), one of the most cited authors in the field of educational differentiation, proposes a framework for differentiation that provides a way for teachers to plan for diversity in a targeted, systematic and purposeful manner. Tomlinson suggests that modifications to the content, process, product and learning environment should be considered in light of the teacher's knowledge about their students' readiness, interests and learning profiles. A brief explanation of each of these elements from Tomlinson's framework will be provided in this section.

*Readiness* refers to the student's ability relative to the specific lesson content. *Pre-assessment* is the way that teachers determine readiness levels. Teachers can gather information about their students' readiness through a number of strategies, including informal diagnostic tests, quizzes, short-answer tests or a quick informal discussion. Teachers should use this information to inform their planning to ensure that they pitch the instruction, activities and assessment at an appropriate level to match the students' readiness.

Knowing students' *interests* is an important element of effective differentiation. Teachers can get to know their students' interests through quick informal surveys, either online or paper-based, where the students identify what they are interested in. Tapping into students' interests (both specific and broad) fosters motivation, and therefore it is important for teachers to find out their students' interests prior to planning a unit of work. Catering for students' interests can include teachers providing opportunities for *choice* of which activities they choose to complete.

*Learning profiles* should also be considered for effective differentiation to occur. Learning profiles can include elements of a student's preference for noise levels or their preferred way of learning (for example, whether the student likes to work individually when conducting experiments, or whether they like to work in pairs to write their science investigation). Knowing students' learning profiles can allow the teacher to purposefully provide opportunities for students to work in ways that the students prefer, which may increase their engagement, motivation and efficiency.

When teachers know their students' interests, readiness and learning profiles, they can use this information to inform their planning to match the instruction, activities and assessment. Decisions regarding the *content* (the curriculum and how it is presented), *process* (how the students learn the content), *product* (how the student demonstrates what they know and understand) and *learning environment* (both the tone and climate of the classroom and the physical learning environment) should be made based on the teachers' knowledge of their students' interests, readiness and learning profiles where suitable. It is important to note here that teachers do not need to differentiate for content, process, product and learning environment for each lesson, or for each student. Differentiation should be planned when it is needed. Differentiation is about teaching the same curriculum, but presenting it in different ways and, where appropriate, allowing students to choose which activities they complete and how they present what they know and understand. Some students can be given more time to complete activities, some can be given set time limits, and others, such as gifted or highly able students, may be allowed to work at their own pace.

## ASSESSMENT

Assessment is an important component in the teaching cycle. Pre-assessment, often referred to as diagnostic assessment (see Chapter 9), should always take place, whether informally or formally, to determine each student's readiness as previously outlined. Diagnostic assessment is consistent with teaching that is underpinned by a constructivist epistemology (see Chapter 3). Once this information has been gathered and analysed, the instructional level should be determined and used as a starting point for planning. Every class is heterogeneous, even when classes are streamed, and therefore there will always be diversity among the students that you teach. As a consequence, diversity should be explicitly considered and reflected in your planning, instruction, resources, activities and assessment.

Diagnostic assessment of readiness, which takes place prior to planning, can be conducted in several ways as previously explained. If students can use digital technology, another option is an online survey that allows the teacher to gather information quickly using online-survey tools. All too often, teachers plan lessons and units of work without gathering information on their students' prior knowledge relative to the content. This usually means that the lessons or unit of work may be at an inappropriate instructional level, which can result in students being bored, poorly behaved or frustrated due to the content being pitched either too low or too high in terms of challenge. With appropriate diagnostic assessment and analysis of the results, the teacher can proactively and purposefully plan for the diverse readiness levels in their class. This should enable the teacher to engage the students and provide all students with opportunities for success.

## INSTRUCTIONAL STRATEGIES TO ALLOW FOR DIFFERENTIATION

Differentiation is not a prescriptive list of instructional strategies; it includes a variety of instructional strategies that allow for differentiation, for example menus, tiered activities, cubing and choice boards/tic-tac-toe (Heacox 2012; Tomlinson 2017). Teachers can also implement differentiation by providing opportunities for students to make choices (choosing activities, resources, how they work and what variables they use) and opportunities for each child to be successful at learning something new or progressing in their understanding of a science concept or skill. Often, simply providing alternative pathways to the same content, skill, activity or assessment can mean that barriers are removed and opportunities for success are increased. One example of this is when a teacher provides students with the choice to use speech-to-text assistive technology, which removes the barrier of writing. This supports many students, including those who are learning English and those with dyspraxia or low literacy levels.

Piggott (2002) provides an example of what a differentiated science classroom may look like. Students 'can work in different ways: some might be discussing a problem and drawing up a joint set of notes; others might be trying out small sample experiments; others drawing cartoons of the major points; others still composing a poem or song' (p. 68). Three instructional strategies, specifically related to the teaching of science, will be presented in more detail below: tiered activities, menus and choice boards, all of which support experiments and investigations.

# EXPERIMENTS AND INVESTIGATIONS

## Tiered Activities

Planning a tiered activity involves the teacher facilitating different levels of activities to meet the diverse needs of the students within the classroom, while still addressing the same curriculum content. These levelled activities can be tiered according to students' readiness, interests or learning profile; however, the most common reason behind tiering is readiness. All of the activities should be interesting and challenging. The teacher can provide three levels of activities that students can choose from; the teacher can set which task the students need to complete, or this can be negotiated between the student and teacher.

# THE ART OF TEACHING SCIENCE 3RD EDITION

An easy way to tier a lesson in science is to provide three activities where all students are working on the same experiment, with each activity having different levels of support, challenge or reading ability. This can be achieved by simply increasing the number of variables to provide more challenge, or by using scaffolded or modified investigation guides (see Chapter 8), where different levels of information are provided depending on the students' readiness (Piggott 2002).

Maeng and Bell (2015) provided an example of how tiered activities were used to teach chemical sciences. 'All the students were tasked with the same goal: identify the unknown solutions through their patterns of mixing. All of the students, regardless of whether they had four or eight unknowns to identify, had to use their knowledge of solubility rules and observation skills. The variation in the tiers was in the degree of scaffolding' that the teacher provided (p. 2081).

Read the example provided in Snapshot 10.1, which outlines how one early-career teacher implements tiered lessons and activities.

---

**SNAPSHOT 10.1:** Tiering using the chilli method

I use the chilli system quite a lot in my classes. I provide three different activities, which all cover the same content, just at different challenge levels. I think a lot of people think that this means a lot more work, but I just use Bloom's taxonomy to differentiate the different challenge levels. The activities at one chilli are at the recall level, and I usually get these questions from a textbook. The activities at two chillies can involve extended answers or putting the information in a table or diagram, perhaps with some application to another similar context. The activities at the three-chilli level can include tasks where the students are asked to create a series of questions relevant to the topic and then find answers to their questions, or the questions of a peer who is also working at this level. Another activity at this level can include analysis of an article where the content is presented at a more complex level or in a different context.

## Menus

Teachers can plan to cater for diversity and provide opportunities for students with choice in the science curriculum through the use of a menu. As the term implies, the students are provided with a menu of options that they can choose from in order to meet the specific learning criteria. The teacher can provide items that students must complete, perhaps as an entrée so that all students start with the same knowledge, understanding or skill base. Points or similar can be used to ensure that all students are completing enough activities to adequately cover the content.

All items on the menu should be interesting and have a level of challenge, with activities being provided at all levels of Bloom's taxonomy (Heacox 2012). For example, the knowledge and recall activities may be worth fewer marks, so that the student may be required to complete more of them; alternatively, the activities that require higher levels of thinking at the synthesis and analysis level may be worth more points, so that the student has to complete fewer activities. Snapshot 10.2 below outlines how a teacher implemented a menu, including the task instructions.

**SNAPSHOT 10.2:** A menu using formative assessment that caters for readiness and interest

### Teacher's reflection

One of the best activities that I have included on a menu was a formative assessment task, where the students were required to create a set of possible test questions and then an answer key. For example, for my Year 9 physics class we had just focused on learning about sound. This activity was broad enough so that students of all ability levels could complete it to their own ability, and yet it was interesting for everyone.

The students with lower ability in that area did straightforward calculation questions. The higher-ability students came up with some bizarre scenarios and questions, and spent ages trying to figure out and refine the problems they wrote as well as writing

> suitable answers. Actually, that was one of the best activities that I did, and it required basically nothing on my part other than walking around, encouraging them and utilising the *think aloud* strategy to model how I might go about answering the questions they came up with.
>
> **The task on the students' menu**
>
> You are required to demonstrate your knowledge and understanding about sound, which we have been covering over the last two weeks. You need to create a test and an answer sheet that could be given to students studying the same topic. As per the instructions on the menu, you need to have at least five questions, including one multiple-choice question, two short-answer questions and two questions that require the test-taker to either draw or illustrate their answer.

## Choice Boards

Teachers can provide students with choice and flexibility by allowing them to select which activities they would like to complete from a board with nine options. The nine activities should all be based on the same essential content or curriculum. By providing students with a choice of which activities they would like to complete the students' engagement and motivation should increase.

The central square can be left as a student choice, where they can propose an activity that they would like to complete and negotiate this with the teacher. Specific criteria or instructions should be provided (for example, students must complete three activities in a row, either diagonally, vertically or horizontally). With careful planning and acknowledgement of the students' interests, readiness and learning profiles, the teacher can purposefully position activities within the choice board to ensure that each student will be sufficiently challenged, interested and successful with the content.

# ADDRESSING CONCERNS ABOUT DIFFERENTIATION

Teachers, students and parents often raise concerns about differentiated approaches to teaching and learning. The most common of these concerns are listed below, with a response provided for each concern.

- *How will the other students respond when some students are given different tasks?* Teachers should explain clearly to their students that, in their classroom, students will often be given a choice of different activities to complete, and that at other times the teacher will choose which activities the class completes.
- *How can I manage a classroom where there are different activities, resources or materials?* Careful and proactive planning by the teacher is essential to the effective management of any classroom, and a differentiated classroom is no different. If teachers proactively plan to cater for diversity in their lesson planning, students will be more engaged and successful because more opportunities for success are provided for all students.
- *Students will often choose the easiest activity.* In every classroom, there will always be some students who choose not to work to their full ability level; conversely, there will often be students who choose activities that are above their ability. Some students will choose the perceived easiest activity; however, in a truly differentiated classroom, the various activities should all have elements of challenge and interest, and therefore this problem should be minimised. If you feel that students are not making good choices, in relation to their readiness or interests, then guide the students to a more suitable option.
- *Parents will question why their child sometimes has different work to complete than their peers.* Parents should know that you plan to make the content more accessible and relevant for students, and that at times students will be given choices in how they work, how they learn and how they demonstrate what they know while still addressing the same curriculum and assessment criteria as their peers.

- *How can I give students grades when they are doing different activities?* The different activities should all be based on the same curriculum or learning goals, and therefore the assessment criteria should be the same regardless of how the student demonstrates what they know and understand. (See Chapter 9 for more information on assessment.)

## SUMMARY OF KEY POINTS

Every class that you teach will be diverse; students in your classroom will have diverse cultural and linguistic backgrounds and different interests, abilities, motivation levels and learning profiles. It is our job as teachers to embrace the diversity and proactively plan to cater for this diversity by differentiating either the content, process, product or learning environment based on our knowledge of our students' readiness, interests and learning profiles. Differentiation can include minor adjustments, such as providing levelled texts, a vocabulary list or offering students a choice. Or differentiation can include major modifications, such as providing a variety of different activities, providing options for products/assessments or allowing students to work at their own pace. In the teaching of science, experiments can be presented in different formats, explanations can be provided in different formats, investigation sheets can be scaffolded for different ability levels, vocabulary lists can be provided, students can be given options with regard to how they present their knowledge, challenge can be adjusted and flexibility can be provided in the pace that students work through the content.

Early-career teachers should be conscious of not planning and teaching in the one-size-fits-all model, as research has shown that this does not cater for the diversity of students in classrooms. You need to take the time to get to know your students, their interests, their preferred ways of working and their readiness relevant to each content focus so that you can provide optimum opportunities for success for all students.

## ACKNOWLEDGEMENT

Thank you to the pre-service and classroom teachers who shared their thoughts and experiences and gave permission for these to be shared for the purpose of this chapter.

## DISCUSSION QUESTIONS

10.1 Discuss ways that you could differentiate specific secondary-science lessons for students who are learning English. For example, a practical lesson on refraction, an outdoor lesson on plants in the local environment, a theoretical lesson on the chambers of the human heart, or an experiment on acids and bases.

10.2 Choose one instructional strategy from this chapter and describe how you could implement this instructional strategy to teach a particular science concept, such as genes and DNA, gravity, acceleration or atoms and molecules.

10.3 How will you manage the science classroom when you are differentiating for different readiness levels?

## REFERENCES

AITSL (2011)—see preface for full reference.

Commonwealth of Australia, 1986, *Human Rights and Equal Opportunity Commission Act 1986—Declaration of the United Nations Convention on the Rights of the Child*, <www.legislation.gov.au/Details/F2009B00173>, accessed 28 August 2018.

Commonwealth of Australia, 1992, *Disability Discrimination Act 1992*, <www.legislation.gov.au/Series/C2004A04426>, accessed 10 July 2018.

Commonwealth of Australia, 2005, *Disability Standards for Education 2005*, <www.legislation.gov.au/Details/F2005L00767/Download>, accessed 10 July 2018.

Commonwealth of Australia, 2009, *Convention on the Rights of Persons with Disabilities Declaration 2009,* <www.legislation.gov.au/Details/F2009L02620>, accessed 28 August 2018.

Heacox, D., 2012, *Differentiating Instruction in the Regular Classroom: How to Reach and Teach All Learners, Grades 3–12,* Minneapolis, MN: Free Spirit Publishing.

Maeng, J.L & Bell, R.L., 2015, 'Differentiating science instruction: Secondary science teachers' practices', *International Journal of Science Education,* vol. 37, no. 13, pp. 2065–90.

Piggott, A., 2002, 'Putting differentiation into practice in secondary science lessons', *School Science Review,* vol. 83, no. 305, pp. 65–71.

Tomlinson, C.A., 2017, *How to Differentiate Instruction in Academically Diverse Classrooms,* 3rd ed., Alexandria, VA: ASCD.

# PART 3
# EXTENDING THE ART OF TEACHING SCIENCE

CHAPTER 11

# A Toolkit of Additional Teaching Strategies and Procedures

Jennifer Donovan, University of Southern Queensland

## GOALS

The goals for this chapter are to support you to:

- Understand the different functions of teaching strategies and procedures
- Understand the importance of using a variety of teaching strategies and procedures
- Attempt to use the strategies and procedures presented here with your classes

Australian Professional Standards for Teachers—Graduate Level:

- Standard 1: Know students and how they learn (Focus area 1.2)
- Standard 2: Know the content and how to teach it (Focus area 2.1)
- Standard 3: Plan for and implement effective teaching and learning (Focus areas 3.3, 3.4)

# INTRODUCTION

Let's start with a question. *Do you think concept maps and brainstorming are teaching strategies OR procedures OR activities?* Yes, that question is tricky, isn't it? I am guessing that you have probably encountered all of those terms, even at this early stage in your teaching career. Now, I could ask you to read 20–30 papers and come to your own conclusion about these terms. Surely, you would find a consensus, clear definitions that separate these out, along with examples that illustrate the differences? To spare you that much reading—and the confusion that would result—there is *no consensus in the literature* as to the differences between these three terms. In fact, these terms have been used in different ways already in this book, so all I can present here is a distinction that makes sense to me!

However, before I do so, let's ask another question. *Does it matter?* Well, in one sense no, as long as you know what you're doing. Maybe it doesn't matter what you call it. However, I think the distinction can be useful, as it forces you to think about your teaching and plan for it at different levels. Ultimately, this depth of thinking and planning benefits your students, plus it should also benefit you. Like many things in life, successful teaching is about good preparation. The more deeply you prepare, and the better your classes go, the more you will enjoy teaching. Also, if things don't work, you have different levels that you can interrogate to see where the problem might lie and how you might improve for next time. So, how do I see these terms as different? I think of them in a hierarchy from bigger to smaller, as seen in Figure 11.1.

Other chapters in this book have discussed theory (particularly constructivism) and approaches (particularly inquiry). Some strategies (and procedures) have also been discussed, although not necessarily following this hierarchy of naming. These include jigsaw, gallery walk, brainstorming, concept mapping, cooperative group work, Predict–Observe–Explain (POE) and effective questioning. How many more strategies and procedures can there be? Answer: a lot! There are many ways to teach science; the best teachers have a large toolkit of ways, and they know when to choose and use each tool. I hope that you will gain some of that knowledge in this chapter, but you will need to apply this knowledge to your practice to gain mastery.

**FIGURE 11.1:** A possible hierarchy of teaching terminology

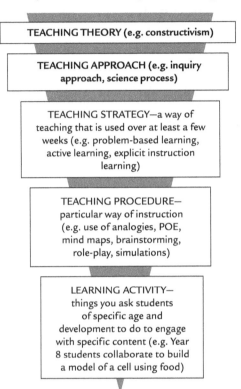

# TEACHING STRATEGIES

In this hierarchy, teaching strategies are ways of teaching that usually occupy a few weeks, maybe a term. The term *strategy* has a meaning referring to *tactics*, and that is a useful context here. The question you are trying to answer by thinking about strategy is: Within the overall approach (for example, inquiry), what tactics can you employ that will achieve broad goals such as:

1. to improve students' problem-solving skills;
2. to improve students' engagement in class;
3. to enable students to appreciate connections between scientific disciplines;

4. to foster students' skills of cooperation and working together;
5. to encourage students to study a topic in depth; and
6. to allow students to experience authentic science?

These broad goals are unrelated to particular science content, but are desirable attributes for students to develop. Broad goals require a strategy that lasts for a few weeks or a whole term to be effective. Some strategies are listed below.

A. Active learning
B. Blended learning
C. Citizen science
D. Distance education
E. Explicit instruction
F. Flexible time
G. Group problem-based learning

As Figure 11.1 suggests, all of these strategies can be used within an inquiry approach.

## Strategy A—Active Learning

This is characterised by the students taking responsibility for their learning by actively participating in a wide range of activities. Reading, writing, discussion, problem-solving, science inquiry, practical activities and experimentation are just some of the possible activities that aim to promote depth of understanding of content and higher-order thinking such as analysis, synthesis and evaluation. This can be combined with other strategies, such as collaborative learning and problem-based learning, to good effect. The use of learning stations—designated areas of the classroom with different resources and materials that groups of students work their way around—is a common way of managing the logistics of an active-learning strategy.

More information about active learning is available from the Center for Research on Learning and Teaching (CRLT 2016). This includes a downloadable pdf that describes many ways of doing this—termed *approaches,* but in Figure 11.1's hierarchy, these would be procedures.

## Strategy B—Blended Learning

This refers to a blend between classroom activities and online activities. The degree of blending is up to the teacher and the nature of the science content that is being covered. The *flipped classroom* is one example of blended learning. Essentially, activities that are *normally* done in class—such as engaging with essential content, taking notes, reading and listening to the teacher—are *flipped,* so they are done online as preparation for the class. Class time is spent in active learning, applying the knowledge gained from the online activities, wrestling with problems, having discussions, debates and other productive classroom talk, and possibly completing some activities that would *normally* have been done as homework, such as practice exercises.

This strategy can be helpful when the content is not easily able to be experienced in the classroom (for example, work on the Solar System). Specific tasks can be accomplished online, with the degree of scaffolding (supply of websites and directions) varied according to the age and maturity of the students. This strategy can also be very helpful when teaching in rural and remote areas where students may not always be able to get to school, as long as the area is served by the internet. Having activities available for students to work on from home can keep them going when things are busy on the farm, or when extreme weather conditions make it difficult to get to school. Challenges include students who come to class without having completed the pre-class work, and the workload for teachers in preparing all of the resources. Debbie Morrison (n.d.) has helpfully collated a great range of resources on blended learning on her website.

## Strategy C—Citizen Science

When used in science teaching, this strategy aims to promote an authentic experience of science. Citizen science has been growing in popularity and involves citizens who are not professional scientists participating in scientific activities, such as gathering data, analysing data and reporting their findings to scientists. Early examples include amateur birdwatchers reporting their sightings to biologists and American volunteers collecting rainwater samples across the United States to raise awareness of acid rain.

> ### SNAPSHOT 11.1: Stargazing as an example of citizen science
>
> In 2017 and 2018, a stargazing program was broadcast on television over three nights in the Australian autumn, part of which encouraged citizens to examine data to search for solar systems (2017) and supernovae (2018). Both of these yielded successful discoveries, subsequently published, and in 2018, a new world record was also set for the number of simultaneous stargazers (over 40,000, though they gazed at the moon). Professor Brian Cox is quoted as saying:
>
> > It's great to break the world record for the number of people stargazing simultaneously, but I think this is only half the story. The real value is that many thousands of Australians have been introduced to the wonders of the night sky, and many of those will be children. They will develop a lifelong interest in astronomy and science, and the impact of that will be felt in decades to come. Perhaps the first Australian to walk on Mars will have been inspired by this spectacular night. (https://tvtonight.com.au/2018/05/stargazing-live-breaks-world-record.html)

Citizen science can accomplish tasks that are too time-consuming or too expensive for scientists to achieve alone. In science classrooms, citizen science usually operates in partnership with a particular scientist or group of scientists. Scientists and teacher discuss possibilities for cooperation so that the needs of both the students and the scientists are met. It is preferable if such discussion results in a few possibilities, so that the students themselves can select their preference, increasing their engagement in the project. Or it might be possible for the class to divide into groups, with each group taking on a different aspect of the project. The CSIRO offers a

A TOOLKIT OF ADDITIONAL TEACHING STRATEGIES AND PROCEDURES

program called STEM Professionals in Schools, and such a partnership can lead to a citizen-science project for your students.

Searching for citizen-science projects will yield many hits for projects all around the world. Not all are suitable for school students, so check them out carefully. An example of an Australian project that can feed into a global project is Aussie Backyard Bird Count, which can feed into eBird. To learn how citizen science has been used in classrooms in South Australia, see Paige, Hattam and Daniels (2015).

## Strategy D—Distance Education

This is learning that occurs remotely from the location of the school. Today, this is mostly accomplished online or using other technology such as radio (for example, School of the Air), allowing teachers to provide distance learners with authentic learning experiences, more closely aligned in outcomes to the experiences of students in classrooms. Video-conferencing technology is always improving and can bring remote learners into a classroom while a lesson is happening, allowing them to see and hear the lesson and to contribute their ideas. However, be wary about making recordings of classroom lessons available online as the sole substitute for learners who cannot be involved in the class itself. This can result in them feeling even more isolated, as it is very difficult to get clear vision and audio of everything in a busy classroom. The sense of missing out when a teacher's discussion with a small group is inaudible on the recording can be profound.

Another common problem with distance-learning programs is that face-to-face materials are simply reproduced online without due regard for the pros and cons of online learning. For example, just replicating notes used in classrooms for online use often lacks the personal touch, leaving learners disengaged. Rewriting the notes in a more personal style and incorporating regular touchpoints as learning activities can greatly enhance engagement. Being creative about resources that students probably have at home and which can be used for activities can promote active learning and hands-on, minds-on science. It may also be possible to create resource

THE ART OF TEACHING SCIENCE 3RD EDITION

kits for a term of science learning that are posted out before the term starts and are posted back at the end of term. Remember that distance learners are often supervised by their parents, who are not necessarily skilled teachers, particularly science teachers, so more instructions regarding risk assessment and safety may be needed for science activities to be completed at home, on camps or on field trips.

## Strategy E—Explicit Instruction

This strategy is often wrongly equated with a *transmission approach* to teaching, bringing to mind passive learners in their seats while the teacher expounds from the front of the class. This is not an appropriate model for explicit instruction. At its core, the focus is clear explanation using unambiguous language, but this should be supported by activities to consolidate the learning. An effective approach is to limit a period of explicit instruction to around ten minutes and then immediately follow it up with hands-on (and minds-on) activities to illustrate the principles that have just been explained. For example, explicit instruction on the structure of an eye, naming all of the parts and explaining their functions, could be followed with the dissection of a sheep's eye or the use of a model that comes apart, and the conducting of visual tests using the Snellen eye chart or the Ishihara colour-plate test for colour blindness.

The skill of explanation is one that must be practised and developed, but here are some helpful guidelines:

- General to specific—start with the big picture and then narrow in.
- Simple to complex—start with simple ideas and build gradually to complex ideas.
- Concrete to abstract—begin with concrete ideas that students can visualise and/or handle, such as concrete models, and progress to abstract, intangible ideas.
- Chunking—divide a large topic into separate chunks that are presented in an appropriate sequence so students do not reach cognitive overload and have time to master each chunk.

- Using visuals—these aid explanation, but only if they can be interpreted by students; do not forget to explain diagrams and model how you arrived at your interpretation.

For more information on explicit instruction, read Archer and Hughes (2011).

## Strategy F—Flexible Time

Traditionally, classrooms run in a lock-step manner—all students have the same amount of time for learning. However, students learn at different rates. A way of differentiating for this is to free up the time constraints and adopt the principle of mastery learning. Students only move on when they have mastered the current step. This is how practical skills—such as swimming, dancing or playing a musical instrument—are taught, yet we rarely apply this strategy to formal subjects (such as science) in the classroom. This is a challenge within the crowded curriculum, where the demand is for all students to complete tests and assignments at the same time, but technology can allow flexible access to materials.

Students can move on when they are ready, not necessarily when others are ready. Capable students can go further in breadth and depth, so they are also stretched. Flexibility in timing is a key recommendation of the recent review into education (Department of Education & Training 2018). The review recommends a shift from our current industrial model of education to a flexible model that allows each student to achieve to their maximum capability, recognising that this will require considerable change in current educational structures that are locked into age and grade.

## Strategy G—Group Problem-based Learning

Problem-based learning relies on supplying students with trigger material about a problem they have come up with that needs to be solved. Students work together in groups to acquire the information they require to solve the problem. Scenarios are a popular choice for trigger material in science. This strategy is particularly useful for exploring aspects of *Science as a Human Endeavour*, especially the nature of science. Problems should be scaffolded in science classrooms to include practical hands-on experimentation activities as well as information research.

Another possibility for a practical hands-on approach to problem-solving is to incorporate design technology with science to attack particular problems. For example, a Year 9 class could be challenged to build a working model to simulate how the movement of tectonic plates causes earthquakes. The design-technology problem then becomes a series of questions. *What materials do we have available that are suitable for our model? What processes must the model represent?* Clearly, students will need to encounter geological information about the Earth's crust, plate structures, boundaries and possible movements. They will need to research seismology, including earthquakes and their measurement scales. Some of this information may be provided by a procedure called *Just-in-Time Teaching*, where content is only taught when the students indicate a need for it. Students will also need to exercise creative thinking concerning the resources available with which to build the model, and some trial and error and other experiments to determine the most favourable resources. This type of problem requires a lot of hands-on and minds-on science to solve, and the teacher can manipulate the degree of scaffolding required as the students work through the process. Torp and Sage (2002) show what problem-based learning looks like in classrooms.

These are by no means all of the strategies available to teachers, even within the definition from Figure 11.1. However, it is a good selection that will whet your appetite for trying new strategies. It is important, though, to use them purposefully, not just for novelty. Think carefully about the broad goals you want to achieve (the six listed earlier in the chapter are not the only possibilities) and what content you want the students to learn, and then decide on the tactics that are most likely to achieve those goals. Combine strategies if necessary to achieve your aims. The success, or failure, of many strategies rides not only on careful selection but also in the way you introduce them to students. Some students are creatures of habit and routine, and they may react unfavourably to sudden

A TOOLKIT OF ADDITIONAL TEACHING STRATEGIES AND PROCEDURES **185**

changes in classroom activities and expectations. So think carefully about how you might engage students in the need to change things and do them differently. Monitor your implementation of the chosen strategy/ies carefully and be prepared to modify, adjust level of scaffolding (teacher assistance) or even abandon a strategy depending on how well it is working (or not). Remember, though, that whether it works or not is context-dependent. It is not necessarily a *bad strategy* if it did not work—it may have been simply an unwise choice for that time, group of students, work involved or even time of year.

# PROCEDURES

Within the hierarchy presented in this chapter, *procedures* are methods of instruction used within individual lessons. Teachers may use these *off the cuff* (for example, when trying to explain a concept, a teacher may use an analogy—'think of . . .'). However, it is preferable to plan for the procedures you will use during a lesson, so you can select the best one for the purpose and be aware of any caveats on its use. For example, all analogies break down in some way— they are not perfect analogs (matches) for the target concept—so planning for the use of the analogy should include a reminder to explain where it breaks down. Some procedures are described below for your consideration.

## Analogies

An analogy has two parts—the *target concept* is what you want the students to learn, and the *analog* is the familiar concept you introduce to help them understand the target concept. Analogies can be simple similes, such as 'a tectonic plate (target) is like a moving walkway (analog)', 'a cell is like a factory', 'an atom is like a tiny solar system' and 'space–time is like a rubber sheet with the big astronomical objects like bowling balls rolling around on it'. All of these may be helpful IF the analogs are meaningful to the students. Some classic analogies—for example, 'the eye is like a camera'—are no longer useful, as cameras today are rarely black-lined objects with light-sensitive film at the back of them. This is why planning analogies ahead of time is important. One of the seminal papers on teaching and learning with analogies is Harrison and Treagust (2006).

## Models

Models may be purely physical resources such as a replica (for example, a skeleton; balls and sticks for atoms), purely conceptual (for example, natural selection) or both, with the physical model assisting students to construct an appropriate mental model. Whether physical or conceptual, models are a type of analogy, used with the same aim of making the unfamiliar more familiar and understandable. Younger secondary-school students may still be primarily concrete thinkers, and the capacity to physically manipulate a model can be very helpful for them to begin to develop a mental model of the target concept.

However, as with metaphors, similes and analogies, teachers must be aware of models introducing alternative conceptions. For example, students often experience the so-called *volcano reaction* as an example of a chemical reaction (mixing sodium bicarbonate with vinegar). Some build elaborate volcano-like structures to contain the reaction and may even colour the mixture red. However, this reaction has little to do with how volcanoes actually erupt, which is due to changes in pressure and movement of molten magma. Carbon dioxide gas is released in both cases but not due to the reaction of the same substances, so the model can be misleading. Some of these models may still be useful for motivational or other purposes, but it is important for the teacher to be clear with the students where the model isn't the same as the real thing.

## Role-plays

Science role-plays can be simple or elaborate, but at their core they involve the students themselves enacting scientific processes. Role-plays can be entirely scaffolded by the teacher, be a product of collaboration between students and teacher, or can be entirely produced by students. Equipment can be as simple as strips of card with paper clips forming headbands to identify what each student represents, or as elaborate as a fully costumed play. They are particularly useful for clarifying dynamic processes rather than single concepts. Here is a short list of processes for which role-plays can be advantageous.

a) Particles of matter—students represent the particles and demonstrate arrangements of solids, liquids and gases by movement within the container/classroom.
b) Atoms and simple covalent bonding—students are identified as atoms of various elements, such as H, C, O and N, and are asked to join hands to form simple covalent compounds to clarify the concept of valency.
c) Cell membrane—students form two lines to represent the lipid bilayers of the membrane, with embedded proteins. Other students represent different substances that try to move through the membrane, with their passage through being determined by their identity.
d) Nerve impulse—students line up to represent the axon of a neuron, with the teacher at one end as the cell body. To simulate impulse transmission in grey matter, the teacher starts a timer and passes a baton (or whispers a few words) to the first student; the baton/words are passed one by one down the line.
e) Planets in the Solar System—after some rigorous mathematics to work out appropriate distances, students can assemble on the school oval to represent relative planetary distances from the sun. This can be extended by having students rotate in the same direction that their planet does.

## SUMMARY OF KEY POINTS

This chapter presented a hierarchy of terminology to guide planning at different levels. The main focus of the chapter was on strategies—tactically employed over an extended period to pursue a broader educational goal. Seven different strategies were offered as

THE ART OF TEACHING SCIENCE 3RD EDITION

a means to extend your teaching toolkit. In addition, three procedures—methods of instruction used in individual lessons, including role-plays and analogies—were described.

## DISCUSSION QUESTIONS

11.1 Can you cross-match the broad goals with appropriate strategies? Is there a one-to-one correlation, or could some strategies be used to achieve different goals? Are the strategies mutually exclusive, or could some of them be used together?

11.2 Quality of data is often raised as a concern with citizen science. What are the ethical issues involved in participating in citizen science?

11.3 What are the essential considerations of a teacher who is facilitating distance education for science students?

11.4 What educational structures do you foresee would need to change to adopt a flexible time and mastery learning strategy for education in Australia?

11.5 Do you regard problem-based learning as a way for students to encounter authentic, real-world science? Why or why not? What is the teacher's role in a class that is undertaking problem-based learning?

## REFERENCES

Archer, A.L. & Hughes, C.A., 2011, 'Exploring the foundations of explicit instruction', in A.L. Archer & C.A. Hughes, *Explicit Instruction: Effective and Efficient Teaching*, New York, NY: Guildford, pp. 1–22.

Center for Research on Learning and Teaching (CRLT), 2016, *Introduction to Active Learning*, <www.crlt.umich.edu/active_learning_introduction>, accessed 10 October 2018.

Department of Education & Training, 2018, *Through Growth to Achievement: Report of the Review to Achieve Educational Excellence in Australian Schools*, Canberra: Commonwealth of Australia.

Harrison, A.G. & Treagust, D.F., 2006, 'Teaching and learning with analogies', in P.J. Aubusson, A.G. Harrison & S.M. Ritchie (eds), *Metaphor and Analogy in Science Education,* Dordrecht: Springer, pp. 11–24.

Morrison, D.A., n.d., *Resources for Blended Learning: K–12,* <www.debbiemorrison.net/blended-learning-resources.html>, accessed 10 October 2018.

Paige, K., Hattam, R. & Daniels, C.B., 2015, 'Two models for implementing citizen science projects in middle school', *Journal of Educational Enquiry,* vol. 14, no. 2, pp. 4–17.

Torp, L. & Sage, S., 2002, 'What does problem-based learning look like in classrooms?', in L. Torp & S. Sage, *Problems as Possibilities: Problem-based Learning for K–16 Education,* 2nd ed., <www.ascd.org/publications/books/101064/chapters/What_Does_Problem-Based_Learning_Look_Like_in_Classrooms¢.aspx>, accessed 10 October 2018.

# CHAPTER 12
# Science and Safety Inside and Outside School Laboratories

Siew Fong Yap, Kingsway Christian College

## GOALS

**The goals for this chapter are to support you to:**

- Identify types of science experiences facilitated by school science classrooms/laboratories
- Cultivate an informed awareness of the Occupational Health and Safety Guidelines and how to manage safety in the school science laboratory and other contexts

**Australian Professional Standards for Teachers—Graduate Level:**

- Standard 3: Plan for and implement effective teaching and learning (Focus areas 3.3, 3.4)
- Standard 4: Create and maintain supportive and safe learning environments (Focus areas 4.2, 4.4, 4.5)

## INTRODUCTION

What's special about science? For many students, their most positive memory of school science experiences is *doing prac*. It follows, then, that science in schools should be hands-on wherever possible. This reflects the work of scientists who understand and explain the world through many processes, including experimentation, observation, measurement, calculation, modelling and other systematic activities. The quintessence of science education lies in providing opportunities for students to learn about both the process and content of science. Effective use of resources and facilities in purpose-built science classrooms or laboratories and out-of-classroom learning environments constitutes an important part of students' learning of science.

This chapter describes science laboratories and their uses, with a focus on safety. It is essential that facilities and laboratory procedures comply with state and national legislation and standards, and that the safety of your students underpins everything you do. The chapter also offers suggestions for some out-of-classroom learning contexts and environments and ways of connecting with outside institutions to consolidate students' learning experiences and apply them to contexts beyond the school setting. Photographs and snapshots illustrate and demonstrate how some resources can be used in middle-school and upper-secondary science classrooms.

# THE SCIENCE CLASSROOM/LABORATORY

Science classrooms are usually specially configured so the room can be used for both theoretical and practical science learning. Most schools refer to the science classrooms as the *science labs,* which are often physically and culturally separated in their own purpose-designed building, the *science block.* Housed in the science block, mostly in storage and preparation rooms, are many specialist resources: books, chemicals, equipment, glassware, specimens and instruments. Offices and meeting areas for technicians and science teachers may also be located in the science block.

The science classroom or laboratory can provide students with learning experiences utilising both manual and intellectual skills. Laboratory work may be structured to help students understand new concepts, acquire habits and capacities, gain practical skills, appreciate the nature of science and develop scientific attitudes. Types of laboratory activities include guided-inquiry, discovery-based, confirmatory, problem-based and open-ended investigations. Confirmatory activities (replicating known experiments) have a place in training students in procedures and in concept consolidation, but students should experience other types of practical activities that allow them to exercise their intellectual skills and satisfy their curiosity. Thus, teachers' choices of instructional strategies, students' opportunities for active involvement individually or collaboratively, student motivation and attitudes to learning are key factors that drive the outcomes of laboratory work. Logistical constraints, such as the availability of equipment, materials, laboratory allocation and the duration of the school allocated period (in other words, the timetable), must also be factored in.

In some schools, all science classes are timetabled into a science classroom, allowing flexibility in running practical work at an optimal time. These rooms can usually be configured for different purposes. However, in some schools, classes are only rostered into a science room once or twice a week, so practical work must be fitted into this schedule. In older labs, furniture was often fixed in place, but modern labs have movable tables and chairs that can be cleared to allow space for large-scale activities, such as student presentations or modelling a scientific phenomenon using role-play. Activities requiring still more space may be conducted outdoors or in a hall or gymnasium (explored later in this chapter).

## Equipment and Safety in Science Laboratories

Most laboratories have fixtures such as sinks, storage cabinets, gas taps, electrical outlets and benches. Safety comes first in science, so the first thing a teacher should note when entering a new science room is the location of the master controls for gas, water and electricity. Next is the location and operation of all safety equipment—from personal protective equipment (PPE) such as safety glasses, coats/ aprons and gloves, which are to be used routinely, to emergency equipment such as fire extinguishers, fire blankets, first-aid box, eye rinses and emergency eyewash, safety showers, evacuation procedures and assembly points. Students should also be made aware of the location and operation of the emergency equipment, and the need for the use of PPE during practical classes.

To promote safe movement around a science laboratory, there should be safe storage for students' bags so the floor is clear, as tripping becomes extra dangerous if students are carrying glassware or hazardous chemicals. Students should also understand the requirement of wearing protective enclosed shoes, tying long hair back and securing any dangling clothing such as sleeves and ties. Figure 12.1 shows a Year 12 student appropriately dressed in a laboratory coat, safety glasses and disposable gloves, and with hair tied back ready for a dissection lesson in a biological science lab.

Figure 12.2 shows the essential safety features (laboratory safety rules poster, first-aid instruction booklet and first-aid procedure chart) and equipment (fire extinguisher, fire blanket and first-aid

**FIGURE 12.1:** Laboratory safety for a dissection

box). Figure 12.3 shows the emergency shower and eyewash next to the fume cupboard, in which any experiments that may release toxic fumes **must** be conducted.

Students **must** report injuries, spills and broken or damaged equipment to the teacher immediately. They are more likely to do so if they are not frightened of being reprimanded for injury or breakages and if they understand that their safety and that of their fellow students depends on reporting such incidents. As hot and cool metal and glassware look exactly alike, minor burns are the most common injuries and should be treated immediately with cool running water. Tongs and safety mitts should be available for safe handling of hot items. Never handle hot items with rubber or plastic gloves as they may melt, making it harder to treat the burn. Liquids squirted into the eye should be flushed out using the emergency eyewash. Any injury involving broken skin should be treated by a health professional such as the school nurse, or by an adult with first-aid training. Teachers should be aware of the health issues of

**FIGURE 12.2:** Laboratory safety features and equipment

**FIGURE 12.3:** Emergency shower, eyewash and fume cupboard

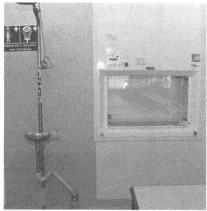

SCIENCE AND SAFETY INSIDE AND OUTSIDE SCHOOL LABORATORIES 195

specific students, as some materials (for example, latex) may cause skin irritations or trigger allergic reactions.

Laboratory equipment is only safe if it is used and maintained properly. Sinks and gas taps are prone to clogging, either by unthinking disposal of inappropriate wastes or by deliberate action. They should be checked regularly, particularly before any practical activity in which they will be used, and students should be briefed about what constitutes acceptable laboratory practice and safe disposal of waste. Benchtops should be kept clean and as clear of other items as possible during practical activities (for example, minimise books, writing equipment and electrical items; allocate one student/group the role of recorder of the data). Once reported, spills should be mopped up promptly and safely, with appropriate disposal of the mopping agents. Beware of colourless fluids that may resemble water but are dangerous to touch (for example, many acids and bases).

Most laboratories have an assortment of glassware, originally designed for chemistry experiments but now used across all sciences. Test tubes and beakers are standard receptacles for small and medium quantities respectively, of liquids, powdered solids and biological samples. Glassware has the advantage of being readily available and completely transparent, and the disadvantage of being brittle and easily broken or chipped. Tools such as a dustpan and brush for safely cleaning up broken glass should also be readily available.

Heating equipment in laboratories commonly includes Bunsen burners, heatproof mats, tripod stands, gauze mats, test-tube tongs, test-tube racks and retort stands. Bunsen burners connect to a gas supply, with outlets usually around the periphery of the laboratory or spaced along fixed benches. Students must be trained in the safe use of Bunsen burners, particularly the different types of flames produced by adjusting the vent hole. A yellow flame is more visible than the hotter blue flame produced by an open vent. Heatproof mats protect the bench surface from damage by hot material or glassware. Tripod stands provide a stable support for gauze mats, which in turn support larger glassware items such as beakers or conical flasks. Always heat substances in glass or Pyrex test tubes

THE ART OF TEACHING SCIENCE 3RD EDITION

or beakers. Lessons should be timed so that hot items can cool down before they need to be handled and put away.

Teachers and technicians should be aware of all chemicals to be used in science classes. Material safety data sheets (MSDS) are available for all chemicals and should be consulted prior to a practical class to check particularly on toxicity and safe handling of each chemical. In compliance with WorkSafe and Chemical Safety Legislation Policy as set by Australian/New Zealand Standard AS/NZS 2243:2006 Safety in Laboratories, all experiments are to be risk-assessed by each teacher and laboratory technician before conducting them in the school laboratory. It is a common practice in most schools to complete an equipment order form and the risk-assessment form simultaneously before handing over to the laboratory technician for preparation and set-up. Some schools opt for a more streamlined approach using *RiskAssess* (www.riskassess.com.au), which provides consistent and authoritative advice concerning all aspects of school-laboratory safety, management and design.

There are various ways to distribute equipment effectively to students, the choice being contingent on the layout of the laboratory, ease of moving around and the nature and potential hazards of the equipment to be used. Equipment may be in trays on a side bench for one student from each group to collect and return, it may be placed on students' benches before class begins, or the teacher and/or technician may move around and deliver the equipment as required. No matter what method is used, all equipment distributed for student use should be pre-counted and counted back at the end of the class. Thefts are not necessarily common but they do occur, and absent-mindedness could also result in equipment (for example, scalpels) leaving the classroom. Science equipment could be dangerous in the wrong hands, and it is also expensive for the school to replace.

Teachers often choose to display eye-catching and motivational items such as models of molecules, models of body parts, skulls, skeletons, science kits, geological sections, posters, potted plants, aquariums and terrariums. Ideally, they should be relevant to the current topic, and should only stay as long as they are clean and in good condition. Posters and models are relatively easy to rotate between laboratories, so students can see a different display from time to time. Excessive clutter and items that jut out into walkways should be avoided. Figure 12.4 shows a display of student-created models, such as cell models, DNA models, digestive-system board games and the periodic table, which may be used for teaching purposes.

## Planning for Safety in Science Laboratories

First, although this seems obvious, you need to be familiar with how each practical works. Not all experiments accessed online or in a textbook may work as expected. Discussions with laboratory technicians and trials of the experiment can pick up missing instructions, unintended hazards and experiments that just do not work. This also helps with risk assessment and devising any modifications needed to suit your laboratory context or constraints, such as limited equipment or reagents. If keeping live specimens, such as chickens or guinea pigs, you must comply with animal-ethics regulations. Table 12.1 provides a list of useful websites to ensure work

**FIGURE 12.4:** Student-created models as teaching aids

# THE ART OF TEACHING SCIENCE 3RD EDITION

standards and laboratory-safety regulations are kept, and records are updated for registration purposes.

**TABLE 12.1:** Useful websites for science teachers and laboratory technicians

| Name of organisation | URL | Type of support |
| --- | --- | --- |
| Workplace Safety Australia | www.worksafe.com.au | Professional knowledge base and support for safe work practices, meeting legal compliance and certification. |
| LABNETWEST Inc. | www.labnetwest.asn.au | Interaction between science technicians, to promote ideas and solutions to practical problems and to facilitate professional development and a support network. |
| Animal Ethics Infolink | www.animalethics.org.au/legislation/other-australian-legislation | Provides schools with advice on changes to physical facilities/procedures that should be made to cater for the needs of the animals used. |
| Science ASSIST Australian School Science Information Support for Teachers and Technicians | https://assist.asta.edu.au | Expert, up-to-date online advisory services and information on quality science teaching and learning resources; consistent and authoritative advice on all aspects of school-laboratory safety, management and design |
| Radiological Council, Government of Western Australia | www.radiologicalcouncil.wa.gov.au | Advice for the regulation of radiation and for meeting standards for registration and licensing. |

## SCIENCE AND SAFETY INSIDE AND OUTSIDE SCHOOL LABORATORIES 199

| Name of organisation | URL | Type of support |
| --- | --- | --- |
| Material Safety Data Sheets Compliance Management Systems | www.msds.com.au | A modular, cloud-based system that provides a suite of tools to address compliance requirements for chemical usage, handling, and storage within all organisational structures. |
| RiskAssess Risk Assessments for Schools | www.riskassess.com. au | A web-based tool that makes performing risk assessments and meeting legal obligations for science quick and easy for teachers and laboratory technicians. |
| CLEAPSS Consortium of authorities on practical science and technology | www.cleapss.org.uk | Information for science teachers and laboratory technicians on all aspects of secondary science, including bulletins, hazards, and practical procedures. |

The teacher or laboratory technician should demonstrate procedures immediately before students carry out the activity. This is especially important when producing toxic fumes such as chlorine or iodine in a fume cupboard, handling corrosive reagents (for example, acids, alkalis or strong oxidants) or very hot or very cold objects, using sharp items (such as probes, forceps or scalpels) or using mains-voltage electrical equipment. **Check with your laboratory technician when using any dangerous substances** for the latest guidelines and requirements for safety.

Where safety is problematic, consider alternatives to student experiments. Restricting the activity to a demonstration may be preferable to allowing students access to the reagents or equipment. Potentially explosive chemical reactions (such as adding sodium to water) should always be demonstrated behind a perspex safety screen with safety glasses and protective clothing. Conducting a dissection is exciting for some students but triggers a cultural sensitivity in others. A lack of familiarity with dissecting equipment and the features to be observed suggests that a careful demonstration and commentary by a skilled practitioner might result in better learning outcomes.

## Safe Behaviour in Science Laboratories

Many students are not naturally safety-conscious and, if left to themselves, they tend to use reagents, specimens and equipment with little care for consequences. As the teacher, you are responsible for maintaining a safe environment for the students and yourself.

Having completed planning and preparation, the teacher must maintain adequate safety awareness during laboratory work. Watching students attentively is critical, as practical classes can become chaotic with movement and talk. As laboratory work is usually conducted in groups, teachers must be aware of each class's working dynamics and different levels of collaboration between certain individuals (for example, students with special needs). When interacting with an individual group, a teacher must regularly sweep the rest of the room with their eyes, much like a new driver learns to check the rear-view mirror. If students see you doing this, it can quell some tendencies to misbehave. A code of appropriate behaviour (a more positive framing than *rules*) is essential (an example is given in Figure 12.5). Most students are capable of contributing to such a code, and doing so makes them much more likely to follow it. Your responsibility is to ensure that they have foreseen all reasonable situations, and that they obey their code while in the laboratory.

# OTHER RESOURCES

## Human

Many schools have technical-support staff, ranging from a part-time laboratory assistant to two or three full-time laboratory technicians. Technical-support staff are creative, trained professionals who do a number of complex tasks, including assembling equipment,

SCIENCE AND SAFETY INSIDE AND OUTSIDE SCHOOL LABORATORIES 201

**FIGURE 12.5:** An example of a laboratory code of behaviour

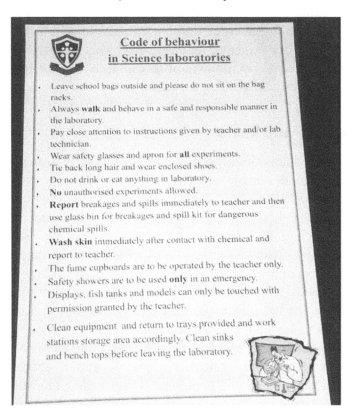

preparing reagents, distributing materials to teachers and classes, putting the equipment and reagents away and disposing of any wastes. Laboratory technicians play a vital role in supporting teaching staff, especially in identifying potential issues on the workability of experiments and offering plausible alternative set-ups to overcome equipment limitations or unavailable resources. Hence, establishing a good rapport with the laboratory technicians will strengthen a teacher's instructional effectiveness in the laboratory.

To allow laboratory technicians time to order, prepare and distribute equipment, it is customary to pre-order it at least a week, or even weeks, in advance. Order forms typically require fairly detailed information about what is needed, and when and where it is to be used. Less forward planning is usually required for *standard equipment* such as preserved specimens of animals; weighing balances; glassware; electrical equipment, such as power packs, ammeters and voltmeters; stock solutions, such as dilute hydrochloric acid and sodium hydroxide; and dry reagents, such as marble chips, copper sulphate and alum. This type of equipment or reagent is usually stored in prep areas, for security, safety and space reasons.

## Technology and Texts

Integration of increasingly sophisticated technology in the science classroom provides many opportunities for science teachers and their students. Interactive boards or whiteboards with digital projectors have become standard features in most laboratories, allowing teachers to seamlessly transition between hands-on and digital resources. Handheld devices or tablets may be made available in trolleys or brought in by students themselves. These devices must be protected from accidental damage during practical activities. Chapter 13 has information on how technology and software can be used to advantage in science classrooms.

Science textbooks are widely used in science instruction, despite some experts advising against a textbook-centred approach to science teaching. Textbooks sometimes have considerable influence on what and how teachers teach, and what and how students read and learn. It is important to use textbooks to supplement a number of resources and not let the one source dominate your approach to teaching and learning. A good text is one that (a) provides clarity and helps students understand the content or concept better (that is, it is pitched at an appropriate level of reading difficulty), (b) poses questions that stimulate students' own thinking process, and (c) encourages students to consolidate the content being taught (in other words, students can identify key points and also reflect on their learning process as a whole).

## Outside Resources

When relocating a class to an alternative venue, such as the library, an oval, hall or the gymnasium (for example, for an egg-drop experiment or a physiology-based investigation), you may have to book space at that venue in advance. You must inform administration where your class will be and leave a notice on the door of your now-vacant laboratory to redirect latecomers to the appropriate venue.

Outdoor areas can provide opportunities for authentic science activities. Natural areas of the school grounds lend themselves to biology and ecology—it is worth befriending the school gardener to ensure appropriate areas are managed well and ready for investigation. The gardener may also be able to cultivate useful plants, such as examples of mosses, ferns, lichens, cycads, conifers, a range of monocots and dicots, pea plants for genetics, and *Tradescantia* or *Senecio* species for leaf epidermal peels to study stomata. Other outdoor areas allow for activities that require a lot of room, such as modelling distances between planets in the Solar System or using drones. Figure 12.6 shows the use of drones in a problem-solving *rescue mission* in a Year 9 science and technology session.

**FIGURE 12.6:** A drone in action on the school oval

## Excursions and Field Trips

There are a multitude of out-of-school activities related to science, including field trips or excursions to a farm, zoo, aquarium, science museum, nature reserve, science discovery centre, industrial or university laboratory, planetarium or industry-sponsored event, as well as local, regional or national science forums, festivals and camps. Using these resources usually requires transport by bus, incurring significant costs, so they may have their own separate budget. They may disrupt classes other than science and generally require a higher staff-to-student ratio than for ordinary classes. School systems have a checklist of procedures to assist teachers to plan off-site educational delivery and to ensure legally acceptable standards of supervision will be provided. Start planning months ahead of the actual time of the out-of-school experience. Fortunately, many excursion sites provide detailed excursion management plans for schools.

To maximise learning outcomes, pre-excursion activities should prepare students for what is to come. For example, students could do a simple transect in the school grounds to learn the procedures before a visit to a beach or granite outcrop. Post-excursion reflective and evaluative activities complete the process. Read King and Glackin (2014) for more information on learning in out-of-school contexts.

Possible links between industry, education, science and technology include industry tours and excursions; sponsorship of events, activities or curriculum materials; teacher placements in industry; industry-staff placements in schools through incursions such as *STEM Professionals in Schools* (www.csiro.au/STEM-Professionals-in-Schools) programs; and the use of donated science and technology equipment and facilities. Snapshot 12.1 illustrates how industry experts can expand students' understanding of the work of scientists.

School–industry partnerships provide a wealth of resources that confer wide-ranging benefits for teachers, students and industries. These partnerships can improve teaching quality and provide curriculum enrichment for teachers; enhance the knowledge, skills

## SCIENCE AND SAFETY INSIDE AND OUTSIDE SCHOOL LABORATORIES

**SNAPSHOT 12.1:** A lesson outlining the use of an industry partnership in a secondary-school science class

Skype Interview with Research Scientist—Capturing Whale Snot Using Drones

Photographs illustrating some aspects of the activity

### YEAR 8 SCIENCE

**Curriculum:**

*Biological science*—Multicellular organisms contain systems of organs carrying out specialised functions that enable them to survive and reproduce (ACSSU150).

*Science as a Human Endeavour*—Science and technology contribute to finding solutions to a range of contemporary issues; these solutions may impact on other areas of society and involve ethical considerations (ACSHE120).

Skype Interview with Research Scientist—Capturing Whale Snot Using Drones

Photographs illustrating some aspects of the activity

## YEAR 8 SCIENCE

**Activity/Skills:**

In this example of a post-excursion activity, students had met the research scientist at a Fame Lab competition a week before. Students now work in groups of three (researcher, scribe and speaker) via a forum on the school's e-learning platform and face-to-face discussion to agree on two or three questions to pose to the research scientist on Skype. A speaker from each team then takes turns to ask their questions, taking about 30 minutes for the entire Skype interview. Learning is made visible by the type and range of questions posed to the scientist. Students are challenged to think beyond the biological concepts of body systems (namely, immune system), marine conservation, and the use of cutting-edge technology to solve contemporary global issues.

and attitudes of students; improve the range and quality of learning environments available to schools; widen the applicability of teaching and learning strategies that value teamwork, interpersonal skills and problem-solving; and enhance the ability of teachers to counsel students about career and future subject choices. Teachers benefit from updating subject knowledge, and students increase their perceived relevance of science and technology through the use of real-world problems and examples. Industries benefit by influencing the formation of skills in the workforce as well as improving product and company image in the community.

## SUMMARY OF KEY POINTS

In summary, comprehensive knowledge and effective use of science resources inside and outside classrooms and laboratories can contribute towards a positive and profound influence on students' science learning and teacher confidence. Rennie, Howitt, Evans and Mayne (2010) maintain that teachers need deep content and pedagogical knowledge to effectively implement their instructional practices with the use of appropriate resources. By working closely with laboratory technicians and fellow teaching staff, teachers can work towards engaging, productive and safe science activities. This will also contribute to fulfilling the pedagogical goals of students developing conceptual understanding and positive values through exploration, inquiry, discovery, questioning and discourse.

## DISCUSSION QUESTIONS

12.1 Outline the safety practices or checks that a science teacher must undertake before and during an experiment where students are required to use an acid or dissect a heart. How would you involve your laboratory technician or your head of department in this process?

12.2 Write a laboratory code of behaviour for a Year 7 science laboratory. What extra features would you include for an upper-secondary school science laboratory (for example, chemistry, physics or biology)? How could you involve your students in developing a code of behaviour for their class?

12.3 Plan an outdoor experiment/activity/excursion that involves all classes in a specific year group. Map out a timeline for the steps you need to take before, during and after the event. (Hint: keep in mind the school diary of events.)

12.4 Using the given snapshot example, outline how you would utilise industry-partner resources in a year group of your choice in your school context. What are the challenges and opportunities you need to address to fulfil your proposed learning outcomes?

## ACKNOWLEDGEMENT

Special acknowledgement to Kingsway Christian College secondary school staff and students for their kind participation in the photographs for this chapter.

## REFERENCES

King, H. & Glackin, M., 2014, 'Supporting science teaching in out-of-school contexts', *Research Into Practice Briefs From Enterprising Science Paper 06,* <www.kcl.ac.uk/sspp/departments/education/research/research-centres/cppr/research/currentpro/enterprising-science/es06-king-and-glackin-2014-supporting-science-learning-in-out-of-school-contexts.pdf>, accessed 10 October 2018.

Rennie, L., Howitt, C., Evans, R. & Mayne, F., 2010, 'Do-it-yourself astronomy: Getting the best out of a science kit', *Teaching Science,* vol. 56, no. 4, pp. 13–17.

# CHAPTER 13

# Teaching and Learning Science with Digital Technologies

Matthew Kearney, University of Technology Sydney, and Wendy Nielsen, University of Wollongong

## GOALS

**The goals for this chapter are to support you to:**

- Describe categories of educational technologies that could be used for science teaching and learning
- Distinguish between techno-centric and pedagogical arguments for selecting digital resources and for rationalising the use of educational technologies for science teaching and learning
- Appreciate the range of digital pedagogies available to science teachers
- Describe and illustrate how behaviourist and social constructivist learning theories might inform digital pedagogical approaches in secondary-school science education

**Australian Professional Standards for Teachers—Graduate Level:**

- Standard 2: Know the content and how to teach it (Focus area 2.6)
- Standard 3: Plan for and implement effective teaching and learning (Focus area 3.4)

# INTRODUCTION

Educational technologies have been regularly hailed as a *game-changer* in schools. From the introduction of film and radio in the early twentieth century to more contemporary digital technologies such as mobile devices and associated applications (or *apps*), educational technologies have frequently been promoted as a panacea for student-engagement problems in classrooms. However, there has also been an alarming gap between these *hyped* claims and evidence of enhanced teaching and learning. This chapter explores ways that secondary-school science teachers and students might use digital educational technologies—or what we also refer to in this chapter as *learning technologies*—to support learning effectively. Throughout this chapter, we refer to specific examples of apps and websites. It is important to note that these are current examples of high-quality resources, and new ones are constantly in development. Key online resources are superscripted in the text and listed at the end of the chapter.

# THE LEARNING TECHNOLOGIES LANDSCAPE

Learning technologies may include hardware such as laptops and game consoles, peripherals such as wearable devices, and software such as educational games and simulations. A wide range of discipline-specific and generic educational software and apps can be used for science learning. Science-specific applications include data-collection apps, visualisations, animations and participatory simulations, which might actively immerse students in realistic scientist roles or support rich experiences of authentic, community-based science projects. For example, *nQuire* allows science learners to join a scientific mission that might involve a science experiment or data gathering using a mobile device. Apps such as *iSpot, Frog Spotter and Platypus Spot* focus on learning about the natural environment, enabling students to participate in ongoing, collaborative research and conservation projects. Other examples of science-specific applications include simulations such as the *Wind Tunnel* app that allows physics learners to experiment with principles of aerodynamics and test different shapes in a virtual wind tunnel. The best of these science-specific software programs and apps position learners in relevant, stimulating science activities that give them a chance to participate collaboratively in meaningful science inquiry projects.

Other types of educational software and apps are more general in purpose, and can be used in any curriculum area to support learning. Examples of broad categories include augmented reality, spreadsheets and databases and online social software—commonly called *Web 2.0* applications, indicating a more sophisticated level of interactivity and social connectivity beyond the passive, static nature of *Web 1.0* web pages. These categories can be further grouped into sub-categories. For example, Bower (2015) outlined 14 different types of Web 2.0 applications for education (see Figure 13.1).

A good way to examine the complex learning-technologies landscape is to consider *how* specific software, apps and other educational technologies might be used by teachers and learners, and for what educational purpose. In this way, teachers can go beyond shallow, techno-centric discussions to consider critically the benefits for teaching and learning. Revisiting the general-purpose case of Web 2.0 applications and the groupings in Figure 13:1, collaborative mind-mapping or image-based tools could allow groups of students to engage in concept mapping (for example, to elicit students' prior knowledge and provide feedback to teachers). Web 2.0 tools can also be used to support students' reflection and authentic *assessment for learning* (see Chapter 9) through digital portfolios, or they could be used for digital storytelling and expression, or for peer collaboration using blogs, wikis or other website-creation tools. Bower (2017) describes many other interesting examples of Web 2.0 applications in education to support students' communication, creation and sharing. We present illustrations showing *how* other learning technologies might be used in science education for various pedagogical purposes in the snapshots later in this chapter.

A challenge for science teachers is to evaluate and select high-quality learning-technology resources, both generic and science-specific (for example, from the plethora of apps in the education category on iTunes). There are resources to assist with

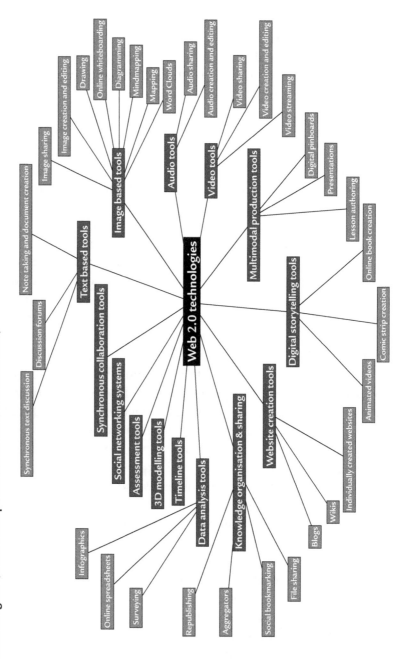

**FIGURE 13.1:** The 14 sub-categories of Web 2.0 technologies, one of the many broad categories of learning technologies (used with permission from Bower 2015)

this task, including various rubrics[1] for critically examining apps. There are also rubrics that focus on the *pedagogic potential* of apps, including one that is specifically designed to evaluate science apps (Green, Hechter, Tysinger & Chassereau 2014). Another rubric[2] evaluates the pedagogical value of mobile apps.

## TEACHING AND LEARNING SECONDARY-SCHOOL SCIENCE WITH TECHNOLOGY

Planning technology-supported science-learning tasks involves many decisions about the learning outcomes to cover, technologies to use and how students might use them to optimise their learning. Some of the technologies and associated teaching and learning strategies will be science-specific, and thus science teachers need to draw these together with their subject expertise. Availability of different software and hardware tools will vary considerably by school, as will both technical support and internet access, so it is important to understand the pedagogical purposes as well as affordances and limitations of the technology in decision-making and planning.

### Digital Pedagogies

We introduce the term *digital pedagogy* to describe the art of teaching and learning with contemporary educational technologies. The broad categories of learning technologies introduced in the previous section offer a place to start in considering technology-mediated science learning. However, secondary-school science teachers need a theory of learning to drive their digital pedagogical decision-making and planning. In the contemporary context, where high-quality digital resources and hardware are readily available, teachers are expected to move beyond traditional approaches to more fully realise the potential of using learning technologies to support science teaching and learning in more progressive ways.

For many years, the dominant learning theory influencing the design and use of educational technologies has been behaviourism. Early technologies—such as Skinner's teaching machine[3] in the 1950s, 1960s' technologies such as the overhead projector, and instructional television shows and videos in the 1970s—were typically associated with behaviourist and didactic approaches to teaching. Current approaches to teaching and learning in technologically rich environments still tend to be traditional and transmissive. Teachers often use mobile devices and apps in ways that replicate lecture-style modes of teaching, such as their use of YouTube, screencast apps and digital pens for presenting information to students for rote-learning purposes. One reason for this tendency is the underpinning behaviourist educational design of popular software and apps. For example, in the education section of the iTunes store, a large majority of apps, including popular educational games, are simply drill and practise in nature, focusing on content and information delivery.

Despite this persistent tendency, education reformers in the past four decades have explored more emancipative, progressive approaches and designs that give learners more agency through inquiry, analysis and problem-solving with digital technologies. Professor Seymour Papert was a pioneer in this movement during the 1980s, and, like Professor David Jonassen in the 1990s, used constructivist theory to develop more open-ended software to support students' creativity and critical thinking. Critical-thinking applications, or what Jonassen labelled *mindtools*, include concept maps for collaborative planning, spreadsheets for problem-solving and modelling, and simulations for hypothesis testing. Papert's classic 1980 book titled *Mindstorms: Children, Computers, and Powerful Ideas* and Jonassen's 1996 book titled *Computers in the Classroom: Mindtools for Critical Thinking* are highly recommended as an introduction to contemporary student-centred digital pedagogies.

In this section, we aim to push beginning teachers to think beyond the dominant behaviourist approaches to teaching and learning with technology to consider exploring digital pedagogies through the lens of social constructivism, with an emphasis on learning *with* (rather than *about* or *from*) technologies to enhance students' articulation, representation and exchange of ideas. This social constructivist position highlights the social dimension of science-learning activities, as developed elsewhere in this book (see Chapter 3), and emphasises learners' use of digital technologies to enhance discussion, questioning and sharing of meaning among peers and teachers. The snapshots presented below depict technology-supported inquiry or design-based approaches to learning. Guided by a social constructivist perspective, these examples include more participative, autonomous student roles, with teachers acting more as consultants, supporters and monitors of students' learning.

## Social Constructivist Digital Pedagogies

Following social constructivist theory, pedagogies need to give students the opportunity to realise their own background knowledge, challenge prior conceptions and build new meanings through learning experiences. An emphasis on the social aspects of learning means that experiences need to be planned so that students build collective knowledge both in the learning process and the artefacts they produce. Supporting these experiences with digital technologies then opens up a range of possibilities to help students develop their science-content knowledge and skills. Each of the following three snapshots describes pedagogical approaches driven by a social constructivist theory of learning and depicts students' use of contemporary digital technologies to support collaborative learning meaningfully.

**SNAPSHOT 13.1:** Technology-supported science-learning procedures

A straightforward way to use technology in designing constructivist science teaching is to consider well-known science-teaching procedures such as Predict–Observe–Explain (POE), a strategy discussed in Chapter 4. The purpose of a POE activity can range from eliciting pre-instructional understandings, possibly provoking cognitive conflict, to a more deliberate constructivist learning strategy designed to support students' meaning-making. Technology can assist in the prediction and observation phases. To provoke the *predict* phase of the POE, a short online video-based scenario (for example, a snippet of a dangerous, time-consuming

THE ART OF TEACHING SCIENCE 3RD EDITION

or expensive demonstration) could be presented for learners to consider, before using the video controls (slow motion, rewind and so on) to scrutinise the outcome. Close observation of the science phenomenon can provoke peer discussion, leading into the explain phase. Also, data loggers can be used during the observation phase (for example, to measure temperature or flux).

Importantly, technology can be used to guide pairs or small groups of learners through the POE procedure and facilitate more autonomous, collaborative learning (Kearney 2004). Online editors such as the *Learning Activity Management System* (Lesson-LAMS)[4], interactive video platforms such as *Edpuzzle* or even a carefully planned sequence of *Google Slides* can be used to scaffold students' engagement in each step of a POE task and allow them to exchange ideas and progress at their own pace. Digital technology can also support the seamless collection and collation of students' responses in each phase of the POE process to inform later instruction. Importantly, student responses may provide insights into their alternative conceptions and may also provoke additional questions from the learners as new points of interest. Thus, student questioning during POE procedures can lead discussions in many new directions. Templates and examples for designing a technology-supported POE are available from the Learning Designs website[5]. Other reference materials, such as the procedures available from the Project for Enhancing Effective Learning (PEEL)[6], offer robust, research-based ways to design learning activities that can be readily adapted for use with digital technologies.

## SNAPSHOT 13.2: Inquiry-based science learning

As developed in Chapter 7, inquiry as a teaching approach gives students the opportunity to explore a question of interest to them. Curriculum scholars have developed several inquiry frameworks, but Bybee's (1997) 5E model is among the most popular (see Chapter 7). There are particular focal points for each E (Engage,

Explore, Explain, Elaborate, Evaluate); working through each of these mirrors the work of scientists in conducting an inquiry and can be supported with various technologies. For example, a 5E inquiry could focus on a community science project investigating local fauna. Here, students could use their mobile devices during the early phases of the inquiry to explore the phenomenon and generate areas of interest and project goals. In a similar way to real scientists, students can use apps to communicate in real time, collect data *in situ*, and co-write and share findings. Teachers could arrange to have students liaise with an expert *biologist-in-residence* in a real-time video chat to discuss the project goals and seek guidance for data-collection procedures. In later stages of the inquiry, they could travel to a range of local areas, collecting multimodal artefacts *in the field* (including photos and videos) and making annotated notes to share among themselves, the teacher and the scientist.

As part of a team, the students in this scenario could use networking tools and social-media apps such as Facebook groups and Instagram to pose questions and share their predictions and interpretations with peers doing similar projects in other local or more distant neighbourhoods, or with other scientific experts. In this way, the mobile activity enables the students to think and behave as part of a real scientific community and act as co-constructors of knowledge through authentic activity. Sharing materials on a social-media platform means that the mentor biologist also has access to their shared notes and *real-time data*, and can give feedback *on the fly*. The students can then co-write a brief report in Google documents and share their findings with the science community in the Elaborate and Evaluate phases.

## SNAPSHOT 13.3: Digital explanation

A designed-based example of a digital-learning experience for science students is *student-generated digital media* or *digital-*

> *worked examples* where students develop an explanation of a science concept for a specified audience. For example, learners can generate an animation to represent conceptual knowledge or interpretations of dynamic relationships. Movie-making programs such as iMovie allow easy upload of still images, video and other digital-media forms, and support development of a progressive sequence of representations that can be edited and narrated to make a mini-movie to explain the science concept to others. Other software or apps allow students to easily create a variety of animations (see the *Slowmation*[7] or *DigiExplanations*[8] websites).

Developing an explanation of a science concept for others is a good way to learn science content, because in order to explain something, the creator needs to understand it. So, in creating a digital explanation, students consider the science content, choose what will be represented (and how) and then work with a range of digital tools to communicate their science understandings. These short, stand-alone mini-movies can be very engaging as a student task, and making them lets students work with science content in a more open-ended way than traditional forms of working with texts or transmissive, didactic teaching strategies, such as passively viewing a teacher-made video lecture. The process of developing a digital explanation can also help students to develop new media skills and digital literacies, because students both learn from and produce multiple representations as they learn about the science and work to produce an accurate explanation. Research in this area has productively demonstrated the value for a range of science learners, including pre-service teachers (Hoban, Nielsen & Shepherd 2013).

## Developing Your Science Digital Pedagogical Knowledge

This chapter cannot begin to cover all of the possible digital pedagogies that teachers can use to teach science effectively. However, through the teacher-education program and later through career-long professional development, beginning teachers will develop a variety of approaches to exploit the affordances of different technologies. Fortunately, there are many ways to keep current with new and emerging learning technologies and associated digital pedagogies. Well-known education bloggers such as Kathy Schrock[9] and Richard Byrne[10] help teachers keep current with the ever-growing list of learning technologies and associated teaching approaches. There are also many professional organisations, such as the Australian Council for Computers in Education (ACCE) and the International Society for Technology in Education (ISTE) in the United States, which produce pertinent publications and other resources for teacher professional development.

The Australian Science Teachers Association (ASTA) and state-level science teachers' associations hold annual conferences that are great networking opportunities to share and discuss innovations in teaching, including science digital pedagogies. Attending teacher conferences and developing a professional learning network (or PLN) incorporating links with other teachers and organisations, both locally and globally, helps teachers connect to others interested in similar questions of teaching and learning. For example, many teachers attend TeachMeets and then use social media to continue their professional-learning conversations in spaces such as Twitter (for example, using #ozscied, #aussied and #edtech hashtags) and Facebook.

## LEARNING SPACES FOR SECONDARY-SCHOOL SCIENCE EDUCATION

Science teachers also need to consider the growing range of physical and online contemporary learning spaces and environments when designing technology-mediated learning tasks and enacting digital pedagogies. Formal physical spaces may include classrooms, laboratories and school theatres, while virtual spaces may include more structured class blogs or school-learning management systems. Semi-formal physical spaces may include school playgrounds,

# THE ART OF TEACHING SCIENCE 3RD EDITION

*break-out* spaces and excursion sites such as science museums, while semi-formal online spaces could include science chat sites, other online communities or even *virtual tours* and field trips (for example, *Google Expeditions*). In these formal and semi-formal spaces, students' learning experiences are typically designed and mediated by a teacher or external expert such as a museum tour guide.

With the availability of mobile devices and accompanying educational apps, there is a growing range of informal learning spaces that students might use for learning science. These spaces could include buses, cafes and spaces at home, all of which are appealing because the spaces are typically more convenient and intimate for learners. Informal virtual learning environments are connective, participative spaces such as social-media networks and immersive online worlds that can be accessed using mobile tools anywhere and anytime. Designing science-learning activities for these new types of physical and virtual learning spaces, some of which are learner-generated and therefore unpredictable, is a new and exciting challenge for science teachers.

Teenagers are comfortable moving and learning across multiple learning spaces—formal and informal—for example, when carrying out science projects. Some educators describe this *boundary crossing* between learning spaces as *seamless learning* (for example, connecting learning in classrooms and science museums); it provides a *bridge* between lab-based inquiry and more realistic settings for investigations, such as *in-situ* collection of data from a beach or forest. Mobile devices and associated learning technologies can mediate this flow of learning between formal and informal contexts (for example, through students' use of social media, online role-playing or cloud-based applications such as *Google Sheets*).

## A FEW CAVEATS

A chapter on using technology to support science learning would be incomplete without a few caveats. Drivers as well as enablers and barriers will continue to evolve, even as they shape the landscape of educational technology in secondary-science education.

## Enablers and Barriers to Integration of Technology in Secondary School Education

Both enablers and barriers of technology adoption and integration in schools have been well documented. First-order factors include access to technology, school budgets, technical administration and support, as well as time for planning and professional development. Second-order factors are arguably more critical and include teacher beliefs, digital competencies and pedagogical approaches (Ertmer, Ottenbreit-Leftwich, Sadik, Sendurur & Sendurur 2012). Teachers' pedagogical beliefs are perhaps the most important influence on the way learning technologies are used in and beyond the classroom. If teachers have strong behaviourist beliefs, they tend to use educational technologies that support didactic, transmissive teaching approaches (for example, the use of PowerPoint for *teaching by telling,* or the use of a lecture-style podcast to *transfer information* for students' rote learning). In contrast, teachers with strong constructivist beliefs will design more student-centred, collaborative, expressive and creative technology-enhanced science-learning tasks. Notably, such constructivist approaches are consistent with contemporary directions in both learning theory and curriculum and provide extensive opportunity to utilise learning technologies in creative and engaging ways.

## Drivers of Technology Use in Secondary School Education

Many learning technologies, such as interactive whiteboards and laptops, have been introduced into schools via a *top-down approach* under the influence of metalevel drivers, including external bodies such as governments and corporations such as Google, Microsoft and Apple. An economic rationale is typically central to arguments driving investment, such as preparing students with 21st-century skills that are relevant to tomorrow's workplace in a rapidly changing global economy. An example from state-level government is the 2011 NSW Connected Classrooms Program, which spent A$23 million on 4300 interactive whiteboards for classrooms.

THE ART OF TEACHING SCIENCE 3RD EDITION

Professional organisations, regulatory agencies and curriculum designers are also influential. The national-level government in Australia recently instituted regulations in the form of the Australian Professional Standards for Teachers (APST), with three standards addressing the effective and safe use of technology for teaching: Standards 2.6, 3.4 and 4.5 (see Illustrations of Practice for these standards at the AITSL website[11]). A curriculum example is the *general capabilities* section of the Australian Curriculum (ACARA 2018) that explicitly states students should develop Information and Communication Technology (ICT) capability and use it to develop conceptual understandings, research science concepts and communicate findings. The Technologies curriculum also specifies a range of skills and knowledge for learning about and working with technology.

More recently, the use of learning technologies—such as cloud-based software (for example, *Google Docs*), digital video-editing software and many education apps—has been introduced and promoted in schools. Arguably, these more *bottom-up strategies* have had a greater impact, because they are under the influence of smaller-scale drivers such as pioneering teachers and school leaders, parents, local authorities or school systems. For example, more locally developed school-based laptop or *Bring Your Own Device* (BYOD) policies have positively influenced practices and students' access to technology.

## SUMMARY OF KEY POINTS

Teachers' beliefs about teaching and learning critically influence the way that science students use educational technologies. Social constructivism is a useful theory for beginning science teachers, as it allows them to consider more progressive digital pedagogies that emphasise students' learning *with* technologies to support discussion and exchange of ideas, open-ended questioning and co-construction of meaning. Collaborative technology-supported design and inquiry-based activities are highly suitable for these purposes. Science teachers also need to think about where and when science learning might take place and how the use of mobile technologies and associated apps might leverage new physical and virtual learning spaces for science students to think, co-create and investigate.

## DISCUSSION QUESTIONS

13.1 Where do you need to focus your own professional learning to develop your repertoire of digital pedagogies? How could your PLN help you?

13.2 You are teaching in a school with a BYOD policy. Design a science-learning activity that exploits the *anywhere, anytime, any pace* flexibility of learning with a mobile device. How could the notion of *seamless learning* across contexts inform your design? Use this short YouTube video[12] as a stimulus for your planning.

13.3 Use one or more of the evaluation rubrics flagged in this chapter to compare and contrast two of your favourite science-learning apps.

13.4 Video-based examples of science lessons informed by a constructivist perspective are available at the University of South Florida's well-known Technology Integration Matrix (TIM)[13]. Choose and view a science example that is tagged *Collaborative*. How is peer collaboration supporting student learning in the lesson?

## REFERENCES

Australian Curriculum and Assessment Authority (ACARA), 2016, *General capabilities*, Canberra: ACARA, <www.australian curriculum.edu.au/f-10-curriculum/general-capabilities>, accessed 10 July 2018.

Bower, M., 2015, 'A typology of Web 2.0 learning technologies', EDUCAUSE digital library, <https://library.educause.edu/ resources/2015/2/a-typology-of-web-20-learning-technologies>, accessed 10 October 2018.

Bower, M., 2017, 'Design of Web 2.0 enhanced learning', in

M. Bower (ed.), *Design of Technology-enhanced Learning: Integrating Research and Practice,* West Yorkshire: Emerald Publishing, pp. 159–217.

Bybee, R.W., 1997, *Achieving Scientific Literacy: From Purposes to Practices*, Portsmouth, NH: Heinemann Ertmer, P.A., Ottenbreit-Leftwich, A.T., Sadik, O., Sendurur, E. & Sendurur, P., 2012, 'Teacher beliefs and technology integration practices: A critical relationship', *Computers & Education,* vol. 59, no. 2, pp. 423–35.

Green, L.S., Hechter, R.P., Tysinger, P.D. & Chassereau, K.D., 2014, 'Mobile app selection for 5th through 12th grade science: The development of the MASS rubric', *Computers & Education*, vol. 75, pp. 65–71.

Hoban, G., Nielsen, W. & Shepherd, A., 2013, 'Explaining and communicating science using student-created blended media', *Teaching Science,* vol. 59, no. 1, pp. 32–5.

Jonassen, D.H., 1996, *Computers in the Classroom: Mindtools for Critical Thinking*, Eaglewoods, NJ: Merrill/Prentice Hall.

Kearney, M., 2004, 'Classroom use of multimedia-supported predict–observe–explain tasks in a social constructivist learning environment', *Research in Science Education,* vol. 34, no. 4, pp. 427–53.

Papert, S., 1980, *Mindstorms: Children, Computers, and Powerful Ideas,* New York, NY: Basic Books.

## RESOURCES

1. www.ipads4teaching.net/critical-eval-of-apps.html
2. www.mobilelearningtoolkit.com/app-rubric1.html
3. https://youtube/jTH3ob1IRFo
4. www.lessonlams.com
5. www.learningdesigns.uow.edu.au/index.html
6. www.peelweb.org/
7. www.slowmation.com/
8. www.digiexplanations.com
9. www.schrockguide.net/
10. www.freetech4teachers.com/

11. https://legacy.aitsl.edu.au/australian-professional-standards-for-teachers/illustrations-of-practice/find-by-career-stage
12. https://youtube/9zxlZvJ-3Aw
13. https://fcit.usf.edu/matrix/matrix/subject-area-index/

Resources 1–13 from this chapter can also be accessed online at: http://bit.ly/kearneynielsenresources

# CHAPTER 14
# Integrating STEM

Linda Hobbs and John Cripps Clark, Deakin University

## GOALS

**The goals for this chapter are to support you to:**

- Understand ways that STEM can be integrated into schools
- Discover how teachers can collaborate to plan and deliver innovative STEM programs
- Appreciate the issues that schools and teachers can face when teaching STEM
- Find solutions for making STEM work

**Australian Professional Standards for Teachers—Graduate Level:**

- Standard 2: Know the content and how to teach it (Focus areas 2.1, 2.2)
- Standard 3: Plan for and implement effective teaching and learning (Focus area 3.2)

## INTRODUCTION

Secondary schools are largely organised into subjects, and teachers are traditionally prepared as specialists in one or a number of subjects. However, the introduction of STEM (which stands for

Science, Technology, Engineering, Mathematics) into schools is allowing us to rethink this traditional subject-bound approach to curriculum, teaching and learning. STEM emphasises the knowledge, skills and capabilities found within the science, technology, engineering and mathematics disciplines, which are increasingly in demand in our fast-changing world. The interrelationship between these disciplines provides the impetus for integrating the subjects in schools to encourage deeper and more authentic engagement in all four disciplines.

The move towards looking for the relationships between science, technology, engineering and mathematics in STEM has challenged the acceptance and usefulness of subject-bound knowledge and skills and is giving greater prominence to subjects that are often considered less *academic*, most notably the technologies. This is a relatively new change in Australia, and schools are looking towards existing programs in Europe, the United States or the United Kingdom for ideas and resources. In Australia, there are a growing number of schools that offer STEM as a subject or are integrating STEM subjects to provide more authentic learning experiences. This chapter outlines some of the different models for teaching STEM that have been used successfully in secondary schools.

The following sections describe how STEM can be framed by schools, the different teacher-collaboration models that are emerging in schools, how to make STEM integration work in schools and how to overcome the issues that may arise.

## WHAT IS STEM?

Science, technology, engineering and mathematics are disciplines in their own right, but the call for STEM has ignited a flurry of political, professional and business discussions, and this has significant implications for education. The current STEM education agenda is driven by the belief that STEM skills are crucial to innovation and development in our contemporary, technological, knowledge-based, competitive global economy (Office of the Chief Scientist 2016). Education has been positioned as important in preparing a

*STEM-literate* society, and this has led to a number of education policies (for example, Education Council 2016) to which schools are responding.

STEM is not a school subject in Australia, so there is a need for teachers to first identify what STEM is and can be for their school. This unique characteristic of STEM as not yet being tightly defined or constrained by state or national curricula in Australia is a challenge for teachers; it is also an opportunity, because schools can draw on teachers' expertise to develop STEM curricula that meet each school's unique needs and available resources. STEM is becoming a useful tool for attending to challenges facing today's schools (for example, student disengagement, decreased enrolments in senior STEM subjects and student resilience).

How schools frame STEM will depend on the expertise, funding opportunities and leadership direction of each school. In turn, the way schools frame STEM will determine how and which teachers will work together to develop a new curriculum, as well as what adjustments are needed in timetabling. It also determines the teacher learning needed to develop new knowledge of content, new teaching approaches and new ways of working with young people, such as building student persistence while learning to problem-solve. As a beginning teacher, it will be important for you to work with colleagues to consider the various possibilities for integrating STEM, and to recognise that curriculum innovation is a product of these many factors.

As you develop your philosophy of teaching science, it is worth thinking about what will make your teaching identifiably *STEM*. As a teacher, you can make decisions about:

- the scale of innovation at either the individual-teacher or whole-school level;
- the way you work individually or with other teachers;
- the connections you make within and between the disciplines; and
- the pedagogies you use that could be identifiably *STEM*.

## Mapping STEM to the Australian Curriculum

The subjects of science, technology and mathematics are normally taught separately, particularly science and mathematics, which are considered core curriculum. The technology curriculum is currently split into design technologies and digital technologies within the Australian Curriculum, but each of these areas has held various positions within the state and territory curricula over the years, sometimes as cross-curriculum priorities and sometimes as discrete learning areas.

This repackaging and repositioning of the technologies curriculum illustrates its marginalised position within schools, compared to the well-accepted and clearly delineated science and mathematics curricula. In this context, some schools are using STEM to give greater prominence to technology.

# FRAMING STEM

The first step for schools in designing and implementing a curriculum that fosters STEM thinking is to work out what STEM means. STEM is emerging in schools, either as separate subjects or in existing science and mathematics classes, through:

- an increased emphasis on digital and information technology, coding, computational thinking and robotics;
- the introduction of design and technology processes into new learning experiences as STEM or design challenges;
- the introduction of real-world problem-solving, in either individual or multiple subjects, taught by individual teachers or teams of teachers;
- an emphasis on 21st-century STEM practices, often linked to cross-curriculum priorities; and
- a rethinking of traditional subject boundaries, with the introduction of integrated units or activities.

There are different ways of thinking about STEM: a set of skills across a number of subjects; the intersection of different subjects;

or a combination of these two options. Hobbs, Cripps Clark & Plant (2018a), for example, provide three different conceptualisations in Figure 14.1. STEM can range from including all of the practices and interconnections in all disciplines (Holistic model) to, more narrowly, including only those generic practices (soft skills) common to all disciplines as a metadiscipline (Amalgamated model).

Science has always worked closely with both mathematics and technology. There are countless examples where a technological or mathematical discovery has led to new scientific knowledge and vice versa. However, there is increasing recognition that the *wicked problems* (Timms, Moyle, Weldon & Mitchell 2018) that we face in our world, such as global warming, food security or newly emerging diseases, are not confined to any one discipline but will need ideas and resources from across many different disciplines to solve them. Increasingly, we need to think and work in multidisciplinary teams. For example, Elizabeth Blackburn, the Australian winner of the Nobel Prize for discoveries in molecular biology in 2009, led a multidisciplinary research team that provided better understanding of the relationship between chronic stress, ageing and cancer (Trounson 2010). Blackburn said that each of the scientists with whom she collaborated had deep knowledge of their respective

**FIGURE 14.1:** Models of *STEM in education* (used with permission from Springer, STEM Education in the *Junior Secondary: The State of Play* by R. Jorgensen & K. Larkin [eds], copyright 2018)

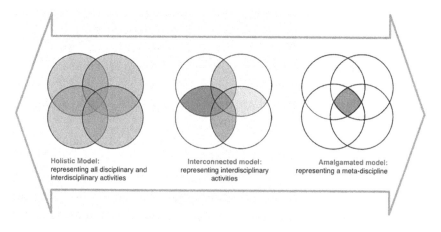

fields, and the collaborative process was crucial to the success of the research (Trounson 2010).

Research has shown that high-quality integrated curricula for students of the 21st century include a high degree of balance between disciplinary and integrated knowledge, and a high degree of connection between local and global knowledge (Rennie, Venville & Wallace 2012).

## STEM Skills and Practices

Different groups have promoted various STEM skill sets. Industry bodies emphasise the skills needed for contemporary workplaces, while educationalists emphasise academic skills that can be more easily linked to the curriculum. The STEM skills and capabilities that different schools promote are often locally determined, depending on the learning needs of their students. Figure 14.2 shows various STEM skill sets that can be used within schools.

Some schools have identified the importance of particular skills, such as resilience or problem-solving, and developed *learning progressions* for these skills. This enables teachers to share a common understanding of these skills and to identify how they look at different levels. These learning progressions can be generic in nature and so can be applied to STEM tasks for assessment purposes. The scope and sequence charts of the *general capabilities* developed by ACARA (2016) as part of the Australian Curriculum resources are useful in identifying progressive development of some STEM skills.

At the most basic level, introducing STEM skills into your own classroom can be as simple as changing a recipe-style experiment to more authentic data gathering, where students use the evidence to solve a problem; or linking science ideas to contemporary industry practices. A more complex approach is to apply STEM skills—such as critical thinking, creativity and problem-solving—anywhere that opportunities arise within, across and outside of the STEM learning areas (see the Amalgamated model in Figure 14.1). For example, a teacher who had participated in STEM professional development was awakened to the possibilities of STEM, stating that: 'STEM is now my default style of teaching. I see STEM teaching opportunities

**FIGURE 14.2:** Skill lists promoted as 21st-century skills, *STEM skills and general capabilities* (used with permission from Springer, *STEM Education in the Junior Secondary: The State of Play* by R. Jorgensen & K. Larkin [eds], copyright 2018)

## 21st–century skills[1]

### Learning and innovation skills
- Creativity & Innovation
- Critical thinking & problem solving
- Communication
- Collaboration

### Life and Career skills
- Flexibility & Adaptability
- Initiative & Self direction
- Social & Cross-cultural skills
- Productivity & Accountability
- Leadership & Responsibility

## STEM Skills[2]

### Flexible reasoning skills
- Problem solving
- Critical thinking & Creativity
- Question generation

### Adaptable use of disciplinary practices and knowledge
- Flexible use of conceptual, digital & physical tools of the discipline
- Application of practices & knowledge to new contexts

### Engage in disciplinary language
- Understanding & engagement with the disciplinary representations & ideas
- Knowledge of the language
- Sharing & communication
- Team work

### Understand the nature of evidence
- Collection of real data in a variety of situations
- Use of evidence to validate a solution to a problem or justify a decision
- Make judgements about the accuracy & reliability of information

## General Capabilities[3]

### Critical and Creative Thinking
- Inquiring – Identifying, exploring & organising information
- Generating ideas, possibilities & actions
- Reflecting on thinking & processes
- Analysing, synthesising & evaluating reasoning & procedures

### Personal and Social Capability
- Become confident, resilient & adaptable
- Communicate effectively
- Work collaboratively
- Develop leadership skills

1. Partnership for P21 (2007)
2. Hobbs, Cripps Clark and Plant (2018)
3. ACARA (2016)

INTEGRATING STEM 233

everywhere' (Hobbs et al. 2018b p. 2). For this mathematics and science teacher, STEM offers a way of learning based around solving complex problems, and so he could see this being implemented in many situations.

**SNAPSHOT 14.1:** Using an integrated approach to teaching STEM

Science, mathematics and technology teachers from G College (as reported in Hobbs et al. 2018a) began incorporating STEM as a multidisciplinary unit delivered to about half of the Year 8 classes. In small groups, students designed a vehicle that they hoped would travel the furthest distance down a ramp, and they represented their learning in a portfolio that was assessed in the three subjects. Teachers explicitly made links between the subjects. Over five weeks, students examined the following:

- *Science:* the properties of materials, forces, friction and speed;
- *Mathematics:* scale (for drawings), circles (for preparing the wheels), percentage (of materials in cars), ratios (for calculating speed), measurement (of distance and time) and decimals; and
- *Technology:* LEGO technologies, collaborative generation of ideas, design (drawings), prototyping, and construction and testing (of the vehicle).

Students visited three local businesses, where they saw contemporary design and production, the testing of prototypes, and advanced manufacturing. The challenge culminated in a Celebration Day, where prizes were given for the design that travelled the furthest and the best portfolio. The design challenge incorporated the following STEM skills:

1. *Flexible reasoning skills:* problem-solving, generating own questions and creativity within the constraints of the design brief;
2. *Adaptable use of disciplinary practices and knowledge:* technology—prototyping, design and construction, 3-D

> printers; science—experiments with data loggers, thermal-imaging cameras; mathematics—measurement, 3-D Google SketchUp;
> 3. *Engage in disciplinary language and practices:* design, prototyping and advanced manufacturing in industry visits, which were then applied to their vehicle design and construction; communication of designs; data produced through group work; and
> 4. *Understand the nature of evidence:* collecting and using authentic data, validating their solutions and making judgements of accuracy and reliability of information.

## HOW TO STEM-IFY THE STEM SUBJECTS

How can STEM be incorporated into existing learning areas? While STEM is often interpreted as integrating subjects, the individual learning areas can also be *STEM-ified.* Incorporating the STEM skills listed in Figure 14.2 is one way of doing this. Each subject provides different opportunities because of the nature of the disciplinary ideas and practices that are associated with the subjects.

STEM is now being associated with activities and pedagogies that are different from the traditional approaches. This means a move away from learning scientific knowledge from textbooks, and students completing recipe-style practical experiments where the solutions are already known. Instead, complex problem-solving activities that use real-world problems can enhance mathematical and scientific thinking, and increase relevance to students' lives. An example of how this can be done is seen in the Modelling Motion unit from the reSolve project (www.science.org.au/learning/schools/resolve). Other examples of how to STEM-ify subjects are included in the following paragraphs.

In science, using project-based learning, the teacher introduces a scenario based on an environmental issue, where students role-play a mock council meeting. Students work with a water-quality expert and engineer from the local CSIRO to collect data that will inform their role-play. The activity is designed to show how:

1. scientific discoveries rely on technological advances;
2. society can influence scientific discoveries;
3. ecosystems consist of communities of interdependent organisms and abiotic components; and
4. matter and energy flow through these systems.

In digital technology, students complete online coding activities, leading to controlling robotic LEGO devices. Students continue to build coding skills using online courses and then spend a number of sessions on a technology task, such as designing and building a *Mars Explorer.*

In design technologies, students collaborate to:

1. undertake design-based problem-solving tasks, such as (a) build a bridge that holds weight and spans a distance, (b) build a machine to lift a certain weight, or (c) design and construct a small self-propelled vehicle to carry water over a set distance;
2. undertake humanitarian engineering projects (e.g. design a shelter for the homeless or refugees); and
3. participate in, or lead, *maker fairs* where students *do, create* and *design.*

In mathematics, students complete investigations involving complex problem-solving, where students use real-world problems (for example, 'What is the best ramp for wheelchair access to the new deck?' or 'At what times during your school life do you need the most new clothes?'), through the sequence of:

1. *immersion*—understanding the problem and guiding tasks;
2. *mini inquiries*—asking questions through exercises and experiments; and
3. *the big question*—analysis and conclusion through a report and recommendations.

# APPROACHES TO INTEGRATING STEM

Integrated approaches to teaching science aim to engage students in real-world issues of relevance to their lives and to enable them to understand complex, multilayered concepts and problems that are often at the cutting edge of scientific research.

STEM is often promoted as being *interdisciplinary*, although what this means is complicated and can be misunderstood. Vasquez (2015) differentiated between four approaches to integrating the STEM disciplines.

1. *Disciplinary* approaches focus on learning the knowledge and skills of individual disciplines. These can still be STEM-ified by incorporating innovative approaches and STEM skills, as described above.
2. *Multidisciplinary* approaches use a common theme in which students learn concepts and skills separately in each discipline taught separately.
3. *Interdisciplinary* approaches focus on making links between the knowledge and skills of two or more disciplines. This requires teachers to know the content deeply enough to understand where the links are and how to make those links apparent for students.
4. *Transdisciplinary* approaches focus on *real-world problems* that require knowledge and skills from two or more disciplines to solve them.

These models of disciplinary integration have implications for how teachers work together to develop and implement activities and teaching sequences. This was demonstrated in Snapshot 14.1, where teachers from science, mathematics and technology developed a *multidisciplinary* teaching sequence together. Many teacher-collaboration models are emerging in schools, and some of these are demonstrated in Figure 14.3 (Hobbs et al. 2018a).

How teachers select from these approaches to integration and teacher collaboration will depend on whether teachers have time to plan together, if the flexibility of the timetable allows for coordination

**FIGURE 14.3:** Teacher collaboration and integration models (used with permission from Springer, *STEM Education in the Junior Secondary: The State of Play* by R. Jorgensen & K. Larkin [eds], copyright 2018)

S-T-E-M
1. Teach each discipline separately
In science classes, there is a renewed focus on using representations to enhance concept development. In mathematics, teachers use complex problem-solving to challenge their students.

SteM
2. Teach all four but more emphasis on one or two
A teacher integrates mathematics and science through a challenge-based unit of work where students design a vehicle.

3. Integrate one into the other 3 being taught separately
The engineering processes of team work, identifying and investigating a problem, designing a solution, and testing and evaluation are added into some science and mathematics units, but there are limited links across the science and mathematics subjects.

STEM
4. Total integration of all by a teacher
A science teacher integrates T, E, and M into science.
A school introduces a new STEM elective focusing on designing digital solutions to real world problems.

5. Divide a STEM curriculum into the separate subjects
Technology, science, and mathematics teachers design a combined unit and each teacher teaches different components of the unit in their separate subject, and with clear contributions from science, mathematics, and technology subjects in solving a common problem.

of classes, and whether other teachers want to be involved. Other examples of models of disciplinary integration and teacher collaboration include the following.

- In technology classes, students develop and apply programming skills to LEGO EV3 Robotics. In science, students compare and contrast human senses and robotic sensors, and link to the electromagnetic spectrum. (Multidisciplinary: taught by the science and technology teachers.)
- In science classes, students inquire into links between mathematics and science through a series of paper-based or hands-on *curiosity problems* relevant to students. (Interdisciplinary: science teacher supports students to make links across maths and science.)
- In integrated maths and science classes, students combine science (acids and bases, half-life of radioactive elements, microbiology)

and mathematics (indices, powers and exponential change) by exploring three topics from real life (pH levels, radioactivity and the Zika virus) during mini workshops, where students become experts in one topic and share their new knowledge as peer tutors. (Interdisciplinary: maths and science teachers work together to prepare and implement the activities in science and maths classes.)

## Individual Activities Versus Whole-school Approaches to STEM

Teachers and schools can approach integration in different ways. Integration of subjects can be done as individual, locally developed curriculum innovations. For example, a teacher who has an interest in vineyards might develop a *winemaking* unit that integrates science and mathematics. Alternatively, the focus might be on whole year levels or specific groups of students (such as accelerated classes). For example, teams of teachers might deliver the whole curriculum for Years 7 and 8, or a STEM unit might be introduced to all Year 9 students.

At a whole-school level, teachers and leadership may introduce an approach that is adopted school-wide. For example, STEM may be promoted through a project-based learning approach school-wide (see Chapter 11 for information on problem-based learning). Or a school-wide digital learning program may be introduced.

# ASSESSING STEM

It can be challenging to assess STEM learning because STEM is not a traditional learning area and there is no tradition of assessment. As always, deciding what to assess should depend on what you want students to learn: content (for example, science and mathematics content standards) or skills and practices (for example, critical thinking and communication). Some STEM tasks may be assessed using rubrics or criteria that are specifically designed for the task and which deal with content and/or skills. Rubrics are particularly useful for targeting specific standards from the relevant learning areas in the integrated tasks.

What assessment tasks should look like is another question. Given that STEM is intended to make learning *authentic* and relevant to students' current and future lives, the type of assessment tasks and what is assessed should reflect these aims. According to Gulikers, Bastiaens and Kirschner (2004), authentic assessment should:

- include a set of activities that uses the competencies, skills, knowledge and attitudes that are applied through professional practice, but that reflect the learning needs of students from basic to mature skills;
- be *embedded* so that the assessable tasks are also the learning tasks, giving students opportunities to demonstrate their knowledge and skills while they are learning;
- consider the physical context, social processes and products or performance that might emulate professional practice (for example, students can apply what they have learned from a visit to a factory using advanced manufactory techniques in their design of a vehicle); and
- use criteria to judge learning that indicate the value of the practices and levels of performance expected.

Students can struggle to make connections between the STEM tasks and the science learning, so diaries and journals (see Snapshot 14.1) can be a useful way to get students articulating the science behind their designs or solutions. Research has shown that where students are given prompts by the teacher, they are more likely to think more deeply about the solutions and the concepts involved (Puntambekar & Kolodner 2005). When used in this way, diaries or journals scaffold student learning and become useful for:

- *formative assessment*, by informing the teacher and student of progress in learning and where further support may be needed during the teaching sequence; and
- *summative assessment*, for judging how well the student has made connections between the science ideas and their design solutions.

## MAKING STEM INNOVATION WORK

While there is mounting pressure for schools to incorporate STEM, it is not necessarily easy to change the curriculum, develop new pedagogies and change assessment practices. Therefore, you may encounter some challenges, but these can stimulate innovation.

### Feeling Out of Your Depth

With integrated approaches to STEM, teachers can find themselves teaching new subjects or content matter. Successful integration requires teachers to have a strong understanding of how the disciplines connect and how to make these connections visible to students. Science teachers might feel uncomfortable or lack confidence in connecting science ideas with the mathematics and technology ideas and processes needed to solve a problem.

Possible solutions might be to:

1. work in collaboration with other teachers from the other subjects to help you make these links;
2. undertake professional development; and
3. seek out and work with industry experts.

### Recruiting Other Teachers

If a school does not already incorporate STEM ideas and programs, it can be difficult to convince others to introduce STEM. Quality STEM learning can be achieved in your own classroom, but to really impact the attitudes of students towards STEM, it is more effective to give students multiple opportunities to engage with STEM thinking and practice across subjects and year levels. Recruiting other teachers to the *STEM agenda* can be tricky, because it may require them to try something new or relinquish old approaches to teaching, and they may have reservations because of a fear of superficial treatment or loss of content in their own discipline.

Possible solutions might be to:

1. prepare clear documentation that shows (a) how the content from each subject is included, and (b) how to implement the new activity or learning sequence (e.g. student workbook with question prompts, how to differentiate tasks, how a lesson might run);
2. collect data from students to show effectiveness (e.g. student attitudes, achievement data); and
3. communicate to other teachers, leadership and the school community what you are doing (e.g. a five-minute demonstration at a staff meeting). This can show that it is not difficult, and allow you to invite participation and solicit new ideas and support.

## Sustaining STEM Innovation in Schools

Teaching can be a transitional profession, with teachers moving between schools or teachers being allocated to different year levels and subjects. This instability can result in innovations being dropped when teachers with the knowledge and drive are no longer available to sustain the program.

Possible solutions might be to:

1. have a comprehensive approach to incorporating STEM in your school by involving a number of teachers, subjects, year levels and opportunities for student engagement (e.g. core units, elective units, extracurricular activities, whole-school events or as a consistent approach to learning); and
2. ensure that students engage with the range of possibilities that STEM provides by allowing them to explore the relevance of science and mathematics in contemporary and future-orientated contexts and problems, and ultimately opening up the possibilities of a future where young people are positioned as problem-solvers, future-makers and job-makers.

## SUMMARY OF KEY POINTS

This chapter describes the different ways STEM can be framed and incorporated into schools, and argues that a range of approaches is needed to improve student learning. The STEM subjects are aligned with the science, mathematics, engineering and technology learning areas within the Australian Curriculum. Skills relating to STEM, including the capabilities within the Australian Curriculum, can be the focus of instruction in different situations. STEM can be incorporated into the individual STEM subjects and through integration, and there are some suggestions for assessment practices. A number of challenges might arise, and we have mentioned possible solutions that can assist you in deciding how to include STEM in your teaching.

## DISCUSSION QUESTIONS

14.1 Which of the approaches to teaching STEM do you consider to be of most benefit for the learning of your students, and for your own professional learning?

14.2 Consider an integrated curriculum focusing on sustainable houses to be taught in Year 9 science. What discipline-based knowledge or concepts from science, mathematics and technology could be taught in such a unit? How could this knowledge be connected with issues on a local and global scale?

14.3 Describe two ways you might work with other teachers in your school to take a multidisciplinary approach to plan and teach this unit? What difficulties might you face, and how would you overcome them?

## REFERENCES

Australian Curriculum and Assessment Authority (ACARA), 2016, *General capabilities*, Canberra: ACARA, <www.australian curriculum.edu.au/f-10-curriculum/general-capabilities>, accessed 10 July 2018.

Education Council, 2016, *National STEM School Education Strategy: A Comprehensive Plan for Science, Technology, Engineering and Mathematics Education in Australia*, Canberra: Education Council.

Gulikers, J.T.M., Bastiaens, T.J. & Kirschner, P.A., 2004, 'A five-dimensional framework for authentic assessment', *Educational Technology Research and Development*, vol. 52, no. 3, pp. 67–86.

Hobbs L., Cripps Clark J. & Plant B., 2018a, 'Successful students—STEM program: Teacher learning through a multifaceted vision for STEM education', in R. Jorgensen & K. Larkin (eds), *STEM Education in the Junior Secondary: The State of Play*, Singapore: Springer, pp. 133–68.

Hobbs, L., Cripps Clark, J., & Plant, B., 2018b, *Project Completion Report: Successful Students—STEM Professional Development Program*, prepared for Skilling the Bay, Geelong, January 2018.

Office of the Chief Scientist, 2016, *Australia's STEM Workforce: Science, Technology, Engineering and Mathematics*, Canberra: Australian Government.

Partnerships for P21, 2007, *Framework for 21st Century Learning. Partnerships for P21*, <www.p21.org/our-work/p21-framework>, accessed 10 July 2018.

Puntambekar, S. & Kolodner, J.L., 2005, 'Toward implementing distributed scaffolding: Helping students learn science from design', *Journal of Research in Science Teaching*, vol. 42, no. 2, pp. 185–217.

Rennie, L., Venville, G., & Wallace, J., 2012, *Knowledge that Counts in a Global Community: Exploring the Contribution of Integrated Curriculum*, London: Routledge.

Timms, M.J., Moyle, K., Weldon, P.R. & Mitchell, P., 2018, *Challenges in STEM Learning in Australian Schools*, Carlton: ACER.

Trounson, A., 2010, 'Deep specialization key to collaboration', *The Australian Higher Education Supplement*, 24 February, p. 23.

Vasquez, J., 2015, 'STEM—Beyond the acronym', *Educational Leadership*, vol. 72, no. 4, pp. 10–15.

# INDEX

5E model 88, 92, 102, 113–14, 216–17

Aboriginal and Torres Strait Islander students 79, 161
'active learning' teaching strategy 177, 178, 179, 181
affective perspective, conceptual change model 56–7
alternative conceptions 36–9, 39–40, 44, 46, 60, 111, 143, 146, 216
analog, meaning 185
analogy 54, 56, 61, 185–6
animal ethics 197–8
Animal Ethics Infolink 198
assessment
  diagnostic 142–3, 150, 164
  diversity considerations 164
  equitable 152–5, 157
  evaluative 142, 144
  external accountability and 156–7
  formative 100, 101, 142–3, 167, 239
  investigative activities as 148–9

meaning 97, 141–2
oral 147–8
role in teaching 141–2
rubric 153, 154
STEM 238–9
summative 94, 142–3, 239
technology and 211
written 147–8
assessment as learning 142–5, 149
assessment for learning 142–5, 149, 150, 152, 211
assessment of learning 142–5, 149, 150, 152
assignments 147–8
Attention Deficit Hyperactivity Disorder (ADHD) 160, 161–2
Australian Academy of Science 114–15
Australian Council for Computers in Education 219
Australian Curriculum, Assessment and Reporting Authority (ACARA) 85, 93, 97, 231
Australian Curriculum: Science

## INDEX 245

see also curriculum; Science as a Human Endeavour; Science Inquiry Skills; Science Understanding
aims 75
Australian implementation 73–5
content descriptions 80
cross-curriculum priorities 78–9, 161
elaborations 80
Foundation to Year 10 79–81
general capabilities 77–8, 79, 82, 222, 231, 232
organisation 76–9
overarching ideas 76–7
science, definition 8, 10, 16
STEM and 229, 231, 242
strands and sub-strands 76, 123
technology, use of 222
whole-school planning 85–8
Years 11 and 12 81–2
Australian Professional Standards for Teachers 160, 162, 222
Australian Science Teachers Association 219
Australian Tertiary Admission Ranking (ATAR) 82, 156
Autism Spectrum Disorder 161–2
axiology 9

behaviourism 213–14, 221
biology 8, 14, 37–8, 71, 72, 81, 130, 203, 208

'blended learning' teaching strategy 178, 179
Bloom's taxonomy 166, 167
Boyle, Robert 25, 27–8
Boyle's Law 25, 27–8, 31

Center for Research on Learning and Teaching 178
chemistry 8, 42, 61, 71, 72, 81, 90, 130
choice boards 165, 168
'citizen science' teaching strategy 178, 179–81, 188
CLEAPSS 199
code of behaviour in laboratories 201, 207
cognitive conflict, using 59–61, 63, 215
concept maps 118–19, 146, 176, 211, 214
conceptions
  alternative see alternative conceptions
  pre-instructional see pre-instructional conceptions
  student 36–9
conceptual change see also constructivist perspectives
  main issues behind 51–2
  new research findings 41
  teaching for 59–62
  theoretical perspectives 52–9
  views of learning 39–40
constructivist perspectives
  planning and 59, 85, 88, 102

THE ART OF TEACHING SCIENCE 3RD EDITION

social *see* social constructivist
perspectives
technology and 214, 215,
221
theory 36, 40–1, 51, 146,
164, 176, 177
context-based learning
approach 89, 90
controlled variables 124, 134–5
cooperative learning 116–18,
120
Curie, Marie 12–14, 16, 20, 23,
32
Curie, Pierre 12–14
curriculum 71–2 *see also*
Australian Curriculum:
Science
curriculum documents 8,
72–3, 91, 111

data
facts, patterns, law, and 25–7
types of 137
dependent variable 134–5, 136,
154
Descartes, René 23–4
diagnostic assessment 142–3,
150, 164
differentiation 162–3
addressing concerns about
169–70
instructional strategies
164–8
digital pedagogies 213–19, 222
dioramas 149
direct science inquiry 129, 130
disabilities 160–2

Disability Standards for
Education (DSE) 161–2
dissection 129, 182, 193,
199–200
distance education, as teaching
strategy 178, 181–2
diversity among students
160–2, 170 *see also*
differentiation
assessment considerations
164
drawing, as scientific literacy
43–6
dyslexia 160, 161

educational technologies *see*
learning technologies
empiricism 8, 9–10
'envoy' teaching strategy 119
epistemological perspective,
conceptual change model
53–4
epistemology 9
equipment
and safety 192–7
planning for use 200–2
storage 202
equitable assessment 152–5,
157
equity and diversity 161–2
Eurocentric science 8, 23, 32
evidence-based 70, 75, 123,
128, 129
examinations 149–51
excursions 91, 204–7, 208, 220
experiments 7, 148, 165–6
safety in 197–200

INDEX **247**

explanation
argument, distinguished 24
'explicit instruction' teaching
strategy 177, 178, 182–3

fact
data, patterns, law, and
25–7
nature of 20–1
feedback levels 153, 155
field trips 182, 204–7
'flexible time' teaching strategy
178, 183
formative assessment 100, 101,
142–3, 167, 239
Foundation to Year 10,
Australian Curriculum
content 79–81

'gallery walk' teaching strategy
119
general capabilities 77–8, 79,
82, 222, 231, 232
group work *see* cooperative
learning
guided science inquiry 129,
130–1

health and safety 102 *see also*
safety
hypotheses, writing 135–6

independent variable 131,
134–5, 137, 154
Indigenous knowledge 7–8
industry partnerships
204–7

Information and
Communication Technology
(ICT) capability 73, 78,
222
injuries 194–5 *see also* safety
inquiry-based approaches
lesson structure 115–16
teaching 14, 81, 107–13,
118–20, 125, 132, 216–17

'jigsaw' teaching strategy
119–20, 176
Just-in-Time teaching 184

laboratory 191–2
code of behaviour 201, 207
equipment in *see* equipment
safety in *see* safety
laboratory technicians 200–2
laws, scientific 7, 19–20, 24,
25–7, 27–31
learning profiles 162, 163, 165,
168, 170
learning spaces 219–20, 223
learning technologies 210–13
*see also* technology, use in
teaching
lesson plans and planning 73,
85, 86, 97–102
literacy, scientific 43–7, 70,
77, 82, 106–7, 124, 127–8,
137

material safety data sheets
(MSDS) 196, 199
mechanisms in science 23–4
menu of options 167–8

models
  assessment, as 149
  multimodal representations, as 42, 43, 47
  safety, use 196–7
  scientific theory and 15, 24, 28
  teaching, in 61–2, 182, 186
multidimensional perspective, conceptual change model 57–9
multimodal languages 42–3

National Assessment Program–Literacy and Numeracy (NAPLAN) test 156
norms 6–7

observation, role in science 9, 20–1, 22
ontological perspective, conceptual change model 53, 55–6, 63
open-ended science inquiry 129, 131
oral assessment tasks 147–8
Orientating, Enhancing and Synthesising model 88
outdoor activities 171, 192, 202–3, 208

pattern questions 11
patterns
  data, facts, law, and 25–7
personal constructivist perspectives 40–1 see also constructivist perspectives

personal protective equipment (PPE) 192–3
physics 8, 37, 55, 71, 72, 81, 211
portfolio assessment 145, 148, 211, 233
pre-assessment 162, 164
Predict-Observe-Explain sequence 59, 60–1, 148, 176, 215–16
pre-instructional conceptions
  conceptual change and 51–2, 53–4, 55
  planning and 85, 102, 133, 134
  recognising 59–61, 110, 215
presentations 145, 149, 192
Primary Connections program 81, 114–15
problem-based learning
  approach 89, 177, 192
  group 178, 183–5
procedure, teaching 185–7
Programme for International Student Assessment (PISA) 156

questions
  role in science 10–16
  role in teaching 112–13, 151–2
quizzes 110, 149–51, 162

Radiological Council 198
readiness 162–5, 167–8, 169
reflective journal 147–8
report sheets 132

INDEX 249

representational perspectives
43–7
research questions, writing
130, 135–6
RiskAssess 196, 199
role-play 177, 186–7, 188,
192, 234–5

safety
equipment and 192–7
health and 102
planning for 182, 197–200
student behaviour and 200
School of the Air 181
science
definition, Australian
Curriculum 8–9
what constitutes 3–8
Science as a Human
Endeavour (SHE) 76,
79, 80, 82, 93, 123, 128,
184, 205
Science ASSIST 198
Science by Doing program
113, 114–15, 116, 118
science inquiry
approach to teaching
124–8
direct 129, 130
guided 129, 130–1
implementing in the
classroom 131–2
levels of 129–31
open-ended 129, 131
what is 30, 124
Science Inquiry Skills (SIS) 76,
79, 80, 82, 93, 123, 132

Science Technology
Engineering and
Mathematics (STEM)
education
activities 238
approaches to integrating
90–1, 234–5, 236–8
assessment 238–9
Australian Curriculum and
229, 231
skills 231–5
teaching challenges 240–1
what is 227–8, 229–31
Science Understanding (SU)
76, 79, 82, 86, 93, 98, 123
scientific facts *see* facts
scientific laws 7, 19–20, 24,
25–7, 27–31
scientific literacy 43–7, 70, 82,
106–7, 124, 127–8, 137
scientific worldview 24, 76
'seamless learning' 220
secondary-school planning
lessons 97–102
units of work 88 96
whole-school 85–8
simulations 43, 46–7, 149,
177, 210, 214
slowmation 149, 150, 218
social constructivist
perspectives 41–2
digital pedagogies 214,
215–18
sociocultural perspectives 36,
42–3
spaces, learning 219–20
staff, laboratory support 200–2

STEM Professionals in Schools program  180–1, 204
students
discussion  111
involvement  110–1
summative assessment  94, 142–3, 239
syllabus *see* curriculum documents

target concept  185, 186
teaching models  113–15
teaching strategies  118–20, 177–85
teaching terminology  176–7
TeachMeets  219
team jobs, as cooperative learning  117–18
team skills, as cooperative learning  118
technical-support staff  200–2
technology, use in teaching
*see also* learning technologies
barriers  220–1
digital pedagogies  213–19, 222
drivers of  221–2

tests  108, 149–51, 162
textbooks  202
theories in science  19–20, 21, 22, 27–31
theory questions  11
tiered activities  164, 165–6
transmission model  107–9, 182
Trends in International Mathematics and Science Study (TIMMS)  156

units of work, planning  88–96

variables  134–5, 137
video-conferencing technology  181

Web 2.0 technologies  211–13
whole-school planning  85–8, 102
WorkSafe  196, 198
work samples  80
written assessment tasks  147–8

year achievement standard  80
year level description  80
Years 11 and 12, Australian Curriculum content  81–2